EMPIRE IN THE AIR

SOCIAL TRANSFORMATIONS IN
AMERICAN ANTHROPOLOGY

General Editor: Ida Susser

*The Sounds of Latinidad: Immigrants Making Music and
Creating Culture in a Southern City*
Samuel K. Byrd

*Mobile Selves: Race, Migration, and Belonging in Peru and
the U.S.*
Ulla D. Berg

*Citizen, Student, Soldier: Latina/o Youth, JROTC, and the
American Dream*
Gina M. Pérez

Empire in the Air: Airline Travel and the African Diaspora
Chandra D. Bhimull

Empire in the Air

Airline Travel and the African Diaspora

Chandra D. Bhimull

NEW YORK UNIVERSITY PRESS

New York

NEW YORK UNIVERSITY PRESS
New York
www.nyupress.org

© 2017 by New York University
All rights reserved

References to Internet websites (URLs) were accurate at the time of writing. Neither the author nor New York University Press is responsible for URLs that may have expired or changed since the manuscript was prepared.

ISBN: 978-1-4798-4347-3

For Library of Congress Cataloging-in-Publication data, please contact the Library of Congress.

New York University Press books are printed on acid-free paper, and their binding materials are chosen for strength and durability. We strive to use environmentally responsible suppliers and materials to the greatest extent possible in publishing our books.

Manufactured in the United States of America

10 9 8 7 6 5 4 3 2 1

Also available as an ebook

CONTENTS

ACKNOWLEDGMENTS

It is true what they say: writing a book takes longer and is lonelier than you think. But it is also true that the abundant grace of others makes it possible to stay the course. This book found its way into the world because of that benevolence.

I owe a tremendous debt of gratitude to Sonya O. Rose. I cannot imagine a more understanding teacher and mentor. She has commented on countless drafts, listened, and shared her incredible insight during and long after our time together at the University of Michigan. She has raised all the right questions with admirable patience. She has pushed and encouraged me for the better. Throughout, she and her partner Guenter have offered warmth, friendship, and laughter, along with immeasurable support. They continue to make an awesome world of difference.

This book would not be here without the untrammeled imagination of people who participated in the Doctoral Program in Anthropology and History at Michigan, aka Anthrohistory. David William Cohen, Fernando Coronil, and Julie Skurski introduced me to the marvels of radical transdisciplinary curiosity. They explained why alternative ways of thinking, writing, and knowing are possible and necessary. They refused to believe that rigorous study and a sense of creative wonder cannot go together. They opened their homes and shared the love of their families. David, Fernando, and Julie: thank you for teaching by example and with heart. Similarly, Paul K. Eiss, Purvi Mehta, Monica Eileen Patterson, David Pedersen, and Julianne O'Brien Pedersen have been steadfast comrades, interlocutors, and friends. They have kept me going with late-night phone calls, unexpected treats by mail, and random visits when I needed them most. Their incisive criticisms and stunning capacity for exploration made for a stronger book.

I am lucky to have benefited from the goodwill of others I met at Michigan. I am indebted to faculty, postdocs, and fellow graduate students for providing intellectual and emotional support, including Laura

Brown, Elana Buch, Sharad Chari, Frank Cody, Frederick Cooper, Aimee Meredith Cox, Shannon Lee Dawdy, Laurent Dubois, Kevin Gaines, Ema Grama, Zareena Grewal, Edin Hajdarpasic, Karen Hebert, Federico Helfgott, Daniel Hershenzon, Erik Huneke, Mark Hunter, Caroline Jeannerat, Olivera Jokic, Webb Keane, Emil Kerenji, Alaina Lemon, Allison Lichter, Oana Mateescu, Edward Murphy, Vladimir Pavlovic, Bhavani Raman, Natalie Rothman, Bill Schwarz, Julius Scott, Genese Sodikoff, Pete Soppelsa, Jessica Thurlow, and Kidada Williams. I am grateful to Lorna Altstetter, Sheila Coley, and Diana Denney who dealt with all of my questions without complaint. I offer heartfelt special thanks to Gabrielle Hecht. She exposed me to science and technology studies and provided ample feedback and considerable guidance. And thank you, Erika Gasser, and thank you, Mary O'Reilly, for making much of the experience a blithesome occasion. Mary: your dazzling fierce friendship and mind are missed daily.

I am deeply appreciative of the supportive community I have found at Colby College. Colleagues, students, and staff have inspired and invigorated me in innumerable ways, particularly those in the Department of Anthropology and in the African-American Studies Program. Catherine Besteman, Cheryl Townsend Gilkes, and Mary Beth Mills made the tough transition from graduate student to faculty member easier. They fought hard for me more times than I know. They made sure that I had time to research, write, and have fun. Catherine, Cheryl, and Mary Beth, together with Maple Razsa, David Strohl, and Winifred Tate have considerably advanced this project. Britt Halvorson, whom I have known since graduate school, has also furthered this work. Her remarks and trust, as well as her true commitment to serious intellectual play, have delighted and propelled me through the ups and downs of writing a book and living an academic life. Sweet cheers to all of them for building us an active scholarly home. I cannot thank enough other colleague-friends who have created similar homes in other spaces: James Barrett, Kim Besio, Lyn Mikel Brown, Cedric Bryant, Megan Cook, Ben Fallaw, Nadia El-Shaarawi, Bevin Engman, James Fleming, Patrice Franko, Jill Gordon, Walter Hatch, Rebeca Hey-Colón, Noel James, Russell Johnson, Karen Kusiak, Sandy Maisel, Jonathan McCoy, Margaret McFadden, Suzanne Menair, Steven Nuss, Jorge Olivares, Anindyo Roy, Cyrus Shahan, Jay Sibara, Judy Stone, Graham Stoute, Walter Sullivan, Mark Tappan,

Sonja Thomas, Wayne Wilson, and Rob Weisbrot. Wholehearted praise for the expertise of librarians and staff—Bev Boose, Beth Christopher, Karen Gillum, Celeste Lessard, and Marilyn Pukkila. They have rescued this book over and again. Friendships with Sahan Dissanayake, Rabbi Rachel Isaacs, Lydia Moland, Laura Saltz, Betty Sasaki, and Melanie Weiss have been inimitable gifts of strength and love. Lisa Arellano, Tashia Bradley, Julie de Sherbinin, and Carleen Mandolfo have become family.

The magical edges of conversations with students at Colby have brought me ineffable joy. The opportunity to teach and learn from them has been an honor. Thank you, bright gentle thinkers, for taking my classes and inviting me to work with you in other ways. You have taught me how to be a better teacher and scholar. Time and again, the marvelous efforts of students in my black radical imaginations and my senior seminars, as well as those in Students Organized for Black and Hispanic Unity (SOBHU), have reminded me that struggle matters. Thank you! My keen research assistants also deserve exclamatory appreciation for the herculean tasks they did with terrific success: Janelle Baptiste, Diamond Drayton, Tionna Haynes, Tiffany Martin, Debbie Merzbach, and Jemarley McFarlane. Abby Snyder used her magnificent command of language to proofread the entire manuscript. Her notes and generous spirit helped me through the final stages of writing. Hannah DeAngelis made sure that I never forgot the sustaining power of a gorgeous sentence. Her uncanny ability to recommend the right book undid difficult times. Emily Pavelle kept the big picture squarely in perspective with her knack for finding sage amusements and generating smart glee. An earnest note of gratitude for students who have gone above and beyond to stay in touch long after graduation. They continue to enrich my life. I trust they know who they are.

This book would not have happened without substantial funding from Colby's Interdisciplinary Studies Division Faculty Research Grant and the Office of the Provost and Dean of Faculty. A pretenure sabbatical and multiple travel grants were also an enormous help. At Michigan, the Doctoral Program in Anthropology and History; Rackham School of Graduate Studies; History Department; Anthropology Department; Center for Latin American and Caribbean Studies; Center for European Studies; Center for the Education of Women; and International

Institute—supported my research and graduate studies. The Daniel and Florence Guggenheim Fellowship at the Smithsonian Institution; Social Science Research Council and Ford Foundation; Woodrow Wilson Foundation; Tensions of Europe Project; and the Society for the History of Technology—funded long periods of research and assisted with professional development in and after graduate school.

These institutions, foundations, divisions, centers, and networks gave more than money. They allowed me to work in incredible places and with amazing people. Much appreciation to the more than helpful archivists, directors, curators, executives, faculty, librarians, officials, officers, pilots, and the entire staff at the Barbados Concorde Experience; Barbados Defence Force; Barbados Light Airplane Club; Barbados National Archive; Barbados National Library; British Airways; British Airways Speedbird Heritage Centre; British Library; British National Archives (formerly the Public Records Office); Jamaica Archives and Records Department; Liddell Hart Centre for Military Archives at King's College, London; National Archives of Dominica; Special Collections Department at the University of Miami; Smithsonian Institution, especially the National Air and Space Museum; University of the West Indies (Cave Hill, Barbados), particularly its libraries and the History Department; University of the West Indies (Mona, Jamaica), notably its libraries and the Geography Department. During some of the hardest periods of study, three families took me in and accepted and treated me as one of their own. To the Alexander, Payne, and Wit families: my thanks for your gracious care. I would also like to acknowledge the people I cannot name, many of whom are infrequent fliers. I owe them a great deal.

When I started this project nearly two decades ago, only a handful of us in the academic arena were trying to do ethnographic fieldwork aboard airliners in the air. This made the process of researching and writing all the more difficult and the generosity of other folks even more extraordinary. I am fortunate to have benefited from the profound open mindedness of scholars and specialists who took a chance on this project and made it possible for me to learn from them. They have affected my work in significant and powerful ways. Among them are Martin Collins, Jim Davies, R. E. G. Davies, Aviston Downes, Howell Green, Keith Hayward, Rosemarjin Hoefte, Tara Inniss, Paul Jarvis, Daniel Miller, Gijs Mom, Suzanne Moon, Melanie Newton, Anke Ortlepp, Ruth Oldenziel, Gordon Pirie, Dominick Pisano, Douglas Rust, Frank Schipper, Hugh Semple, Elizabeth Thomas-Hope, Robert van der Linden, and David Williams. I am privileged to have had the opportunity to participate in forums, workshops, and seminars including but not limited to the Caribbean Studies History Forum at the University of the West Indies in Barbados; Caribbean Studies Workshop at the University of Chicago; Technology, Innovation, and Society Seminar in the Centre of Innovation Studies at Eindhoven University of Technology; and the Transatlantic Tourism Workshop at the German Historical Institute. The Anthropology Department at University College London and the KITLV/Royal Netherlands Institute of Southeast Asian and Caribbean Studies kindly welcomed me to their community at pivotal moments in the project's development. The collegiality and congeniality I found at each of these places grew this project in more ways than I can say.

⮌

I am very happy NYU Press decided to turn my manuscript into a book. Jennifer Hammer has been an ideal editor. Her intellectual acuity and compassion have been a heartening boon. Thank you, Jennifer, for having confidence in what I set out to do, and for offering much-needed advice, edits, and encouragement throughout the entire process. I am grateful to her editorial assistant Amy Klopfenstein for carrying the manuscript through the production stage with thoughtful diligence. I also thank the anonymous reviewers for their insightful comments and questions, as well as Matt Bolinder for providing me with a place to carefully work through the revisions. And thanks fondly to Eben Wood for being a champion of creative academic efforts.

Portions of chapters 4 and 5 previously appeared in the *Journal of Transport History* and *Transfers: Interdisciplinary Journal of Mobility Studies*. I thank the *Journal of Transport History* for permission to include revised and expanded sections of my article, "Caribbean Airways, 1930–32: A Notable Failure," *Journal of Transport History* 33:2 (December 2012): 228–242. I thank *Transfers: Interdisciplinary Journal of Mobility Studies* for permission to include revised and expanded sections of my article, "Reshaping Empire: Airline Travelers and Colonial Encounters in the 1930s," *Transfers: Interdisciplinary Journal of Mobility Studies* 3:1 (Spring 2013): 45–64. Thanks is also given to the journal *Anthropology and Humanism* and *Curatorial Dreams: Critics Imagine Exhibitions*, a book edited by Shelley R. Butler and Erica Lehrer (Montreal: McGill-Queens University Press, 2016), for providing innovative spaces to experiment with fledging thoughts and for permitting those thoughts to be told anew as ideas in the creative parts to follow in the book "The Alchemy of Flight" in *Curatorial Dreams*, 64–81; and "Passages: Airborne in the African Diaspora," *Anthropology and Humanism* 39:2 (December 2014): 129–144. The British Airways Speedbird Heritage Centre, the National Air and Space Museum (Washington, D.C.), and the Estate of Abram Games have approved the reproduction and inclusion of the images that appear in the book, and for this I am deeply grateful.

Finally, I return to where I began. The abundance of help I received supported and moved this project over many years, from thought to idea to book. If I have failed to mention anyone, please forgive me. The kindness and generosity of others made writing possible; the flaws of the work are my own.

Sacrifices were offered up and endured, and abiding love given by generations of my family and evermore friends. I give thanks to them for working in unspeakable ways to ensure that possibility survived. And to Wendy Singer and Pamela Scully who introduced me to history and historiography as an undergraduate—they put me on the path that eventually led to this book—thank you. Nat and Jules Alexander—many thanks—for listening, caring, and talking me through the knottier parts of that path. And when the path pulled me away, Maria Messina Angelo, Amanda Abresch Harbert, Jennifer Hunt, Cecil Craig Jackson, Katie Peters Tolson, Andrea Walker, and Collette Williams kept our respective friendships going, and for this I am in their debt. My bottomless thanks go to Beth Schiller and Lee Straw for insisting that the spirit of the work be warm, and mine light. And my loving thoughts go to my sisters Kerilyn, Heather, and Kayla, for unearthing old ways to dream; Desmond, my brother, for being uncommonly perspicacious and funny; Alexia, Kathryn, and Laurence for being mischievous, cheeky, out of this world nieces and nephew; and to my beautiful parents, Krishna and Dorothy, to whom this book is dedicated, for continuing to keep possibility going by teaching us to learn, stay curious, love, and let fly.

PASSING

Terminal

1

When Floresa Eglantine Varlack died on Friday, October 13, 1989, most of her children could not attend the funeral. Like most migrants, their reasons varied: money, time, transportation, logistics. Floresa died on Anegada, a British Virgin Island, and the majority of her kids lived stateside.

In the 1980s, the trip from New York City to Anegada went something like this: take a direct flight to St. Thomas or Puerto Rico. Land in St. Thomas, taxi to the waterfront, ferry to Tortola, taxi to the airport, and fly to Anegada. Or land in Puerto Rico, wait in the airport, fly to Tortola, wait at the airport, fly to Anegada. Timing mattered. Back then just two round-trip flights went three days a week between Tortola and Anegada.

When she passed, Floresa had an infection and Anegada lacked a morgue. Her husband did not want to send and store her body in Tortola, a decision that inadvertently made it difficult for some of their kids to find last-minute flights or funds. On Saturday, three siblings washed, wrapped, blessed, and buried their mother, a red hibiscus in her hair. Unable to fly, the other four grieved at a distance.

2

Jimmy Kelenda Mubenga was 46 years old when he died on Tuesday, October 12, 2010, on the runway. That evening, he had boarded British Airways flight 77 at London Heathrow Airport. Escorted by three private security guards, he walked to the back of the Boeing 777, went to the last row, sat in a middle seat, and complained. After sixteen years in Britain, he was bound for Luanda.

Jimmy did not want to go. He said they would kill him. He repeatedly asked for help. Over time, his screams, which cut through the cabin—"I can't breathe." "No, no, no, no." "I have a family."—decreased in vigor.[1]

The guards said little. They were members of G4S and the major security firm had trained them for this. Hired by the Home Office, they pushed and pressed and held the reluctant deportee down. Meanwhile, the boarding process continued and the remaining passengers emplaned. "He'll be alright," a guard explained, "once we get him in the air."[2] The crew prepared for takeoff.

The phrase prefigured the wake of plane and person. In the air: a reference to a place; to culture off the ground; to travel in state; to comfort and calm for many; to resolve, then resignation for one.

Introduction

It's about airline travel. This is my stock answer to a standard question: *What is your book about?* It is simple talk. It is conventional, straight-forward, and considerate. Then people ask why, and the pulse of the conversation changes from polite to political. The shift is slight but palpable. *Why do you study airline travel? Why did you get interested in that? Why does it appeal to you?* In other words: Why would flight matter to someone like me?

Social categories are weird creatures. They are seemingly fixed but totally flexible cultural constellations in which personal histories and historical processes unevenly fuse. Like most folks, I occupy many categories, but many people seem most curious about the confluence of my research topic, race and gender, and my chosen disciplines: aviation, black woman, and anthropology and history.

I am generally grateful when someone is kind enough to ask how I came up with my project. But every so often the question feels like a backhanded way to ask me to explain myself, most notably in academic spaces where colleagues who are not black women are not asked similar questions. Yet not once have I refused to answer the question, despite feeling uncomfortable or exposed.

I have thought about this scenario a lot over the years. At first, I thought that the exchange (the question and my reaction to it) was part of the racism deeply embedded in the academy, which it is. In arenas of power play, such as a conference, my willingness to satisfy this kind of curiosity is, as they say, a deadly encounter; depending on how one locates the players of the exchange, it was curiosity (i.e., racism) that killed (i.e., the question) the cat (i.e., the one who asks or answers, or both) and satisfaction (i.e., consent, spontaneous or not) that brought it (i.e., racism) back.[1]

Such exchanges are not uncommon or new. Curiosity as surveillance has long surrounded, stifled, and suppressed black women scholars and their topics in the academy.[2] Over time, as I wrote this book, I realized that I had missed a key player: the topic itself, airline travel. There is something very interesting about how race and flying are represented, experienced, and (not) discussed in everyday life. By and large, ordinary air spaces, such as the airport and the airliner cabin, are tacitly understood to be 'white' places. Consider, for instance, *Soul Plane*, a movie about a black-owned airline, which arguably calls to mind buffoonery or black nationalism (e.g., Garveyism). Or 'flying while black' stories, which are usually about racial profiling and state-sanctioned violence.[3] And the statement famously put forth by Black Lives Matter U.K. activists as they protested a mass deportation flight due to fly from London to Jamaica in September 2016: "Black people are the first to die, not the first to fly." There are significant differences among these narratives, particularly in terms of circumstance, intention, and meaning. But commercial air travel, blackness, and transgression are among the concerns they have in common. One of the underlying points made in each of them is that black people do not belong in the commercial sky, as a company, consumer, worker, deportee, or otherwise. Passenger flights and black people do not *go* together. The relatively small presence of black people working *in*-flight is another example of the racial landscape of airline travel, especially when seen alongside the substantial presence of black people working *with* flights on the ground.[4]

How racism took to the sky is one of the questions of this book. What brought me to the question, how I searched for answers, and why I wrote the book as an assemblage of fragments and more conventional prose, are central to this work. I am in a way explaining myself. However, this time, I am doing it more of my own volition.

↬

A daughter of immigrant parents, I grew up in a family where access to airline travel seemed to define us. My father is from Trinidad and Tobago. My mother is from Anegada. Like countless West Indians who settled in Canada and the United States in the 1970s, my parents saved to send us to see their parents 'back home': money, vacation days, and eventually, air miles. When we returned to the States, they saved again. Baggage identification tags and used airline tickets merged with birth certificates, expired passports, and other important papers in a combination lock case; it was a carefully selected repository of things that proved we had existed and moved.

The collection made sense in terms of class. A somewhat working-class family on solidly middle-class Long Island, we hardly ever flew, which meant we rarely saw our grandparents. This felt strange for the suburbs, a place that valued relatives visiting and visiting relatives. We saw nearby aunts, uncles, and cousins, but as kids, the overseas away-ness of our grandparents marked us. For me, a stash of airline para-phernalia was profoundly comforting. Plastic pins shaped like wings, branded playing cards, stamped boarding passes, and even logoed nap-kins could briefly change our status. This stuff was more than memora-bilia. It was an asset demonstrating some sort of means. It was leverage.

Except the loot was never enough. When it came to race, these trap-pings were risky. We were black—immigrant, first-generation, black—in a mostly white area. We were an anomaly, and a stockpile of tickets and other objects collected on trips to the Caribbean made us stand out even more: we were not on vacation; it was not a holiday.

As a black girl hell-bent on blending in in the burbs, my relationship to airline artifacts was complicated at best. I experienced privilege, con-nection, and love through them. I endured some of the quintessential hallmarks of racial difference because of them: self-consciousness, ex-posure, humiliation, and betrayal.

Then my grandmother died, on Anegada.

Our options were limited. We did not attend her funeral. I went to school and told a good friend all about it: no money, tricky layovers, no morgue, no time off from work. She was sorry about the death and snide about the fact that we couldn't go. She knew family and flying were inex-tricably linked for us; our inability to fly to the funeral fueled anxieties about who we were and what we could do. It outed and othered us again.

Immobility sparked an acute sense of shame steeped in the subtlety of classism and racism. It was an ambivalent moment, and I split, aber-rant on the one hand and stereotypical on the other. My point is that the situation made me deal with three identities at once: post-colonial, first-generation, and African-American. This is a painful thing to do. Each identity is sharp and unfinished. Each has a hyphen—a dash about breaks and omissions: a stroke, for the missing. For people who were enslaved and colonized, and for their descendants, the convergence of hyphen-identities amasses shards, smashed pieces of personhood. It does not suture the self.[5] We were odd for staying, but we would have been odd for going. We were, 'of course,' the black family who couldn't get it together.

It was around this time that the significance of the trove of travel effects started to shift for me. Pieces were prompts, then portals, and I went.[6] I met ancestors and stumbled on their relocations, generations of lives truncated in the making. I found interruptions and itineraries not taken. I mined cancellations. Personal roots were in the route stuff my parents saved. The artifacts allowed me to cross thresholds, rendering the lowest point the runway's ends. They gave bearings. Present in the presence of a moving past, I learned and lifted a thing or two, and took them back to the ordinary world as a weapon. We were *of course*. We were a black family in the Americas. We were descended from the Middle Passage. We were made out of movement. I wanted to make sense out of that.

⤶

The decision to pursue anthropology and history was easy. History sought differences in similarities. It situated stories about people, practices, and places in time. It created chronologies for them, arrangements that could authorize the contextualization and comparison of experiences and events. History made actual imagined unknowable pasts, like parts of my own past, feel less lonely.[7] Anthropology sought differences too, calling them forth for familiarity's, not similarity's sake. It crossed cultures and contrasted expressions of human creativity. It poked around the everyday and turned ordinary into odd and odd into ordinary. My discomforts delighted in this.

But the disciplines dealt in different domains. History mainly prioritized a then and anthropology mostly privileged a now, though crucial crossovers did happen.[8] The distinction was disquieting. The disciplines seemed to need and thus created otherness, as they studied 'other' times, 'other' spaces, 'other' places.[9] The elsewhen of histories and elsewhere of ethnographies were realms removed from the here and now of their writers and readers.[10] It was a segregation of sorts, and it didn't suit how the ancestors and descendants of the Middle Passage *got* going. In this African diaspora, supposedly separate futures, pasts, and presents coincided. The creative manipulation of time and space was a survival strategy for the muted ways in which racism worked through the mundane.[11] A black girl on Long Island moved mentally through corridors of imagination, met her long-dead Caribbean kin, who then taught her how to live. Alone, the disciplines could not account for lives lived like this. Anthrohistory at once opened up.

The approach of anthrohistory was manifold, labyrinthian in its possibilities and potentials.[12] It was transdisciplinary, "not quite of two disciplines, not quite bridging them, not quite between them, and not quite aspiring to any of these postures."[13] It worked through imagination, an authentic space to play seriously with misfit ideas, awkward practices, and experimental forms. In serious play, archives could be field sites (and vice versa); pasts could be presents, could be futures, and all of them could be long ago, living, and dead. A fragment, a gap, a trace, a rhetorical question, an ambiguous word, or an unfinished moment could be combat matter to disrupt dominant exclusionary ways of knowing and being in the world.

~

The 'almost, but not quite' of anthrohistory is unsettling. It upsets conventions and seeks room, new ways to know and be known. If the market or disciplines insist on turning this much sought-after space into a place, let the walls of the room be "limited only by our imaginations."[14] In a world rife with drones and deportees executed on the fly, one advantage of standing on shaky ground is the ability to apprehend the opening of *up*. Another is the set-up: a little book that is loving because it hopes to be outside—and not just out of—the violence that informs it.

OPENING UP

Level

1

The afternoon flight from Barbados to New York was full of black and brown elders that day. On board the packed plane they sat in the sun and waited on the tarmac for the situation to end. A slightly drunk college-aged white man from the United States was refusing to stow his computer bag, delaying takeoff. The police came. The man continued to insist on keeping his laptop on his lap. Some thirty minutes had passed before the teeth sucking began. The loud, unmistakably West Indian sound was a clear sign that the other air passengers had just about had it. A crewmember told them to be quiet, all the while trying to reason with the man. Imagine if he was black, an old woman said to the person sitting next to her. They would've kicked him off a long time ago. Chances are she was right. But he wasn't, so they didn't.

2

The women, men, and children watch them coming in across the sea to land on their island. They point and say here comes (insert a person's name). They refuse to see black travel in terms of ships of any kind. People and not planes descend from the sky.

1

Groundwork

A Willingness

"The sky grew Caribbean" is tucked away in the poem. In *The Prodigal*, Derek Walcott writes a world for a wanderer who wrestles quietly with the wrath and waltz of history and memory. The traveler is a contemporary Caribbean man who crisscrosses Europe and the Americas. As he moves, he encounters African elements and espies the residue of empires. The history of slavery and colonization slips into living memory; the weights of racial oppression accompany him now. They tint but do not taint his understanding of foreign places. He looks at the Hudson River and beholds a conquered continent. He listens to the canals of Amsterdam and hears mercantilist expansion. He watches the sun irradiate Italy, sees the sky turn Caribbean, and discerns subjugated and slaughtered beings.[1]

The traveler experiences and explains the quotidian transatlantic from the vantage point of the Caribbean. For him and for this book, the Caribbean is a place and a position. As a place, it is an archipelago, islands whose pasts and presents are nested in historical realities like slavery, emancipation, colonization, migration, and liberation.[2] As a position, it is a strategic orientation. It is a way of *sensing* the African diaspora in or alongside events, instances, experiences, and occurrences that appear to have nothing to do with the diaspora; like, for instance, looking at the beautiful Italian sky, perceiving the Caribbean, and recalling past genocides and wars. Resonant with W. E. B. Du Bois's notion of second sight and Fernando Ortiz's concept of transculturation, the act of sensing is subtle, sometimes slight, always suspicious, thus strong. A consciousness and approach forged in but turned against Enlightened thought, it is occasionally suspect.[3]

Yet it is through insecurity that seemingly incongruent stories integrate.[4] A willingness to hold *certain* ways of knowing lightly lets the European-American sky grow Caribbean. It summons Suzanne Césaire's call for "permanent readiness," a plea for imagination as revolt against all forms of domination.[5] It situates the advent of modern airborne mobility in the reverberations of Middle Passage, a goal that defines the focus of this book.

The Stories

This book tells two tales together—stories so ostensibly disparate that one wonders why they should mix. One is about the origins of airline travel. The other is about the terrains of racial oppression. Their pivot: empire, an ensemble of ideas and practices assembled by states for ascendancy.[6]

Early airline travel reshaped the composition and experience of empire. It ushered in new ways to imagine and inhabit space, time, and place. These innovations must be understood in relation to race. Racialist thoughts, tendencies, and transactions influenced the development of the nascent technology. They were also altered by it. The opportunity to gather the history and anthropology of airline travel and the history and anthropology of racial oppression is an opportunity to think differently about current global movements.

Subject Matter

I do things in this work that may disturb. This book is not a traditional history or ethnography. It is an anthrohistory that leans toward creative nonfiction. I splice archival, ethnographic, and other sources together. I slide among futures, pasts, and presents. I prioritize the imagination, occasionally seeing it as a place to do fieldwork. My scope is sweeping on the one hand and constraining on the other. It spreads out to glimpse how racially oppressed people and people in racially stigmatized places have long envisaged and experienced air travel. It zooms in to explore how the relatively recent arrival of commercial aviation changed lives and life chances along the transatlantic corridor of the African diaspora. Britain and its Caribbean colonies are this book's particular focus. British Airways is a focal point.[7]

The motivation to research and write in this manner and on this topic is twofold. First, it stems from the way we have—and have not—

considered the role that race played in the inception of the airline industry. A 'romance of the air' has tended to monopolize popular understandings of aviation in the early twentieth century.[8] Countless books, movies, and other mainstream media have portrayed the period as a golden age: glamorous, luxurious, adventurous, heroic, and white. They have depicted fliers as singular men, women, and companies that battled against and triumphed over nature; that disappeared with courage and died for progress; that became national and imperial icons. These types of narratives have eclipsed other stories. Their pervasiveness has left little room to *sense* how people and places of color advanced aviation at the outset.[9]

There are exceptions. There are accounts of the achievements of black women and men during this time. They have concentrated primarily on the pioneering efforts of military and civilian pilots.[10] They have documented how individual aviators struggled to overcome racial and gender exclusion.[11] Their contributions have been invaluable. They have stood apart, separate from while still part of the general history, like a special topic.

Second, the motivation stems from the emancipatory potential of transdisciplinary exchanges. African diaspora scholarship and scholarship centered on aviation are, undeniably, interdisciplinary bodies of knowledge. Each one contains works from a wide range of fields, a growing number of which draw on multiple disciplines.[12] Both of them revolve around and contend with a similar core subject: movement. They unwittingly share many sources, among them surrealism, science fiction, and futurism. Yet they rarely converge, the space between them signaling ineffable assumptions about who will (or can) research and write about a topic.

But what if they did? What if parallel lines of inquiry let loose, experimented and played openly with each other? For some of us, an assemblage of things such as liberation poetry and the physics of flying may express how we feel the realities of physical displacement. For others, it could explain why they see planes and not people in motion when they watch jets cross through the sky.

The crucible of transdisciplinary exploration is permeable. It acquires and releases storytellers and storytakers from an array of times and places. As one of them, I offer an analysis of early airline travel in this book that includes the Middle Passage and its descendants. The combination illuminates vital links between empire, aviation, and diaspora as lived relations. It provides initial insight into everyday practices and racial subjugation in flight, a relationship whose continuing echoes are still at work today. This book draws attention to the enduring ways in which ancestors taught scions how to soar. The aerial presence of some diasporic subjects—dead kin and dying deportees; black bodies viewed from on high; stowaways falling from the sky—raises a question about what befalls humanity aloft. The search for answers begins by exploring how we got there in the first place.

Empire

In the early twentieth century, the geography and the geometry of empire changed. The emergence of new forms of artificial flight revolutionized the movement of people, objects, and power. The ability to move in three-dimensional space unlocked the degrees of freedom that dictate motion, increasing our capabilities to maneuver from one and two to three sets of direction.[13] The opportunity to rise above the limits of the ground and advance untethered through the air gave empire-states the chance to expand upwards, extend outwards, and execute downwards. The sky, which had long been an imperial frontier, a fictional setting, a sacred space, was now an actual human dwelling place.[14]

Empire is in the air. It would be a mistake to say that empire is air: it is not uncontained, intangible empty space. It is not deterritorialized to the point that it cannot be held accountable.[15]

The idea that aerial empires are political entities found voice in James Baldwin's preface to *Notes of a Native Son*. In the spring of 1984 Baldwin sat in Amherst, Massachusetts, and wrote several pages about his exasperation with structural racism in the United States. He began with a discussion about why he became a writer, a decision fueled decades prior by a desire to make black histories matter. When Baldwin finished the recall, he returned to his present and wondered if race relations had truly changed over time. His thoughts moved decisively from the transatlantic slave trade to the persistence of white supremacy; from the taking, buying, and selling of people and land to the taking, buying, and selling of air. They created a chronology that helped him to conclude:

the foundations of racial oppression had shifted somewhat and super-ficially. As Baldwin put it, "Neither did the savages in Africa have any way of foreseeing the anguished diaspora to which they were about to be condemned. . . . Nothing in the savage experience could have prepared them for such an idea, any more than they could conceive of the land as something to be bought and sold. (As I cannot believe that people are actually buying and selling air space above the towers of Manhattan.)"[16]

Air is territory. Some territories are real. Some territories are imag-ined. Baldwin saw that air, a natural resource, had become commercial space. It was valuable, a commodity not unlike those tied to slavery. But before the twentieth century, before empires and enterprises took the air, the air was refuge for citizens of the African diaspora. It was a place where black people went to escape the tyranny of everyday life.

Diaspora

Vessels helped make, remake, and maintain the African diaspora. Con-versations about mobility in the diaspora have noted the importance of water- and land-based vehicles: the slave ships of the Middle Pas-sage; the freedom tracks of the Underground Railroad; Marcus Garvey's black-owned and -operated ocean liner; Rosa Parks's unwillingness to move to the back of the bus.[17]

I was puzzled when I learned that winged passage had received mini-mal consideration. Black people have long seen the sky as sanctum, cou-pled flight with self-determination, and linked ascension to liberation. People enslaved in the Americas found hope in the Flying Africans, a set of stories about 'New World' slaves with souls that rose up and went home to Africa. The North Star guided fugitive slaves to freedom.[18] Du Bois was "in a region of blue sky and great wandering shadows" when he lived above racism. Toni Morrison created Milkman, a character who understood his blackness best when he was "in the air, away from real life." Sun Ra, George Clinton, and Lee Scratch Perry thrust their way into outer space, the ultimate unfettered place.[19]

The imagination was their means of transportation, much like it was for the traveler in Walcott's poem. It was a human-powered carrier, con-spicuously absent from the usual list of vehicles: ships, trains, cars, carts, bikes, and planes.

Key visionaries of black consciousness used creative energy to stretch the boundaries of diaspora. They used it to include (and reach) the realms of the above. The air, the sky, and the universe were liberating and otherworldly. They were more than conduits, more than mere spaces through which things move. They were inhabitable, emancipated places.[20]

Ancient black aerial culture reconfigures the iconic geometry of the transatlantic slave trade system: the triangle.[21] It outspreads the apex upward to involve the sky in the setting of the Atlantic world. It re-*shapes* power and reroutes us, broadening our ability to discern dynamic systems. Remember these old air dreams of the diaspora. It is important in a book about contemporary commercial flight.

Terms and Conditions

There are two types of aviation: military and civil. For reasons soon to become clear, an imperial history of the former tends to overshadow a colonial history of the latter. Airline travel is a form of civil aviation, though what sets it apart from militarized flight is increasingly unclear.[22]

There are also two types of aircraft: lighter-than-air and heavier-than-air. Lighter-than-air crafts are generally buoyant. They include aerostats such as the blimp, hot air balloon, and dirigible. Heavier-than-air crafts typically gain their thrust and lift from engines. They include machines like the helicopter, space shuttle, and airplane.

The commercial airplane transformed transportation. Access to airspace and accelerated speeds reduced transit times. The decrease in the amount of time required to circulate goods reduced the amount of time capital remained in the commodity form, which quickened the production process.[23]

The commercial airplane also changed communication. Initially, airlines carried mostly mail and other cargo. Increased pace moved information faster. Letters, newspapers, and other documents reached readers sooner. Costly ticket prices and limited seat capacity ensured that few people flew as passengers.[24]

Transportation and communication networks were integral to colonial empires. They helped to build, sustain, and destroy them. Talk about these moving forces often treats the onset of heavier-than-air travel as the foregone continuation of imperial journeys made by water and land. It is almost as if things were different on the one hand (e.g., new technology) but the same on the other (e.g., foreign domination). There is a quiet danger in this line of thought. It leads us to run the risk of describing rather than deconstructing colonization—of naturalizing rather than denaturalizing race. The airplane, literally, relocated empire; it repositioned how and *where* race was made.

I read the history and anthropology of civil aviation and I *feel* the silence that surrounds the construction of race. There is an abundance of critical histories about controlled, powered flight. These histories are committed to the deep interrogation of many significant subjects, including commerce, gender, globalization, identity, invention, labor, modernity, nationhood, ownership, sexuality, and statecraft.[25] They include a small, but growing, set of scholastic engagements with colonial empires, civil aviation, and their entangled pasts. Like recent works about belligerent flight, they are cultural histories that underscore state-driven expansionist urges.[26] They tackle race and avoid the tinge of nostalgia that pervades aviation in the popular imagination. However, a tendency to gaze on blackness and lose an explicit analytical grip on the production of whiteness or conceptual grasp of the category of race remains strong.[27]

Meanwhile, many anthropologists have studied fliers such as witches and spirits. Not many have studied mechanized flight. Those who have have been apt to forgo the past and focus on present-day forms of aviation.[28] They have examined incidents that pertain to the existence of culture aloft. But without historical context, we are left with questions about the emergence of the existence itself. How did culture become airborne? How did airborne movement become ordinary? How did people learn to live with aerial assaults? How did people learn to live, however fleetingly, in the sky?

Full-on anthropological enquiries into air culture are few, but references to air travel in ethnography are many. There are ample descriptions of anthropologists flying to and from field sites. Airports and airplanes turn up in articles and books about migration, human organs, tourism, humanitarian aid, security, empire-making, and waiting.[29] The appearances are brief yet suggestive of aviation's cultural significance. A longer, centered, interpretive look at air travel and its connection to the everyday is needed—if only to shake off the feeling that airline tripping is a means to an end, unremarkable and inherently familiar.

Research

I arrived in Barbados in the early 2000s with the hope that I would write a historical ethnography of British Airways in the Caribbean. My intention was to focus on colonial agency. I wanted to foreground how black West Indians shaped the development of *the* British airline. I wanted to show how people who were colonized both created and challenged a seemingly national technology and its identity.[30]

Barbados was a good place to start. The country was a former colony with an established relationship with the company. It was, for instance, one of the few places to which the famed Concorde flew. I conducted extensive archival research. I spent lots of time in the airport. My research broadened; I went to other islands; I pursued fieldwork *in* the air. I had many conversations, including exchanges with government officials, nongovernmental organizations, private pilots, returned migrants, and airline executives, passengers, and crew. Over time, six of them would shift how I understood my project.

Two were about the experience of flying before and after emancipation from Britain in the 1960s. They called attention to the Americanization of Britain's Caribbean colonies; the affective work of colonialism in-flight. In one conversation, a retired government official contemplated "the great days of Pan Am [Pan American Airways] in this region." He asserted, "Pan Am did more for us than [the] British."[31] In the other conversation, a returned migrant remembered flying from Barbados to Britain in the early 1960s: "It was a great opportunity to start a new life. It was a colonial thing. Colonial experience ties you to Britain. I went by BOAC [British Overseas Airways Corporation] via Bermuda to London to Edinburgh. I remember flying over the red roofs of Edinburgh."[32]

Then there was the airline executive who talked about the Britishness of British Airways. In one instance, she aligned the airline with the nation. "People will fly British Airways because it is Britain on a plane. . . . The expectations are that it is British," she said. In another instance, she aligned it with the empire. We were discussing local operations and regional development when she mentioned that most major international airlines "pulled out" once colonies became nation-states. Her airline stayed. It "divided the [region] into three clusters: North Latin America, South Latin America, Caribbean." Traces of imperialism wove through our time together: the airline as Britain; the geographic manipulation of foreign areas; the strategic study and careful commodification of other cultures. "BA [British Airways]," she proudly noted, "now has a better feel for customs and has worked towards sensitizing its crew towards cultures and cultural differences. The music and entertainment on routes are specifically designed for that route in an effort to promote regional offerings."[33]

Other conversations focused on routes, lingering colonialism, and race. A woman complained about flight patterns and fares. The fact (or feeling) that flying from the Caribbean to London was cheaper than flying from the Anglophone to the Francophone Caribbean offended her. She was "quite upset" that "the colonial routes were still maintained."[34] The air routing of the region also frustrated a man with whom I spoke who directed a nongovernmental organization. The lack of "links between Africa and the African diaspora" concerned him. He wanted a "direct airline linkage between Barbados or the Caribbean and West Africa." He was acutely aware of the material and symbolic importance of uninterrupted air travel in the African diaspora. It meant less journey time and straight, unmediated ties to an imagined homeland. "Right now for Caribbean people to get to Africa," he lamented, "we have to go through either the United States or Britain, a very long journey through Britain." A direct air line was an opportunity for black people to be in the above; to move physically and mentally over, and not just across, the Atlantic Ocean, a place steeped in the history of profound, violent rupture.[35]

The sixth exchange was about the preservation of memory and the production of history. I met with an older man who spoke candidly about his desire to save and share early aviation stories. He talked about death: "I think that the sad thing in our region is that the history of aviation is slowly being lost because it is in the minds of people. Few of us remain. A lot have passed on and that information has gone on with them." He discussed documentation and asked for official papers. The request resonated with the history of people enslaved and forbidden to write. He insisted, "Governments in the region should take stock of the situation and see to it that this history of development is written, is there for the children or grandchildren to have access to."[36]

Needless to say, my project changed, slightly. There were moments in each conversation that inspired me to see British Airways and West Indian agency differently. Some were about the things that happened: Americanization ("the great days of Pan Am"); verticality ("flying over the red roofs of Edinburgh"); postimperial Britishness ("it is Britain on a plane"); and flight paths ("the colonial routes were still maintained"). And some were about the things that were not there: routes ("Right now for Caribbean people to get to Africa") and historical permanence ("the history of aviation is slowly being lost"). What began as a historical ethnography of an airline became an anthrohistory about presence and absence in air culture. In other words: this book examines what is and is not there.[37]

Part of the history of British Airways lies in the Caribbean. It consists of fragments. The pieces are minute, inconspicuous, and sharp. They could sever constructed truths. The airline began as Imperial Airways in the 1920s, turned into the British Overseas Airways Corporation (BOAC) in the 1930s, and became British Airways in the 1970s. When people talk and write about the company in the Caribbean, they often focus on its second and third manifestations. This is understandable. The airline implemented sustained air services in the region after the Second World War.

But operations started earlier, on paper and in plans. The Caribbean played a small yet significant role in the making of Imperial Airways, the airline that would become British Airways. There are piles of archival documents about Imperial Airways. In them, the Caribbean appears here and there, in moments, such as a phrase in a paragraph of a long speech. At first glance, the references seem negligible. The bulk of information concerns airline initiatives in areas that greatly interested the empire-state, namely Asia, Africa, Australia, and the Middle East.[38] Still, the Caribbean was considered. A slow exploration of instances that look short and minor lifts up the significance of these contributions.[39]

There is a section in *On the Natural History of Destruction* in which W. G. Sebald suggests that the erasure of individual moments is part of the perverse violence of aerial warfare and its histories. He offers a careful argument about the immediate and long-term eradication of lived experience. As he reflects on the air raids on Cologne and Dresden during the Second World War and thinks about "destruction, on a scale without historical precedent," he explains: when a fleet drops tons of bombs and causes a single catastrophe, the single catastrophe is forgotten; the next destructive fleet has already arrived and caused another catastrophe. The "annals of the nation" amass the catastrophes and treat them as a generalizable whole. The particular is lost, though not necessarily forever. Sebald tells us that "scarcely a trace of pain" is left behind in the process of generalization. The particular may be minuscule, but it is still there.[40]

Salvage and Restoration

The Caribbean and its fragments occupy an odd and awkward place in the book. At times they feel peripheral to Britain, an entity which convention has taught people to envision as whole. This book is not alone in its unevenness. In his famous Nobel Prize speech, "The Antilles: Fragments of Epic Memory," Walcott describes imbalance as intrinsic to the "restoration of our shattered histories, our shards of vocabulary, our archipelago becoming a synonym for pieces broken off from the original continent." (The "our" refers to members of the Caribbean's African and Asian diasporas.) Through a series of elegant images, he turns love into a diasporic method: love is a way to grasp the slivers of things that survived the destructive nature of colonialism. It begins as perception. "Break a vase," he says, "and the love that reassembles the fragments is stronger than that love which took its symmetry for granted when it was whole." Then, in the context of diaspora, it becomes technique: "The glue that fits the pieces is the sealing of its original shape. It is such a love that reassembles our African and Asiatic fragments, the cracked heirlooms whose restoration shows its white scars." Here, love is a strategy that allows for an imperfect mending of the diasporic past. It is a recuperative act that includes the exposure but not the resuscitation of imperial whiteness.[41]

Love is also an inheritance. "This gathering of broken pieces," Walcott discloses, "is the care and pain of the Antilles, and if the pieces are disparate, ill-fitting, they *contain* more pain than their original sculpture, those icons and sacred vessels taken for granted in their ancestral places."[42] Without a doubt, the love that collects and rebuilds in the archipelago includes, holds, and restricts hurt. It emerged in connection with enslaved and indentured labor. It was akin to what Sidney Mintz identifies as "the process of creolization" in the Caribbean: "an attempt by the victims to respond creatively to their condition," a way for people who were enslaved to "figure out how to retain and restructure their humanity under the most trying conditions in world history."[43] People made music, created poems, and danced in spite of the weight of oppression, their traditions inconspicuously kept, invented, coded, and bequeathed in a phrase, a beat, and a step. They generated lightness, a diasporic gift that has helped Caribbean people to find and write their histories in the residual heaviness of institutional practices that exclude them. "In the grace of this gift," remembers Walcott, "a boy opened an exercise book and, within the discipline of its margins, framed stanzas that might contain the light of the hills on an island blest by obscurity, cherishing our insignificance."[44]

It is through this love that I locate my interpretation of Imperial Airways in one of the conceptual homes of the African diaspora: the black Atlantic. Its transnational approach offers a way to go beyond the conventional borders of a region and un-imagine the Caribbean, Africa, Britain, and the United States as discrete bounded units. Its cross-temporal framework offers a way to bring together, and close the gaps between, far-flung points in time. And the word 'black' makes it difficult to ignore how race fueled the formation—the initial creation and lasting configuration—of airline travel. In combination with 'Atlantic' it also signals a multiverse that includes slave ships en route from Africa to the Americas, progenitors of the African diaspora, generations of their descendants, and aerial life *over* seas.[45]

The black Atlantic is multidimensional. It possesses a spacetime that is, as Michelle Wright theorizes with transdisciplinary wonder, less linear and more "Epiphenomenal" in the twentieth century.[46] Accordingly, it contains a kaleidoscope of relationships that the overlapping fields of African diaspora and black Atlantic studies have seen as what Wright calls vertical (aka hierarchical) and horizontal (aka peer). And yet the "image of ships in motion across the spaces between Europe, America, Africa, and the Caribbean," which Paul Gilroy put forward in a well-known passage of *The Black Atlantic*, stands as "a central organizing symbol."[47] It is an important and powerful image. It invokes the Middle Passage and evokes the transatlantic slave trade. This book does not seek to replace or abandon it. I want to add aircraft to it. The airplane in vertical and horizontal motion through the sky transformed the directions and the dimensions of human movement in the twentieth century. The image of airplanes soaring above ships gliding across the ocean captures the geometry, the physics, the velocity, and other vectors of transatlantic affairs. The image restored to its cultural and historical contexts shows its asymmetrical scars.

The Chapters

This book brings together race, empire, and airline travel. They come together to present the colonial origins of Imperial Airways. The chapters pull together subjects from those six pivotal conversations: identity, diaspora, documentation, skyways, foreign elements, and lives overhead.

Chapter 1 sketches some of the circumstances that surround the start of Imperial Airways. It provides a frame of reference and it is, intentionally, short. It aims to bring context into view without casting it as a fixed condition, a thing of fact that can weigh down, squeeze out, or outright flatten the minutiae of a moment. There was drama in the decision to make a government-backed airline and the transatlantic pops up in it. Too much attention to an overarching 'history' could submerge the drama and puncture the pop, so to speak.[48]

The next two chapters examine what is not there. They are about race, a construction often analyzed in terms of appearance, not disappearance in airline travel. The third chapter concerns speed and the velocity of empire. It aims to understand how speed lost its sense of slowness and became synonymous with fastness. The fourth chapter explores how the first generation of airline travelers experienced distance (i.e., high-speed) and direction (i.e., speed-up). It examines the physical void between people in the air and people on the ground, and discusses the reorientation of human relations. Together, the chapters show how racial inequality came to—and was remade in—the sky. They illuminate the origins of the links between ordinary airline travel and global white supremacy.[49]

Air routes are the focus of chapter 5. The first part of the chapter asserts: paths that connect points of arrival and departure are lines of

power. They indicate agreements and coalitions, which is to say part-
nerships with a past. The second part of the chapter puts this point into
practice. It takes on the creation of a major Anglo-American air route,
an alliance that called for the collapse of a local airline in the colonial
Caribbean. Recalling Walcott, it is a story about the importance of insignificance, the rebuilding of which redefines the concept of failure and
reorients the transatlantic map.

The aftermath of the colonial airline's demise is the subject of chapter
6. The chapter concentrates on the impassioned debates that led to the
government's decision to nationalize Imperial Airways. A close reading
of the parliamentary record reveals that one reason why Imperial Airways became the British Overseas Airways Corporation and eventually
British Airways was in the Caribbean. An exploration of pauses, inter-
jections, and laughs exposes a faint uneasiness with twin obligations:
nation and empire. The concern was that the state had developed the
colonies more than the mother country.

The Conclusion returns to airline travel nowadays. It addresses race
and the remnants of empire in the air. Some of its pieces pertain to British Airways and the Caribbean while other fragments in the book deal
more broadly with the commercial aviation industry. All of them involve
the African diaspora in some way. They gesture toward the resonance
of historical racism enmeshed in the banalities of contemporary flight.
There are uncertain traces that are hard to ignore once they are sensed.
The feeling that airline travel and racial oppression go together is one
of them.

Limit

1

The men are on the sea somewhere near Dominica. They are aboard *Flight*, which is a schooner in Derek Walcott's "The Schooner Flight." A jet zips loudly over their heads, "opening a curtain into the past." One says to the other, "One day go be planes only, no more boat." The other says to him, "Vince, God ain't make nigger to fly through the air." They move on.[1]

2

According to Facebook, he liked two things: AARP NY and American Airlines. That's about right. He worked to retire. He worked to get home. Before he stopped talking, he said he wanted to go to where he came from, which was Trinidad, and that never happened. Born hot in Sand City, he died cold in New York, a jet passing over his head as he travelled then passed. The sky. His limit.

2

Ascent

Artificial flight has captured the Euro-American imagination for centuries. Daedalus and Icarus created wings of wax in ancient Greek mythology. Wayland the Smith covered his clothes with bird feathers and soared in an old northern European tale. Bladud, King of the Britons, fashioned a pair of wings and flew from Bath to London in the ninth century. The Anglo-Saxon monk Eilmer of Malmesbury made a parachute-like device, leapt from a tower, and survived in the eleventh century. Roger Bacon, a Franciscan monk, wrote extensive scientific theories about flight in the thirteenth century. In the late fifteenth century, Leonardo da Vinci designed several aerial contrivances, including an ornithopter, glider, parachute, and helicopter. In the early sixteenth century, Giovanni Battista Danti, a mathematician, used feathered wings and iron bars to make a flying machine. Then, in the late eighteenth century, the Montgolfier brothers launched large, untethered hot air balloons in France; large, untethered hot air balloons floated above French Caribbean colonies by the close of those years. In nineteenth-century England, Sir George Cayley theorized the physics of modern flight and published a set of scientific papers on aerial navigation; William Samuel Henson and John Stringfellow proposed an aerial transport company and patented a steam-powered, fixed-wing monoplane. Across the Atlantic, airborne assaults occurred on a large scale for the first time. During the opening years of the twentieth century, rigid airships flew; a controlled and sustained heavier-than-air powered flight with a pilot finally happened.[1]

The modern airplane was primarily employed for pleasure and military purposes before the end of the First World War. Air races and air shows, the feats of early aviators like stunt pilots, daredevils, and skywriters, helped popularize this form of flight. Brazen aerobatics and occasional deaths turned the airplane into a titillating, twisted spectacle.[2]

The aerial campaigns of the war complicated general perceptions of machine-driven flight. The first-time combination of lighter-than-air and heavier-than-air vessels militarized the skies. Its onslaughts on landscapes and lives shifted the spectacle from thrilling to murderous.[3]

The end of the war was, as Maurice John Bernard Davy witnessed, "the beginning of a new phase" in aviation history.[4] Companies and governments in Europe and the Americas were keen to create systematic commercial air transport services: they were eager to make new markets amid the social, political, and economic ravages of armed conflict. They repurposed bombers and other belligerent machines, refashioned them as passenger planes to be flown by former battalion pilots. Executives "turned their eyes towards air transport as a contemporary method of converting swords into ploughshares," R. E. G. Davies said fittingly.[5]

The United States, Netherlands, Germany, France, and Britain were in the vanguard of commercial flight. The St. Petersburg-Tampa Airboat Line launched the world's first scheduled airline service in January 1914. It was a short-lived company that moved payloads between Floridian cities before the war commenced. After the Armistice, the Dutch airline KLM Royal Dutch Airlines and the German outfit Deutsche Luft-Reederei offered air passenger services. A French concern called Farman also operated passenger services in early 1919.

Airline operations in Britain began when Aircraft Transport and Travel inaugurated a regular passenger service from England to France in August 1919. It was one of the first of its kind in the world: international and scheduled. Over the course of the next four years, other airlines were created in the country. Handley Page Transport launched in September 1919. Instone Air Line got underway in 1921. Daimler Airway started in 1922. The British Marine Air Navigation Company arrived in 1923.

The British government was ambivalent about commercial aviation, notwithstanding that more and more people in the postwar nation liked it. Discussions fraught with unease about government subsidies for the new enterprise developed.[6] The state had long invested, financially and culturally, in the maritime and railroad industries; however, other states had begun to bolster commerce by backing heavier-than-air, civil air transport companies. The Air Ministry was determined to work it out— would British airline travel be publicly or privately owned? It hosted three conferences, convened a committee, and undertook other endeavors.[7] Specialists and experts offered advice. The government made a decision.

The Thing about a Decision

The decision itself was important. But the decision-making process was meaningful too. Conference records and the committee report show that several issues were involved. Some make sense for a postwar government with imperial world power: money, utility, longevity, nation, empire. Others, like civilization and the transatlantic, are slightly more peculiar.

The first conference took place in London 1920. There, the Controller-General of Civil Aviation, Major-General Sir Frederick Sykes, presented a paper on the merits of airline services. He set a mood that felt dour and foreboding. "Let us have no illusions about the difficulties confronting civil aviation," he cautioned grimly. "Never has the need of national retrenchment been greater, and it is clear that financial stringency will increase rather than diminish."

But Sykes was an advocate for commercial flight and the three rhetorical appeals of ethos, pathos, and logos were his persuasive strategy. He pushed for a sensible commitment of funds by promising a rich future to a country presently down on its luck. He carefully described the industry as in "its infancy." It would "wilt" without "visible public support" from the government. It needed backbone—"the British characteristic to persevere in the present"—to grow. It required nourishment to thrive, which he hoped would come in the form of imagination, money, and encouragement. In short: commercial aviation was the nation's baby. It would mature and provide "productive services" if it was raised right by the state.[8]

Two years later, the call for support continued. At the second conference, the conversation expanded to include twin concerns about the status of the nation and the security of the empire, ideas which delegates couched in the racially coded language of advanced social development. "What has civil aviation done for civilization," asked Lord Weir of Eastwood, a former Chairman of the Air Council who proudly saw himself as "intensely pro-aviation." A subsequent string of quick phrases left little doubt. Civilization meant Britain. See, Weir wasn't concerned with what the 'civil' in civil aviation could do for humanity (i.e., possibility). He wanted to know what it would do, was doing, and had done for the country (i.e., certainty). "What is it at present capable of doing," he questioned right after he asked about civilization. "In Great Britain the aeroplane has been unable to demonstrate its practical utility, commensurate with the cost, for any purpose whatever," with the exception of an air service to France.[9]

Weir wasn't the first person at the second conference to mention civilization. The Under-Secretary of State for Air, Lord Gorell, did so during the morning session on opening day. He gave a long paper that put forward the Air Ministry's attitude toward civil aviation. The argument unfolded quietly: his slowness of thought let slip the racism that was there. It began with a declaration. Britain was "an island Empire" with a "natural genius for flying." After that, a discussion came, exploring aviation and "progress in the United States, the chief continental powers, the Dominions and this country." A few words about imperial air services followed. They rendered "the least civilized part of the Empire" unfit for the "expenditure of public money" from the government.[10]

The tale Gorell told chronicled a familiar story with some slight twists. The account was about global inequality, unaltered yet intensifying—the same, changing.[11] The declaration, for example, reinscribed. It revived an old notion, namely, Britain as innately superior and technologically advanced, a conviction used for centuries to enable and excuse the subjugation and exploitation of people, territories, and their resources. The declaration also remapped. It elided deep-rooted distinctions between nation and empire. The latter was no longer out there, in the world, as a thing that Britain owned. It was now not an overseas unit ruled over by an imperial nation. Rather, in this instance, the nation itself was empire.[12]

The idea of Britain as an island empire might have had another meaning. In 1906, around the time when Alberto Santos-Dumont, the aviation groundbreaker from Brazil, launched the airplane in Europe, the prominent British newspaper proprietor Lord Northcliffe famously remarked, "England is no longer an island." He, and others after him, said the phrase to suggest that the airplane had ended isolation, the ideated separateness imagined through the physical separation of an isle from places beyond its borders. It exposed the below from above, imperiled the efficacy of sea power and protection, abiding cornerstones of British influence and identity. Perhaps the discursive turn to island as empire answered and ablated public disquiet about vulnerability with an invocation of supreme political strength. "There is no doubt," noted Gorell, "our national situation has already been greatly changed, and in the future will be still more changed, by the growth of aerial activity, and that it is a simple truism that we have now ceased to be an island."[13]

The discussion then conjoined. It aligned the island empire with particular international forces. These were established and emergent perceived sites of progress: the United States, core European countries, and the dominions. The reference to "the Dominions"—recognized at the conference as Australia, Canada, New Zealand, Newfoundland, and South Africa—was a well-known cipher for the white, self-governing realms of the British crown.[14]

The words that followed *addressed* the colonies.[15] They spoke of and to them; classed, ranked, and valuated them. The colonies—"the least civilized part of the Empire"—were set apart from and worth less than white spaces. The refusal to fund them evinced the modicum of responsibility and obligation the empire-state bore for the formation of commercial aviation in its colonies, if only for a moment. Gorell carried on, insisting that the military finance and operate imperial air services. Paradoxically, he stood firm on the fact that "public money" must not be given. A further complicating matter was that the Royal Air Force fell under his office's authority.

The argument for militarized colonial development, steeped in discrimination, did not go unchallenged. A few men favored plans that culled taxpayer money from military and civil aviation budgets. They warned, "The integrity of the Empire would be most gravely imperiled" without widespread contributions. They reflected on transportation and "the making of nations," remembered roads and the "greatness of the Roman Empire," and reminded the government of its "duty" to country and colonies.[16]

A more muted defense of combined efforts came from Sykes in a measured statement that tendered the colonies a means to an end. His steadfastness to commercial flight, so plainly exhibited at the first conference, persisted intact. This time, though, Sykes invoked the memory of a very specific imperial history as he sought to build a civil aerial nation. Deftly, he worked both sides of the debate. He dubbed himself a "purely detached and uncritical spirit" and pushed for and against commercial aviation in the colonies. He led with a look "at the main problem as to how best to ensure for Great Britain and the British Empire the sovereignty of the air." (The line showed balanced concern for comparable power for both domains.) He kept on speaking. He aimed for supremacy, "like the sovereignty which since the days of Elizabeth she has held upon the seas." The assertion, which directly followed his earlier utterance, summoned old images of an era touted as the great, golden age of *English* exploration and expansion, the progenitorial base of the empire. The nod to origins was subtle; an old school understanding of ownership, hierarchy, and rule metonymically roused. It was a hint of a reminder of British power and its fount: England.

Afterwards, the thoughts expressed continued to couple nation with empire, except that now the 'internal empire' within the British Isles had quietly entered the conversation. Sykes returned to the trope of the child. During the first conference, when he wielded it, he styled commercial aviation as a young one to rear. At the second, he did something similar. Commercial aviation was still "a child as yet." These days, though, he gave it an identity and called it a girl. Sykes mobilized this gendered tweak to "plead for something greater than a measure of financial support." "Freeing her of the blighting incubus of military end-all and be-all" would, he foretold, "allow her to go her own way as a peaceful, not unproductive, sister." It was a labyrinthine claim full of interpretative twists and turns, each one leading out to the same time to come. Commercial aviation: a female sibling or youthful comrade trapped in the dominance of a violent and damaging, somewhat sexualized, masculinized, and demonized, nightmare. Liberated, she would be fertile and constructive, "a potential asset of incalculable value." She would answer the question that followed his assertion, "The air knows no boundaries, and Great Britain and the Empire are therefore no longer protected by their engirdling seas; air power is therefore a necessity. How best can this be attained?"

The colonies were an afterthought. "I have said nothing of what commercial aviation may do within the Empire," noted Sykes near the end of his statement, the reference to imperial interiors a signpost of occupied places with subjected people. He carried on, "of what indirect advantages it may confer by speeding up that all important question of communications." Having remarked on the incidental pluses of flight, he stopped. That was the whole of what Sykes said about the colonies. A single idea, one sentence long.[17]

The first and second conferences were infused with such murmurings and audible silences. The days were undeniably filled with talk about material value, technological constraint, symbolic promise, and political significance for nation and empire. But the version of empire envisioned with the nation while planning was a different kind of global Britain. It was less about imperialism through colonialism and more about imperialism through other means.[18]

The shift in political imagination was pervasive, gradual, and slow. It took hold in and was strengthened by deliberations over the construction of British aviation in general and transatlantic connections in particular. Comments about the Atlantic threaded through the records, often in tandem with sentiments about profitable alliances, urgency, and the United States. Sykes alluded to them at the initial conference. He touched on commercial aviation from "the Imperial point of view" and argued, "The onus of linking up the Empire by air must not rest upon Great Britain alone." "There are within the various countries of the Empire," he acknowledged, "considerable opportunities for practical development," several of which were in the Caribbean. "At present the West Indies are suffering from the lack of inter-island communication, both for mails and passengers, and this can be partially rectified by an air service for the Leeward, the Windward Islands and the Bahamas, and between the Bahamas and the American Continent." Britain would get steppingstones to the United States, people in the Caribbean would benefit some, and colonies in the West Indies would suffer less.[19]

At the next conference, Lord Gorell called attention to transatlantic affairs and necessity. (Remember, he was the one who rallied behind teaming up with international, not colonial forces.) He encouraged the growth of air routes to continental Europe and urged delegates to focus on that first. "This country," he explained to them advisedly, "suffers under certain disadvantages." Location was at the top of his list. Size and weather followed suit. "Unless and until aeroplanes can safely negotiate the Atlantic—expansion of transit by aeroplane is restricted to the south and east." A year later, at the third air conference, during an exchange about routes to Paris, Constantinople, and Moscow, he would make the same point with a bit more bite. "It is along those three arteries that development must take place over the world from England, because England is unfortunately situated in having no possibility, until trans-Atlantic Flight is practicable, of going westward."[20]

The pronouncement was bold. There was a sense of an undercurrent of interest in securing global power, underscoring the importance of the transatlantic, and ensuring the centrality of England. It fit: throughout the course of the conference, there was a substantial amount of conversation about the colonial empire that existed and the noncolonial empire that could be. Spokesmen for the former wanted an "Imperial air route" to and within and through the dominions, protectorates, and colonies. They coveted faster movements, reduced distances, and accelerated communications and trade. They proposed a resolution, which passed, and its terms made the government responsible for the institution of an all-empire airmail system. They wished for an imperial air route with southern legs from London—Paris, the first step; from there, the Middle East, Africa, South Asia, and the Pacific. Spokesmen who gravitated toward the latter mode of sway wanted much of the same. They desired shorter travel times. They aspired to gather speed. But they also pursued a velocity that was at odds with the other vision. The way their imperial air route would carve through space was a marked difference. They pressed for legs from London, with easterly branches forked across continental Europe. The Middle East, Africa, South Asia, and the Pacific would evolve in the wake of essential mainland lines. They didn't deny the foreseeable merits of a southern network of routes. They simply stressed the conceivable magnitude of an eastern one, while they waited for feasible transatlantic flight to begin.

"Develop the air properly," Gorell angled, a tad slyly perhaps, as he compared people traffic to the transport of goods. The instruction came after he pushed for routes "over the world" via Europe. There was a right way to build the air, and it involved the development of a direction. Indirectly but explicitly, the expression was a comment on access—about who or what could travel *that way*.[21]

The Decision

In January 1923, a month before delegates at the third air conference met, the Secretary of State for Air, Sir Samuel Hoare, created the Civil Air Transport Subsidies Committee. He named the president of the Institute of Bankers and deputy chairman of Barclays Bank, Sir Herbert Hambling, chairman. He asked the Hambling Committee, as it was commonly called, "to advise on the best method of subsidising air transport in the future."[22] Their job was to answer the subsidy question.

The committee met fifteen times in two months. It heard from airline operators, consulted with aircraft manufacturers, and conferred with many other groups. A week after the third air conference ended, Hoare received the committee's final report. The recommendations included government acquisition of current commercial aviation operations and the creation of a new airline, an "organization run entirely on business lines" and not "administered under Government control." The company would have a "privileged position" with respect to subsidies and routes.[23] The government would recognize it as "the chosen instrument of the state," and it would function like a monopoly.

Hoare, in his position as president of the Air Council, agreed to the formation of the Imperial Air Transport Company on December 3, 1923. Among the numerous stipulations were four noteworthy clauses. The directors, shareholders, and registered aircraft of the company had to be British. The government had to supply a direct subsidy of £1,000,000 divided up and administered annually for ten years. The company had to operate an air transport service across Europe, east to the Black Sea. It could establish air services within the empire, if it liked.[24]

The company was incorporated on March 31, 1924. Imperial Airways began the next day.

DIRECTION

Speedbird

1

The operational call sign for British Airways, Speedbird, was also the iconic company logo of Imperial Airways. Theyre Lee-Elliott, a noted English artist with a distinctly modernist style, created Speedbird for the airline in 1932. The design was simple: an acute angle with sharp, thin, and straight lines that met in a point, like a chevron. The meaning was straightforward. The symbol stood for the swiftness of flight. Its pointy sleek shape helped Speedbird to look like the common swift, a bird reputed to be among the fastest birds in level flight. Its name called to mind quickness and mastery over nature, which helped to denote power and technological modernity. Speedbird signaled supremacy in the sky.

From Imperial Airways through BOAC to British Airways—from colonialism through decolonization to imperial postcolonialism—Speedbird has endured. The symbol remained relatively intact until the 1980s, when it was redesigned and renamed Speedwing. The new emblem retained the sharp straight lines and point of its predecessor, and had a shape that looked markedly like Speedbird's wing. A decade later Speedwing turned into Speedmarque, which is what is used today. The lines are sleek but curved, and the sharp point is gone. But the overall effect of the image continues to evoke the mark of Imperial Airways.

Over the years, the embodiment of 'speed' has transformed from bird to wing to marque. The call sign, however, has remained the same: Speedbird. Its "spirit," British Airways has said, "lives on."[1]

2

The Errol Barrow statue in Bridgetown is bronze. A couple of thousand pounds heavy, it stands several feet tall. The man it remembers is one of ten National Heroes in Barbados; he was the first prime minister, the famed father of the country's emancipation from Britain. This particular likeness of him is in Independence Square, a solid presence in an open-air public arena. It faces the buildings of Parliament, which are coral limestone and gothic revival. It overlooks what is between them: the waterfront around the Careenage, a place to bring in and let leave commercial goods, including, centuries ago, people who were slaves.

Behind the statue, on the busy road behind the square, is a barely gray multistory building with offices and stores. The roof is flat with an overhang, which juts out just a bit. Along the front of the overhang, large and thick navy blue letters, widely spread and evenly spaced, spell out Speedbird House, which is what the building is called. Two Speedbird icons flank the name, etching Imperial Airways' long-standing logo and British Airways' operational call sign into the capital's center.

Barbados declared its independence from Britain on November 30, 1966. The next day, Speedbird House opened its doors.

3

Speed

The news came on the cover of a vibrantly colored brochure, which doubled as an advertisement. Imperial Airways was "Speeding Up the Empire" (see Figure 1).

The image on the front cover was a scene, active with people on the go. There was *Canopus*, an empire-class flying boat shown on arrival at some nameless, tropical place. The silver and steel airplane was moored. A slew of passengers alighted on translucent blue water, which undulated calmly, and boarded a smaller, but presumably still mechanized, red-trimmed brown boat. Nearby, in an even smaller rowboat, a figure stood and steered with a long straight post. Pink hibiscuses and blood orange flowers, palm-like leaves, and a woman's face in the foreground

Figure 1. "Speeding Up the Empire," poster, 9A00689, NASM.

edged what unfolded on the water. The passengers were white and modern: the figure and the face were black and not.[1]

By the 1930s, which was when Imperial Airways put out the image, a tradition for illustrating the black colonial world was firmly in place. It was well known and long established across Greater Britain, especially when it came to depictions of the tropics.[2] Nineteenth-century advertisements in and out of England liked to portray equatorial lands and their inhabitants as liminal, as well as dark. They were spectacle, their contrived images mingling race and sex with jingoism to sell products like soap. Ads were profitable spaces where "the non-western world—whether the warm South or the sensual Orient—is idealized and eroticized on the one hand as a paradise on earth, and on the other hand rejected and condemned."[3]

"Speeding Up the Empire" drew on these common tropes of "exoticization, racialization, sexualization, commodification, and civilization."[4] It visually marked and marketed airline travel as imperial travel by replicating racially charged conventions. The topography it authored betokened a picturesque, tropical paradise. The romanticized story-bound landscape it described was unmistakable. It was the alluring exotic, the colonial tempting and far-flung. The sunlight, weather, water, and plants appeared unending, hot, lucent, and verdant. The intricate arrangement of beings and things turned some people into black locals, their maybe naked bodies and skin offered up as sexualized counterpoints to those of the commercial air travelers. (They disembarked on arrival fashioned and barely exposed.) The craned neck, crimson lips, and direct coy stare of the black woman enticed and invited onlookers to participate then and there in this familiar strange fiction.

The cover unfolded stories that dealt with history and time.[5] The careful manipulation of orientation and scale transformed the image of three water vessels into two progressive teleological tales. To some degree, they were a history of the present for people back then. One narrative opened chronologically forward, from the perspective of the external viewer. It was a linear account of advanced technological change. The smallest boat kicked off the story. The physical might of a black, presumably native man, was its motor. The idea of him turned the boat into a primitive apparatus. It gave way to the second, slightly larger instrument of travel in the scene. This vehicle was still a boat.

But it seemed more modern than the first. It was in the middle, located between the other two liners. It carried the British civil air ensign; it flew the official flag of the air. The second boat bridged the technological past with its future: *Canopus*. The visual timeline culminated in the Imperial Airways flying boat. Powered by four engines, tagged with the British ensign, *Canopus* was the largest and most modern of the three.

The second story unraveled chronologically backward, from the perspective of the air traveler who was disembarking. It was a circular tale about imperial time. It began with the arrival of the flying boat. As the visual moved from the image of the most modern carrier to the image of the most primitive boat, the trajectory of technological advancement reversed. The airliner had landed in another place; the airliner had entered a past time. Imperial Airways, in other words, sold time travel. It took passengers back. The second boat then was a go-between. It ferried passengers from the modern flying boat to the elsewhere and elsewhen, which the mooring and rowboat represented. But the story did not end with arrival. This narrative culminated in *Canopus*, too. It was the 1930s. The advertisement was for a relatively new transport service. A story about white travel to the black unknown had to conclude with an unseen but implied return trip home.

The pictures joined the airline and the modern. The text linked empire to the pair. The words in the advertisement described empire in two ways. First, it was wherever. Late Victorian and Edwardian period adverts for imperial tourism tended to focus on travel to a single colonial region (e.g., Africa); this ad seemed to suggest imperial air travel gave access to all areas at once. Through letters it mapped the routes of Imperial Airways, some of them to places that were not official British territories. Empire could be almost anywhere in the world, all together reachable by air: "Europe, Africa, India, The Far East, Australia, Bermuda, New York."[6]

The reference to foreign countries and a city as parts of empire was odd. It hinted at several things at the same time, a network of ambiguous tensions possibly among them. The physical borders and boundaries of the current empire could be expanding. The idea behind empire itself could be shifting.[7] A decentered international empire could be developing, key questions about ownership, responsibility, and accountability rising with it. To whom would this empire belong? Would it still be British?

The second way the words in the advertisement discussed the outward extension of political power offered clues. Empire had a rate (a frequency, a price, a pace) and it was speeding up. The cause was not named, though the visuals seemed to say the airplane was the instrument and the airline was the agent. The airliner was literally the driving force for speed, up: the rate an object travels distance (speed), and the rate an object travels distance with direction (velocity). It was also a driving force for speed up: acceleration, the rate an object changes its velocity. The change in speed and direction, *of course*, occurred over time.

But what exactly did it mean for an empire to change direction as it gathered speed? What follows explains why "Speeding Up the Empire" was a consequential slogan, then as well as now.[8]

Speed Empire: Now

We often take speed to mean the rapidity of movement. It is a common synonym for fast, fastness, quickness, swiftness, hurriedness, and haste. Slowness is its opposite. "These days, the whole world is time-sick. We all belong to the same cult of speed. . . . Why are we always in such a rush? What is the cure for time-sickness? Is it possible, or even desirable, to slow-down?"[9]

Carl Honoré asked those questions in a book with two English titles. In the United States, it is called *In Praise of Slowness*; it is named *In Praise of Slow* everywhere else. In the renaming, slowness and slow are interchanged, even though they are not one and the same. (Nowadays, 'slowness' is a noun, a word for a thing. 'Slow,' on the other hand, is a noun, a verb, an adjective, and an adverb—it is a word for it all.) For Honoré and others, the veneration of speed is pandemic. It is driven by what defines it, an unabated appetite for fastness. The addiction to speed feels inescapable and everlasting, a sickness, as Honoré put it. The panacea: the deceleration of everyday life.[10]

References to obsession, violation, and decay frequent the literature on speed in the twentieth and twenty-first centuries. "The New Speed is perceived as the symbol and substance of our new freedom," commented Juan Alonso as he expressed concern for how the persistent hunt for more rapid ways to be alive is transforming humanity. Those who want to go faster search nonstop for instantaneity, to "go faster and faster from here on until Time itself flattens out into an immediate present which never ends." They revere immediacy, endlessly imbibing "darkly dry, electric speed juice," making themselves "feel excitedly on the point of being able to rape Time itself."[11]

The ravage of time has cautious appeal for some. In the early winter of 2002, Klaus Schwab, the founder and president of the World Economic Forum, spoke with David Gergen, an editor-at-large for *U.S. News and World Report*. The topic of conversation was the troubled state of the global economy, which had started in 2001. Gergen asked Schwab if calamities such as recession and terrorism were "just a rough patch, or is something more fundamental going on." "Fragility," Schwab replied as he thought about economic transactions synced around the world in real time. "With globalization we have much more synchronization— this is the first really synchronized world recession. A second factor is speed, time compression, mainly driven by technology advances."

Schwab was concerned about the aftereffects of speed. The contraction of space by time allows the global market to transact simultaneously, without delay. The ripple effects, whether gainful or disastrous, are quick moving. Reverberations from the collapse, crash, or implosion of one country's financial system can instantly go global and grab hold, which was partly what happened in 2001.

Ultimately, though, Schwab tentatively praised speed. He carefully discussed the effects of time reduced and distance obliterated throughout the interview. Gergen posed his final question. He asked him to reflect on the present from the future. "How do you think we'll look back upon the 21st century's early years?" Schwab began positively, "It's the first time in the world when to a large extent we can determine our own and our children's fate. So it depends whether we recognize that we live in a global village, that we must act together as a global community." But he ended ambivalently, "If we do, then I feel we'll look back and say, we are living in a more peaceful world than 20 years ago. If we don't, I think the world will become more and more gefahrlich, which means more and more dangerous."[12]

Awkward relationships with speed overlap with complicated relationships with power. Paul Virilio, in his smart works on the "dromocratic" revolution and wars of displacement, aligned speed and militarization. He questioned why modern states habitually long for acceleration and persistently seek out its technologies. "Speed is the hope of the West," he resolved. It is a strategy loved for its near-instant, immediate facilitation of the subjugation of others. Both its mastery and the mastery over it execute real-time violence no matter the distance. Joysticks moved and buttons pushed in North America steer missiles and drop bombs from drones over South Asia and the Middle East, also without delay.[13]

Speed is private power, too. It is unapparent, intimate, and from within. In 1984, when Italo Calvino thought about writing *Six Memos for the Next Millennium*, he set out to find the indispensable peculiarities of literature. Quickness—"the speed of thought"—was one of the six essential qualities that he found: lightness, quickness, exactitude, visibility, multiplicity, and consistency. Calvino marveled at the agility of the imaginative mind as it jumps from thought to thought, pushes the pace of energy, feeds on the kinetic frenzy of ideas in formation. Mental speed is creative power. It is swift and digressive and at war with mechanical speed. This is "an age when other fantastically speedy, widespread media are triumphing, and running the risk of flattening all communication onto a single, homogenous surface." Clocks and other devices have "forced speed on us as a measurable quantity." Mental speed, Calvino hoped, could be a form of human resistance, "valuable for its own sake, for the pleasure it gives to anyone who is sensitive to such a thing, and not for the practical use that can be made of it."[14]

Speed is biopower, so clearly enmeshed in and exercised through modern transportation modes. New ways to move faster—especially on rails, roads, and in the sky—changed how people felt about and felt distance, movement, and time. Three gendered archetypes of these physical and affective shifts are Wolfgang Schivelbusch's train-man in the nineteenth century, Milan Kundera's motorcycle-man in the twentieth century, and Roland Barthes's jet-man after him. The first two feel the fast pace act on and then in their bodies. (A person who walks or runs feels the fast pace of and in their bodies.) They experience what Kundera called "ecstasy speed," a transcendent state of intense emotion. Speed is something different for the jet-man. It is not "an experience, of space devoured, of intoxicating motion." It is "only a condition." The jet-man moves super fast but feels nothing between taking to the air and coming down to land, turbulence aside. The "paradox," Barthes explained, "is that an excess of speed turns into repose . . . a coenaesthesis of motionlessness (*'at 2,000 km per hour, in level flight, no impression of speed at all'*)."[15]

A sentence slid into Kundera's *Slowness* brings us back to the politics of speed. "There is a secret bond between slowness and memory, between speed and forgetting."[16] That speed means fastness for many people is not very surprising, and neither is the idea that speed goes hand in hand with power. Numerous sources attest to this, including the ones above. That speed does not have a sense of slowness when commonly used and understood is something of note. Speed is a rate, a measure. It can be fast and it can be slow. The predominance of one meaning over the other is peculiar and, perhaps, it unsettles some.[17] A sliver of its processual cultural creation returns to the historical flinders of imperial racism and airline travel. As Michel-Rolph Trouillot said: "Terminologies demarcate a field, politically and epistemologically. Names set up a field of power."[18]

Speed Empire: Then

Our understanding and experience of time and space were dramatically transformed during the first decades of the twentieth century. David Harvey described the years between 1910 and 1915 as the "second great wave of modernist innovation." Around then was when: Albert Einstein published his first and second papers on relativity (1905 and 1915); Émile Durkheim published *Elementary Forms of the Religious Life* (1912); Henry Ford introduced and then used the assembly line (1913); the Paris Observatory, by means of the Eiffel Tower, sent a radio signal to the United States for the first time (1913). Each of these and other works were in that second wave. The first had come with the compression of time and space in the mid-nineteenth century; the second, through the acceleration of time, or speed up. "The fact is that around 1910 a certain space was shattered." It was the year, Virginia Woolf determined, that the "human character changed."[19]

Futurism was central to the widespread cultural shift into speed up. On February 20, 1909 the French newspaper *Le Figaro* printed the first "Manifesto of Futurism" on its front page. Filippo Tomasso Marinetti, a wealthy Egyptian-born Italian poet, wrote it. He outlined the principles of the movement in the manifesto, which he aimed at writers and other artists.[20] Futurism called for a fervent rejection of the historical past. It demanded a total embrace of the modern city, the invigorating energy of industrial society. It trashed everything that smacked of stasis. It welcomed violence, destruction, and the explosive absurd in its stead. It upheld speed while it held speed up as dominion over nature. The first principle announced: "We intend to sing the love of danger, the habit of energy and fearlessness." The second decided: "Courage, audacity, and revolt will be essential elements of our poetry." The third declared: "We intend to exalt aggressive action, a feverish insomnia, the racer's stride, the mortal leap, the punch and the slap." The fourth proclaimed: "We say that the world's magnificence has been enriched by a new beauty; the beauty of speed." The next six: praised invention, applauded poetry, justified aggression, adulated "eternal, omnipresent speed," hyped war, and authorized misogyny. The last one, the eleventh, hailed a long triumphal list of fast technologies. It ended: "the sleek flight of planes whose propellers chatter in the wind like banners and seem to cheer like an enthusiastic crowd."[21]

Speed defined as fastness was ingrained in the movement. Adherents of futurism exalted celerity in their artistic expressions. Their writings, paintings, and sculptures, as well as their musical compositions and architectural designs, worshipped what they saw as the beautiful elegance of high speed. It was religion, blessed and scripted.[22]

In the spring of 1916, during the First World War, Marinetti wrote and released "The New Religion—Morality of Speed." It parodied Judeo-Christian ideals and promised to "defend man from the decay caused by slowness, by memory," like a holy text. It fastened speed to forgetfulness and fixed slowness to remembrance, the precursor of what Kundera said. It toyed with the sacred-profane dichotomy, which Durkheim had introduced four years before in *Elementary Forms of the Religious Life*. The savior, "*Speed*, having as its essence the intuitive synthesis of every force in movement, is naturally *pure*." The devil, "Slowness, having as its essence the rational analysis of every exhaustion in repose, is naturally *unclean*." The scriptures, "After the destruction of the antique good and the antique evil, we create a new good, speed, and a new evil, slowness."

Speed up was god. Futurism was a liturgical faith. Technology was the altar to the "holiness of wheels and rails." There, in supplication, "One must kneel on the tracks to pray to the divine velocity. One must kneel before . . . the highest mechanical speed reached by man." Possession, "the intoxication of great speeds . . . is nothing but the pure joy of feeling oneself fused with the only *divinity*." The pulpit preached and the congregants learned, "If prayer means communication with the divinity, running at high speed is a prayer." To be and go faster without cease was the futurist path to the god speed.[23]

The incessant desire to increase the speed of ordinary life was not separate from the incessant desire to establish the supremacy of people over time and space. Futurists wished for more than the compression or other such manipulations of these phenomena. They longed to *over*come time and space through the divine, speed. Technophiles, futurists were devoted to machines, their vehicles for god. They sought fresh ways to convey mechanized dynamism, the movements—whirrs and hums—and rhythms of trains, cars, ships, and planes. In February 1910, for example, the authors of the "Manifesto of the Futurist Painters" pledged to "breathe in the tangible miracles of contemporary life—the iron network of speedy communications which envelops the earth, the transatlantic liners, the dreadnoughts, those marvelous flights which furrow our skies, the profound courage of our submarine navigators."[24]

Futurism glorified modern conveyances; in particular, it was in awe of aircraft. Its artists paid little attention to lighter-than-air innovations, like the rigid airship. They were enraptured by heavier-than-air, fixed-wing, powered flight. The airplane, which was less than six years old when Marinetti penned his manifesto, was one of their two ever-changing icons of modernity. (The automobile was the other one.) Futurists, forward-looking and fast speed-obsessed, anticipated with excitement the newfangled aerial dreams of the next generation. "Our successors will rise up against us," Marinetti longed. "They'll see us huddling anxiously together besides our airplanes, warming our hands around the flickering flames of our present-day books, which burn away beneath our images as they are taking flight."[25]

The airplane remade mobility in a manner that thrilled these artists and shaped their politics. It was a cutting-edge breed of fast travel, from their point of view. Other modes of transportation shrunk the relative temporal and spatial distances between places through the horizontal manipulation of mostly land and water; the airplane did so through the vertical manipulation of mainly air. Futurists were acutely aware of air travel as more than speed up. They reveled in the fact of the matter: air travel was truly speed high and up.

Adoration of the change in the direction of speed coincided with a belief in a racial hierarchy of speed. A few months after the first manifesto appeared on the front page of *Le Figaro*, Marinetti released a second piece of written work. "Let's Murder the Moonshine" was an orientalist allegory of the high-tech demolition of nature told through a simple story about the slaying of moonlight. It raved about the airplane and the murderous delights it gave. The parable recounted the adventures of the madmen, a hodgepodge of young innovation-devoted Europeans who lived in two old innovation-averse cities: Gout and Paralysis. The men felt trapped by stagnation and decided to flee from inaction. They "crossed the ruins of Europe and entered Asia." There they took trains on military tracks "down one peak and up another, casting themselves into every gulf and climbing everywhere in search of hungry abysses, ridiculous turns, and impossible zigzags." They went "head-over-heels into Hindustan," with "vehement locomotives" which leapt over the Ganges and climbed up the Himalayas. As they in their fast trains caught sight of the Indian Ocean "slowly [stretching] its monstrous profile," a madman begged with urgency (and Marinetti punctuated accordingly): "Hurry, my brothers!—Do you want the beasts to overtake us? We must stay ahead, despite our slow steps that pump the earth's juices. . . . To the devil with these sticky hands and root-dragging feet! . . . Oh! We're nothing but poor vagabond trees! We need wings!—Then let's make airplanes."

The madmen made "futurist planes" and colored them a mimetic blue—"blue, the better to hide us from the watchful enemy and confound us with the blue of the sky." They turned "the ocher-colored cloth of sailing ships" into tail-steered, sky-blue biplanes with eight cylinders, eighty kilograms, one hundred horsepower, and "a tiny machine gun."

The madmen took off, camouflaged. They ascended in "intoxication" and shouted "Hurrah!" from planes, which zipped across and darted above "enemy hordes" on the ground, beneath them. "Look down, straight down, among the masses of greenery, the riotous tumult of that human flood in flight!" They climbed, "up 800 meters! Ready! . . . Fire!"

The European air travelers relished "the joy of playing billiards with Death!" It was high speed, and they were straight, up and over South Asia.

The airplane opened the grave precision of straight-line travel over heads. The fabled madmen in flight basked in their ability to look and fire straight down. Vertical speed and earthbound detachment also pleased them, as did the distance created by the physical gap between people airborne and grounded. "Look!" they ordered. "There are the hordes! There, there, ahead of us, already beneath our feet!"[26] Marinetti via the madmen made these claims about direction, span, and pace before fixed-wing aircraft were rolled out as weapons in the First World War. During the war, he amplified his claims about the significance of air travel and its horizontal straight-line advantage. He boasted: "Tortuous paths, roads that follow the indolence of streams and wind along the spines and uneven bellies of mountains, these are the laws of the earth. Never straight lines; always arabesques and zigzags. Speed finally gives to human life one of the characteristics of divinity: *the straight line*."[27] The airplane didn't appear overtly in the passage; but the passage did plainly appear in Marinetti's treatise on speed and religion-morality. The airplane was in the image of the god speed offering humans the straight line. (Recall: It was the airplane that saved European madmen from "ridiculous turns and impossible zigzags" and let them shoot straight down and kill effectively and efficiently, in "Let's Murder the Moonshine.") Air travel, ripped from the ground, gave three gifts: swiftness, altitude, and a skyline.[28]

Speed Up, Slowed Down

Futurism was more popular in the United States, Russia, and continental Europe than it was in Britain. British artists viewed speed and mechanical power differently, and the movement's affiliation with fascism was a problem for many of them.[29] Wyndham Lewis, a well-known British painter and writer, was one vociferous opponent. His rants were infamous. He railed against Marinetti in his autobiography, which, published in 1937, circulated widely. Early on in the book he described a fight that erupted between them. The men had run into each other in London. It was sometime before the war. Marinetti delivered a lecture, walked into a bathroom, turned to Lewis, and called him a futurist, which pissed off Lewis. Lewis snapped back: "No." "It has its points," he acknowledged, "but you Wops insist too much on the Machine. You're always on about these driving-belts, you are always exploding about internal combustion. We've had machines here in England for a donkey's years. They have no novelty to *us*."[30]

It was bigoted, nationalist talk. Wop was an ethnic slur, an offensive epithet for Italians, and donkey's years slang for a long time: the superiority of British people and English ingenuity was implied.

The social politics Lewis attached to and expressed through his art were similar to those of futurism. Around 1914, on the brink of war, he formed an avant-garde art group whose charge was to show the dynamism of modernity and technology. Vorticism, like futurism, focused on motion, the direction of movement, and speed as themes, though their motivations and methods set them apart. It was not irrelevant the vortex took as their focal point: chaos and kinetic energy as controlled, ordered forces, which meet and fuse at the center, made sense for a British group.

National context shaped the meaning and experience of those themes. The squabble in the bathroom illuminated, for example, the interplay between nation and speed. Lewis claimed to "loathe anything that goes too quickly." He *felt* that acceleration led to absence and blindness. "If it goes too quickly, it is not there," he complained before he continued, "I cannot see a thing that is going too quickly." Marinetti said the opposite. He *felt* that acceleration led to presence and awareness: heightened, it sharpened the senses. He reproached Lewis with national bias: "You have never understood your machines! You have never known the *ivresse* [intoxication] of travelling at a kilometre a minute," he accused before he declared, "It is *only* when it goes quickly that it *is* there!" "You *do* see it. You see it multiplied a thousand times. You see a thousand things instead of one thing," he lobbied. Marinetti called Lewis "a monist" before his last insult landed: "What a thing to be an Englishman!"[31]

Of course, those might not be the exact words. Lewis relayed them in his autobiography, after all. That said, the men bickered a lot about travel and rapidity in public; the point about nation and speed stands. The discussion between Lewis and Marinetti was partly about how fastness related to slowness. Both men were advocates of speed up; however, they wanted different versions of it. The distinctions were framed by, understood through, and signals of the nation. One wanted quickness. His speed was Italian. The other had British speed. He wanted quickness, but he wanted it slowed down. The first version of fastness had no room for slowness, the second one did. In Britain, speed as fastness had a sense of slowness *within* it. This was not quite the case for the colonial empire. There slowness was *outside* fastness. Unequal, they were inextricable.

Apprehensions about extreme fastness remained part of British life through the end of the First World War. These concerns tended to cluster around ideas about travel, much like they did for Lewis and Marinetti during their row. They often involved apprehensions about vehicles and loss.[32] In *The Thirty-Nine Steps*, for example, John Buchan, a Scottish novelist and unionist, had his protagonist Richard Hannay use somewhat slow methods of transport to safeguard military secrets for Britain. Hannay rode an "old bicycle," drove a "40 h.p. car," and took "the slow Galloway train." At one point, he tried to hide in the rural countryside, a place where he found calm and relaxation and felt safe. Hannay, about to lounge around, looked up "into the blue May sky," saw an airplane "climbing into the heavens," and felt his pulse race for two reasons. He thought the plane was after him. He was sure it had destroyed the countryside, a beloved part of British identity and life, "chosen for refuge"— especially for the English. Hannay, maudlin in edgy tension, decided, "Those heather hills were no sort of cover if my enemies were in the sky." "I must," he concluded, "find a different kind of sanctuary."[33]

The plane overhead meant exposure and erasure. It passed across as it moved above the countryside, in ascent, toppling mythical promises and disturbing national symbolism. The idea of the countryside had long been linked to notions of protection, romance, security, tradition, history, and the slow life. The airplane, more than other rapid-transport vehicles, threatened this. The combination of how and where it moved were among the things that made it different. Men, for instance, chased Hannay by train and car, but only the one in the plane made his pulse race. When he encountered the airplane again, after the countryside episode, his body responded to the fast-paced maneuvers and off-the-ground position of the machine. "Just then I heard a noise in the sky, and lo and behold there was that infernal aeroplane, flying low, about a dozen miles to the south and rapidly coming towards me." The plane gave pursuit, and Hannay took flight. "Down the hill I went like blue lightening, screwing my head round, whenever I dared, to watch that damned flying machine." He arrived at a road, which led to a little, narrow river, and entered "a bit of thick wood." (Buchan had him reach that road "soon.") In the dense small forest, Hannay "slackened speed."

The two bodies were both in flight. Their juxtaposition provided a comparison of two versions of fastness in Britain. Hannay as well as the airplane moved quickly: everything about the scene was fast. It was no coincidence that the airplane appeared suddenly, that Hannay reached the road before long, that his slow down happened in sheltering woods, and that "speed" did not denote fastness but referred to rate alone. This was not an instance of contrast wherein the airplane was fast, the man on foot slow. It was a moment when regional and directional differences seemed to matter more: air/land, below/above, up/down, under/over.[34]

Airborne creatures and things have floated in British skies for centuries. Early concerns about them focused less on rate and more on hover and height. They shaped perceptions of airspace in the British imagination. Traces of some impressions have lingered across the years. Early in the eighteenth century, Jonathan Swift dreamed of air attacks and vulnerable skies in his satirical works on state power, reason, and science. In *Gulliver's Travels*, the king of Laputa, which was a floating island in the sky, dropped large heavy stones on his subjects when he wanted to punish them. The vast majority of them lived directly under him, in a dominion on the ground. When they rioted or refused to pay a tax, they were "pelted from above with great Stones, against which they have no Defence." The aerial attack destroyed their houses, the roofs bombed by rocks, "beaten to Pieces." More resistance, and the king threatened "the last Remedy." It was an act that would entail "letting the Island drop directly upon their Heads, which makes a universal Destruction both of Houses and Men."[35]

Expressions of fears about the consequences of violent falls from the sky continued through the nineteenth century, at times as satire or with humor. In August 1802, Mr. Garnerin, a man known for his air balloon excursions, lifted off from Vauxhall Gardens with his wife and another man. When they reached "a considerable height," Garnerin attached a parachute to a cat and dropped it. Its fall from the balloon was "gradual and perfectly safe"—for the cat. It landed in the garden of a Hampstead man, who demanded compensation "for the indemnification of the trespass committed." The cat had intruded on two pieces of private property: the land and the airspace above it. English common law held that a person owned what was above and below as well as what was on the ground of their estate.[36]

Height as measurement, area, and medium fascinated people. It was cruel pleasure for people like Garnerin. It was blended knowledge for others. When James Glaisher, a nineteenth-century meteorologist, rode balloons for atmospheric observations, he marveled at the mix of scientific and cultural knowledge that height gave him: "at a distance of 11,800 above the earth, that a band was heard; at a height of 22,000 feet, a clap of thunder was heard; and at a height of 10,070 feet, the report of a gun was heard."[37]

On top of that, height was strategy. A few years before Garnerin's cat fell down, state-sponsored aerial warfare began. The cultural significance of altitude above ground level—the vertical distance (depth) between an aircraft in airspace and the terrain below—was starting to change. The French were the first to use lighter-than-air crafts as weapons during war. They used balloons for aerial reconnaissance over the Austrian army at the end of the eighteenth century. Then, early in the course of the next century, armed forces throughout Europe and the Americas used balloons to bomb, transport, communicate, and spy. Britain was late to start. Military balloon training didn't begin until the 1880s, and, though it deployed multiple balloon sections during the South African War, the empire-state preferred to use land and sea forces to constitute and maintain supremacy, as it had done for hundreds of years.[38]

Tentative enthusiasm toward actual flight continued into the early twentieth century in Britain. Fascination with altitude above ground level went with it. In time, tentativeness shrank, but fascination did not. Its grip on imagination tightened. The technology of flight advanced: interest in rate grew.

For instance: Large, elongated, cylinder-shaped, rigid bodies of airships captured people's interest, as they wondered and worried with rapt attention about the war dangers and travel delights of these streamlined aircraft. Their remarks often drew attention to features such as buoyancy, lifting gas capacity, and hull span; those about rate were apt to discuss speed as lacking or slow. In 1907, Baden Baden-Powell wrote a chapter for *A Short History of Balloons and Flying Machines*. In it, he described the size of airships with technical detail: "a large airship 164 feet long, and containing 224,000 cubic feet of hydrogen." He used unspecific terms to discuss their speed: "none accomplished a greater speed or distance" and "not attaining any great speed, and usually being carried away by the wind."[39]

The discourse of speed shifted from slowness to fastness alongside the development of the modern airplane. Speed started to eclipse height in the discourse of travel alongside the development of commercial aviation. Meanwhile, altitude above ground level was ensconced—but not indelible—in the public imagination, and it continued to hold fascination for people. Rate and direction were done together, knotted.

This was speed-up. It was an amalgamation of speed, up (rate, direction) and speed up (acceleration). The trifecta of rate, direction, and change helped another three amass power in Britain: airline, speeding up, empire.

"Speeding Up the Empire"

Nearly five months after the Treaty of Versailles was signed, toward the end of October 1919, the first British Secretary of State for Air, Winston Churchill, received a relatively short report from his newly formed Advisory Committee on Civil Aviation. The document, which was six pages long, pertained to the development of imperial air routes. In a couple of years, there would be several, much longer documents on this topic like those from the three air conferences analyzed in chapter 2.

This report was special. It was one of the first to wonder why an empire-state should concern itself with civil aviation in its colonies. (Later ones focused more on would, a word that did not carry the same sense of obligation with it.) It was one of the few to seek answers by taking air itself seriously. The committee's job was to determine "how best to organize Imperial Air Routes." That imperial air routes would exist was implicit in the charge. Nevertheless, the committee asked: Should the empire-state make "use of the air element for everyday commercial purposes?" The report presented readers with doubt.[40]

It was a moment. Air travel was being envisioned as an everyday, commonplace, not unusual occurrence. Ordinary air travel, which was not an actuality, was separate from the cultural cult of imperial oppression. Their union was not predestined, unavoidable, or inevitable: The report was a small, weighty piece of what led to their fusion.

There were eleven men on the committee. Most of them were prominent military leaders, reputed aeronautical experts, or Conservative party politicians. Several would participate in the three air conferences on government-sponsored commercial flight. Some would be well-known figures in aviation history. The chairman was Lord Weir of Eastwood, late Secretary of State for the Royal Air Force, according to the report. The vice chairman was Sir James Stevenson, a member of the Army Council and the Air Council. The others were Lord Inchcape of Strathnaver (chairman of British India Steam Navigation Company and P&O Steam Navigation Company), Sir Arthur Robinson (Secretary of the Air Ministry), Colonel John Moore-Brabazon (member of parliament), Charles I. de Rougemont (chairman of Lloyds Bank), H. White-Smith (chairman of the Society for British Aircraft Constructors), L. Bairstow (professor of aerodynamics), Air Marshal Sir Hugh M. Trenchard (chief of the Air Staff), Major-General Sir Frederick H. Sykes (Controller General of Civil Aviation), and F. G. L. Bertram (Air Ministry and secretary for the committee).

The men set out to figure out what advice they would give as a committee. Speed-up was key, as they explored whether Britain should use air for empire, and if so, how. For them, air was not a surface *on* which to act, as with water or land. It was an element *in* which to act *through*. And, for empire, "the element in which the air has the advantage over other means of transport," they agreed, "is speed."

The committee was clear about air. "There is a future for the development of the air as a new means of civil transport and communication." Air was a medium, and it was an area to occupy—*move into*, take over, inhabit.

The committee was less clear about empire. The report began with a statement of clarification: "The Committee understand the designation, 'Imperial Air Routes' to mean routes which will enable the new transport element, namely, air, to be made use of in speeding up communication between the various portions of the British Empire." That the second sentence supplied a definition was not remarkable. That the definition was so overtly discriminatory was. A route was imperial when air could be used to speed up some—but not all—parts of empire. The committee was of the opinion that the state should pursue "flying supremacy" with the formation of imperial air routes between Britain and the dominions, aka the white empire: Canada, Newfoundland, South Africa, Australia, and New Zealand.[41] It added India and Egypt to the list. The first had secured limited self-government as of that year. The second, a protectorate of strategic importance, had demanded independence, as protests erupted throughout the year. Britain had bans on civil aviation in both places. The committee wished the bans removed and main trunk lines established between the brown empire and Britain.

Colonial routes were not imperial routes. The converse was also true. They could, however, be feeder routes. The committee prescribed: "Such trunk lines would no doubt in course of time be supplemented, if not preceded, by local lines connecting up the various Dominions and Colonies internally, and with other Dominions and Colonies."

It was a carefully designed, intricate network of temporal and spatial hierarchies. The committee thought the dominions and colonies should create domestic operations on their own. These would be two-pronged intra-empire services: colonies—dominions; dominions—Britain. The imperial routes would feed on them.

The plan did not promise equal portions or fair shares. A linkup between Britain and a colonial portion of the empire could happen, but it wasn't guaranteed. It hinged on the dominions. Colonies that could afford to partner with dominions could then use the air element to reach Britain. Britain, by way of its imperial air routes with the dominions, could reach the colonies on the cheap. The dominions could simply refuse to participate in the scheme.

There were no direct air routes between Britain and the colonies; there were no direct air lines of communication or commerce between Britain and the black empire. Direct access to speed-up was denied, according to plan.

The committee wanted a specific kind of speed for the empire-state. After the men claimed that the special benefit of air for transport was speed, they compared "the time occupied in transit" between Egypt and

India by sea and by air. At first glance, the comparison appears to have been one of rate. (This is particularly true when we look at it through the prism of the present day.) The committee found that transit times were less by air. It appreciated the reduction, embraced fastness, and welcomed the chance to expedite "the carriage of mails by air." The concept of speed and travel time as interrelated is unsurprising: The ongoing refinement of the railroad in the nineteenth century had overhauled perceptions of the relationship between speed and time.[42]

Understood in its cultural context, the comparison appears to have been one of rate, direction, and change. The report dealt with two things at once, sometimes with candor in the foreground, sometimes with indistinction in the background: air as medium *and* area; change as acceleration *and* deceleration via the direct air route. (Acceleration: Britain—dominions—Egypt—India; colonies—dominions. Deceleration: Britain—colonies.)

The committee wanted speed-up for the empire-state. It was something to own and use. Speed-up was time: "*the time* occupied in transit." It was somewhere to be. Speed-up was space: "the time occupied *in transit*." It was something to do. Speed-up was takeover: "the time *occupied* in transit."[43]

Airline travel afforded all of that. It took speed-up, and sold it as speed.

Speed-Up

The hyphen is important. It reminds us to remember. Air travel is speed. Air travel is up. Air travel has a straight line. The hyphen is a bar that connects: the mark of a hyphen is a horizontal line. Bars can sometimes have space below/above, under/over them. The hyphen disrupts the rush to forget slowness when speed is taken to mean fastness. The hyphen is also a dash.

The acceleration of everyday life feels ubiquitous and seems unaccompanied, but it's not. Part of the perverse cultural work of speed is its ability to cue its sense of fastness in ways that obscure its sense of slowness. Some people in certain places experience airline travel as a normal part of ordinary, everyday life. The imperial turn to speed-up is part of how they learned to live like that.

Speed-up reoriented as it redirected. Air travel opened up, which helped reposition the vectors of empire. Airline travel allowed the empire-state to use the air element to route, and to forge and use imperial bonds in that everyday way it so wanted. It placed some people plus stuff high up above in the sky, and kept others low down below on the land: aircraft over terrains had vertical distance and depth between them. Airline travel was separation with connection.

Imperial Airways showcased nearly all those effects in "Speeding Up the Empire." The juxtaposition of boats—flying, motor, human-powered—showed the slowness in the fastness. Names of places mapped the high-speed lines of empire. The destination was part of the map too—unnamed, less than. The black woman in the foreground provided perspective: depth and a bird's-eye view. She looked up at the viewer, the seductions of her fixed stare tempting them to look down, past flowers, leaves, and her, at the scene below. Her head blocked the tailfin, which tied her to the plane; the viewer looked down *on* the action, their gaze moving from the woman to the arrival of the plane, from the plane to the smaller motorboat, from the smaller motorboat to the smaller rowboat. The italicized slogan explained the whole thing: empire with airline travel was, after all, rather new.

Over time, through cultural work, such slogans would not be needed. Airline travel, speed-up, and empire would be unseen because their dynamic would be understood. The confluence of the three ensured that people in some places would exist in different dimensions. A willingness to recall the slow in the trio's fast, even for a split second, crooks the straight line: in 1919, imperial air routes were drawn up in Britain, and Marcus Garvey and the Universal Negro Improvement Association prepared to sail the African diaspora back to Africa from the Americas on the ships of their Black Star Line.

Uprising

1

The English author Virginia Woolf chronicled a woman's first flight in "Flying over London," an undated short piece that she most likely wrote in the late 1920s or 1930s.[1]

The airplane journey began. There were fifty to sixty airplanes grounded "like a flock of grasshoppers" in a shed, a Moth plane among them. The propeller engine started and the pilot made the plane "roar." The Moth took off, sped-up, and the air travelers ascended.

They flew high above England. With vertical distance extended, the physical gap between the people in the sky and those on the ground expanded, deepened, and grew. The woman saw houses, gardens, streets, and animals "swept into long spirals and curves of pink and purple," from on high. "Everything had changed its value seen from the air," she observed, "assembling things that lie on the surface," like a "game."

They flew over "the poor quarters." She looked down and examined the bodies and lives of the people beneath them. The people on the ground appeared to be looking up at them. She considered "the expression on their faces." She found the countenance of the poor to be "complex. 'And I have to scrub the steps,' it seemed to say grudgingly. All the same they saluted, they sent us greeting; they were capable of flight."

The open-carriage biplane turned fast, slanted downward, and the woman, riveted by direction, movement, and high speed, watched in awe as "the fairy earth appeared" to shoot up from under them. She noticed how the land "rose towards [them] with extreme speed, broadening and lengthening." She scrutinized the landscape as it grew closer and became clearer, and was exhilarated. She caught sight of a galloping horse and found that "all speed and size were so reduced that the speed of the horse seemed very, very slow, and its size minute." She was fast, larger than other lives. "Millions of insects moving" turned quickly into "men of business," as she moved. "One could indeed now see the tops of the heads of separate men and could distinguish a bowler from a cap," she noted, "and could thus be certain of social grades—which was an employer, which was a working man." The woman struggled to be at ease with the power of speed-up; it made people on the ground seem far less than human. The plane flew up, down, and forward, and she thought "one had to change perpetually air values into land values." "So we had not flown after all," she concluded. She was starting to push back.[2]

The flight did not happen. Virginia Woolf never flew.

2

The Trinidadian author C. L. R. James wrote a short pamphlet advocating for the emancipation of the British West Indies, early in the 1930s. In *The Case for West-Indian Self Government*, which was excerpted from his longer work, *The Life of Captain Cipriani: An Account of British Government in the West Indies*, he argued that colonialism had ripped West Indians from "the natural course of events" and their inevitable "rise to power and influence." They should "be free to make [their] own failures and successes." He concluded, "Governors and governed stand on either side of a gulf which no tinkering will bridge, and political energy is diverted into other channels or simply runs to waste. Britain will hold us down for as long as she wishes. Her cruisers and aeroplanes ensure it." The rather prophetic statement followed thirty-one pages of sharp careful argumentation for self-determination, on the last page as a final point. Emancipation would happen on one plane; the continuation of oppression would come by way of two others: water and air. With liners on the ocean and liners in the sky, British influence in the Caribbean could come from all directions, and last forever.[3]

In 1933, Hogarth Press, which was owned by Leonard and Virginia Woolf, decided that it was time to publish *The Case for West-Indian Self Government* in Britain. James had sailed from Trinidad and settled in England the year before.

4

Planes

A "thousand pens have described the sensation of leaving earth," Virginia Woolf said in "Flying over London."[1] One imagines she drew on these accounts to imagine the experience and power of aerial mobility, especially since she had never flown. One imagines C. L. R. James, a radical Pan-Africanist who was acutely aware of the long-lasting marriage of transportation and oppression, did not need to.

Travel stories from first-generation airline passengers shed light, however subtle, on the entangled promotion of commercial aviation and state violence. In particular, they show how practices used to incorporate air travel into everyday life worked together to further and maintain racism. There are different types of first-generation stories; there are different ways to take flight. There are stories from the first airline passengers and ones from first-generation migrants and their children. People in the first group told the stories shared in this chapter. Someone from the second has claimed and is retelling them.[2]

During the research and writing of this book, and in my everyday life, I realized that people who have access to flying love, or feel obliged, to swap airline travel stories. The ones I hear (or overhear) in airports or airplanes about in-flight experiences intrigue me the most. I am often struck by the wild assortment of details strangers share with one another; by their willingness to participate in the act of storytelling itself; and by the assumptions people make in order to tell their story to a fellow passenger. (Stories told to people who work on flights or in airports are different.) The storyteller often assumes that their experience is simultaneously unique and shared—that listeners will 'get it' because they also fly. Sometimes they talk about a passenger on board *their* flight acting out or not knowing the rules for acts such as reclining one's seat or using both armrests, as if there are scripts and rules. Sometimes they recall the days before airline deregulation and remember when air travel was, in their opinion, better for everyone, with unknowing wistfulness for an exclusive social world in the sky.

Stories such as these involve thick-layered assumptions about class, about race, about gender, about citizenship, about ability, about sexuality: about belonging. They came from somewhere and somewhen. At some point, people learned how to be airline passengers. They learned standards; learned how to be appropriate, ordinary, and acceptable, in the air. They developed expectations; they learned to expect other passengers to be appropriate, ordinary, and acceptable, on the fly. They learned to revise or unlearn those lessons as well.

The sky is what Teju Cole has called "unquiet."[3] There is an uncanny resemblance between the airline travel stories people tell now and the ones that were told when the airline industry began. The first airlines and airline passengers started to build a grammar of flight. Their travel narratives help to illuminate how ordinary people became part of what Peter Fritzsche coined "a nation of fliers."[4] Each one is jam-packed with explications, assumptions, and descriptions of expectations, perceptions, sensations, and experiences. They are full of exclusions: things not done, places not visited, people not there. Outlines of these old rules have hung around. A story is one place to find them.

The Inflight Magazine

Imperial Airways sought to create an empire, as well as a nation, of commercial fliers in the aftermath of the aerial horrors of the First World War. For the chosen instrument of the state to succeed, the image of the airplane would need to shift from deadly weapon to safe journey.[5]

Imperial Airways set out to transform the meaning of air travel in the public imagination. The goal was to establish sustained appreciation for commercial aviation throughout the British world. It was a colossal undertaking, though Imperial Airways did not have to do it alone. Newspapers, exhibitions, books, and circuses were among the cultural aids helping to redefine air travel. There were social events arranged by the Post Office, British Empire Film Society, and other state-funded organizations helping to spark public interest in commercial aviation. Government-subsidized fares for "joyrides" afforded working-class children and adults the opportunity to learn about the airplane firsthand.[6]

Slowly, the discourse of flight was changing, as Imperial Airways got under way.

As part of its efforts, the airline created a monthly magazine called *Imperial Airways Gazette*, which ran from the summer of 1928 to the fall of 1939.[7] Each issue was fewer than ten pages, and each of those pages boasted a variety of items: travel schedules, route maps, company plans, advice columns, how-to manuals, aerial photographs, destination guides. The publication, which was known as the "official organ" of the airline, promoted and sold the advantages of flight.[8]

The *Gazette* was more than an entertaining magazine. It was an education. Through carefully selected materials, readers of the magazine turned into tourists. Like a guidebook, the *Gazette* told them where to go, how to get there, what to do, how to see. Curated images of nation, empire, and nature spoke of selfhood, otherness, and trade. The newness of airline travel and the rawness of airline passengers were never taken for granted. The *Gazette* taught manners and etiquette, both of which it invented. The lesson: how to be in the sky and British through the air.[9]

It is hard to know who exactly read the magazine. Subscriptions were free. Adults could receive a monthly subscription by contacting the company's publicity office. The airline encouraged schoolteachers and headmasters to request copies for students. *Aeroplane* and other popular British publications sometimes included the magazine as a supplement. Imperial Airways also gave copies to its employees.

It is also difficult to know if the *Gazette* circulated outside Britain for extended periods of time. Workers staffed the airline's colonial and foreign offices, though it is unclear if the airline considered all or some of them as employees. Articles and announcements in the magazine periodically targeted readers who were not in Britain. There were snippets about dentists in South Africa with *Gazettes* in their waiting rooms; occasional paragraphs about trips that didn't start, stop over, or end in England; and a smattering of ads for "intending travellers by Imperial Airways from Europe and the Empire."[10] Infrequent pieces such as these suggest the magazine circulated outside Britain once in a while, at the very least.

Uncertainty about readership or circulation does not diminish the importance of the magazine as a repository and record. The *Gazette* published a wide range of authors. Some wrote original pieces for the magazine while others had their works republished by the *Gazette*. Some were famous authors and others ordinary passengers with letters, testimonials, diaries, and long tales to share. Their stories help us to sense perspectives, sentiments, inclinations, and attitudes. They enable us to see, even if only slightly, how first fliers flew, and why people inhabit commercial airspace in certain ways.

Like any story once told, these are not inviolable, pristine sources. They were published in the company's magazine, an instrument to make commercial aviation an ineffaceable part of ordinary, everyday life. That the airline manipulated—selected, edited, printed, distributed—them is not insignificant. The documents are tricky to interpret, no matter how mindful the reader. Then and also now, readers slid into *emergent* airscapes, which were imagined and material worlds engendered by the cocreation of new "global cultural flows" and the commercial aviation industry, and in formation.[11] There, authors moved and wrote in a manner that was not altogether new. Tales to recount trips abroad were hardly a novelty in Britain, especially those about colonial encounters. For centuries, travelers had described sensuous journeys in vibrant detail. They captured what appealed to them: smells, tastes, sounds, touches, sights of people and places. Many of their creations animated imperial culture. Those vibrant detailed passages documented and recreated colonial adventures for people back home.[12]

Airline travelers descend from that tradition. Those who wrote and published in the *Gazette* retained aspects of the old style, and they revamped them. In particular, they participated in exoticism as they noticed and chronicled 'difference' while moving through the world, like those before them. Airline travelers, however, were transfixed by the *experience* of sight in a very different way. First-generation fliers had lots to say about what airborne mobility let them see.

A note about who flew and saw, and who wrote: Airline travelers were not prevalent in the late 1920s and early 1930s. The sumptuous ocean liner and reliable train were established forms of mobility, and an expanded steamship market enabled an increasing number of workers, tourists, and itinerants to sail amid a dire postwar economy. By the late 1930s, there was growing public interest in dreaming about and debating the airplane as a form of mass transportation. Air-mindedness was shifting. Payloads were rising. The bulk of cargo was mail and freight.[13]

Airline transport was elite travel, particularly on what government officials and company executives touted as the "Empire Routes" of the "Empire Mission." They were long-haul flights along the imperial air routes, which officials and executives had designed to ensure "the future of civilisation" for Britain, its dominions and protectorates, and its colonies. Officials and executives imagined the white British businessman as the ideal frequent flier, as they advertised for what they wanted: improved communication flows for a new global Britain, which is where the first story begins.[14]

Airmail

This is a story the airline told the public. Imperial Airways was asking people from different social worlds to help advance communication flows in Britain, throughout the empire, and across the world. Promotion of airmail and freight services was an integral part of the campaign. Most people could not afford to travel by air but, they were told, their stuff could. In nearly all issues of the *Gazette*, Imperial Airways printed at least one article about the power and magnitude of airmail. Airmail, a "vision of cheap and rapid delivery," was a "contribution to Empire corporate unity."[15]

The message was simple enough: use airmail, strengthen the communal and economic bonds of empire, do your part for Britain. Marketing it to the general public was somewhat more complicated. Trust in the safe conveyance of property and persons by road, water, and rail was strongly established. British women and men were not convinced airlines could rival and eclipse the railroad, ocean liner, or on-road vehicle, and become the dominant form of public transportation. By the time Imperial Airways was launched in the mid-1920s, the railway journey symbolized function and reliability; the car represented privilege and prestige; and the steamship embodied the modern.[16] By the mid-1930s, as public opinion about airborne mobility shifted, the Air Ministry found that people still preferred to use surface transportation systems. Many of them felt those methods were "already highly developed," a commonplace set of ways to move valuable personal matters such as mail. At the same time, the Ministry found that the public was drawn to the "greater convenience and speed" of air travel. Although trust in surface transport was strong, speed-up was enticing.[17]

Imperial Airways decided to showcase speed-up to garner trust. It focused its attention on shifting the public's perception of airmail in two areas: confidence and protection. Its goal was to normalize airmail. One of its lures was weight.

Stories about the mighty weight of airmail filled the *Gazette*. In the February 1933 issue there was an article about the growth of the airmail industry. It featured an elated Postmaster General applauding British patrons for setting a new airmail traffic record. He praised them for a 20 percent increase in the amount of mail sent: "52 ½ tons" of letters flew from Britain to the colonies in 1931. The next year, "64 tons." "Christmas mail dispatched to India by air during December amounted to about three tons; the mail of 10 December alone weighed over a ton." The Postmaster General communicated the significance of the accomplishment by describing heaviness, which he did by using numbers. In a two-column chart, he compared airmail letter traffic from 1931 and 1932. An organized list of numerical figures revealed the "117,350" pounds of letters flown in 1931 and the "143,000" pounds of letters flown the following year—a "record weight of letters" had traveled by air.[18]

Weight meant significance. The Postmaster General's focus was on tonnage. The mark of triumphant success was the bulk of the letters; heaviness set the record. (The Postmaster General could have measured increased airmail traffic by the number of letters flown.) The heaviness of the mail was a sign of protection, as it implied that tons of letters safely flew Imperial Airways. It was the combination of speed-up, long distances, heavy weight, and tonnage that helped set the airliner apart from the steamship as a symbol of modern travel.[19]

The numerical depiction of capacity and distance was also used to build confidence. In the inaugural issue of the magazine, the airline noted the nearly 78,000 passengers, 3,000 tons of freight, and 3,500,000 miles it had flown since services began.[20] Numbers—the quantity of people, accumulative weight of freight, and accretion of miles—worked to construct an image of the chosen instrument of the state as durable, established. The belief in numbers as truth, fact, and evidence helped to *prove* that the airline was established and safe.[21] The alignment of protection and verticality was another way the airline tried to build confidence in air transportation. The airline insisted that altitude evaded the hazards of transshipment. Mail was invulnerable and secure because, airborne and fast, it was untouchable. The notion of speed-up as a form of safekeeping was a difficult message to convey. In the early 1930s, an ad for airmail in the *Gazette* drew a sharp contrast between surface and air transportation (see Figure 2). It conjoined speed-up and guardianship. The meaning of the headline and the message was clear. The headline:

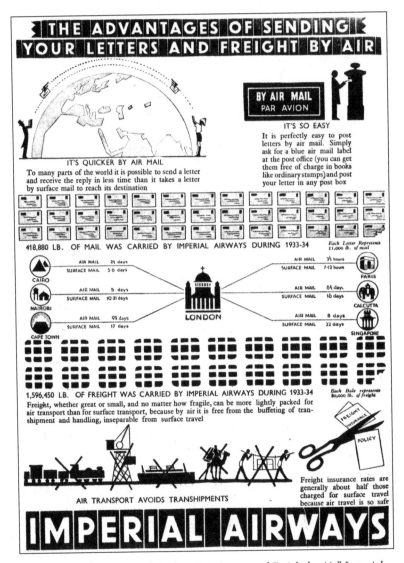

Figure 2. "The Advantages of Sending Your Letters and Freight by Air," *Imperial Airways Gazette*, July 1934, 8.

"The Advantages of Sending Your Letter and Freight by Air." The message: Airmail was "quicker . . . so easy." It was "so safe."

The lesson being taught was more opaque, leaving itself open to interpretation and accessibility. Two graphic tales were told. In one, letters and freight traveled the world by surface transport and transshipment. They left from London; the postbox, top hat and tails, and St. Paul's Cathedral made that clear. They went by train, rig, ship, camel, native, and arrived in Paris, Calcutta, Singapore, Cape Town, Nairobi, Cairo. Cargo moved on land and by water, which meant senders needed insurance. The second tale spoke of letters, freight, and their journey by air. They left from London, like the first ones did, and went to Britain's colonies and dominions, signaled by landmarks and an imperial uniform. Magic moved the cargo: no airplane was shown. Senders posted mail. The posted mail was given wings. It flit across the globe, confidently, because it was safe. No insurance was needed. Scissors cut the policy up.

Instructions were among the tales. The ad showed people how to prepare and pack airmail parcels; like a manual, it told them how to use the new postal system. "It is perfectly easy to post letters by air mail. Simply ask for a blue air mail label at the post office (you can get them free of charge in books like ordinary stamps) and post your letter in any post box."[22] The instructions came over and again. Imperial Airways distributed pamphlets, sponsored exhibitions, and handed lecture materials to schools about how to send mail by air.

There were other directives, more political ones. The airline tethered airmail to three concerns: global ethics, imperial unity, and national obligation. In the *Gazette*, pieces linked airmail to internationalism. They stressed that fast communication networks among colonies, dominions, Britain, and other nation-states made for peace. In one issue, the chairman of Imperial Airways, Sir Eric Geddes, remarked on the importance of the "Empire Mission" first to shareholders and guests at an annual meeting and then to readers of the *Gazette*. "To-day we reside in a world which is very disturbed," he explained. "But there is a majority amongst intelligent people who do realize that the future of civilisation depends upon the spreading of a closer international understanding." "The essential link in such a bond is transport," Geddes concluded.[23] Airmail could close gaps and bring calm to future global relations. The rhetoric of a civilizing mission was invoked.

Airmail could be a conduit for amity and cultural exchange. The airline hammered this point throughout the 1930s, as tensions between nation-states intensified. An article from 1937, "The World Travels By Air," pitched airline travel as the quickest way to the "happy state." The happy state was a riff on a place imagined by the British poet Samuel Butler in the seventeenth century. For the poet, it was a state of being. For the airline, it was a place to be in. The happy state was a destination, and its motto was cultural contact: "The more people see of each other the less likely they are to disagree," Imperial Airways expounded, carefully. It defined mail as cultural contact, and cultural contact as "the spread of knowledge," the maker of "goodwill." The airline stressed, "Contact can only be gained by communication in some form or other." Then, it asserted, "It is essential that the methods of communication should be continuously improved throughout the world because the easier and the quicker people can see and correspond with each other the less likelihood there is of a misunderstanding." By the end, Imperial Airways had established itself as the carrier of all four: mail, cultural contact, knowledge, and goodwill—the happy state.[24]

"Why don't you fly? Why don't you post by air? Why don't you send freight by air?" Imperial Airways once asked readers. They were aggressive, perhaps even accusatory, questions. They were at the bottom, as the finishing lines of a full-page ad for "The Growth of Imperial Airways" on the last page of a *Gazette*. Above them were three sets of symbols: silhouettes for passengers, envelopes for mail, and angels for freight. Under each set were numbers for what was carried: bodies, ton-miles of letters, and ton-miles of freight. The message: join the crowd, do your part. The lesson: airmail lets ordinary people be passengers too.[25]

The Frequent Flier

The frequent flier is made. The commercial sky is made for them.

The chosen instrument of the state did not want to carry everyone. The type of rich white businessman the airline sought was one who appreciated luxury, leisure, and the nuances of imperialism. This was how it tried to get him.

Imperial Airways billed its services as cutting edge. It made the airliner seem similar to but better than the ocean liner. It often compared the prestige of the airline's fleet to that of the steamship companies in the columns, advertisements, and photographs of the *Gazette*. It was a bold, slightly risky strategy; the companies and their steamships were revered as emblems of empire and nation. Imperial Airways did not hold back. In one comparison in July 1936, it dubbed a new fleet of flying boats, "Queen Marys of the Air." The Queen Mary was one of the fastest transatlantic steamships, owned by the famous Cunard White Star Line. It was beloved, iconic. As enticement, Imperial Airways pointed out that its fleet of twenty-nine planes was like the Queen because it was expensive, luxuriant, and intended for transatlantic crossings. The thing was, its fleet was faster than the Queen's.

Sometimes rootedness defined the cutting edge. There were times when the airline imagined itself as loyal to the British nation and the British people. It shared accounts of British workers building flying boats in Britain as a reminder of the job, pride, and dream the airline had given them. One such narrative was about a journalist visiting a factory in Rochester and touring its facilities. The short story began: The journalist walked through the factory yards, and stumbled. He saw "a remarkable sight, the impressive spectacle" of three thousand men building ten flying boats. He noted how many men it took to make a handful of planes, then continued. The journalist was soon transfixed as the "buzz of steady activity" overwhelmed him. He watched workers "busy building the new Empire"—the flying boat—and was proud. He admired how they interacted with and cared for metal; they tenderly "bent and hammered and bored and filed, fitting small piece to small piece with the most loving care." He marveled, as the workers became little boys riveted in model sets: "There must be thrill in this work; the men looked as though they took a joyous pride in it. I envied the apprentice boys, whose faces shone as if they were in some angelic dream as no doubt they were!"

A guide led the journalist deeper into the factory. The visitor wound through rooms, occasionally stopping to inspect piles of duralumin and stainless steel, or "long wings" shaped around circular petrol tanks. His eye caught "silvery shining metal hulls" and the "absolutely smooth" skin of the plane, which he liked. Near the end of the tour, he arrived at a full-size model of an 18 ton flying boat. The journalist went inside and wondered, "Like a ship?" He walked around the interior, which "decidedly" resembled a steamship. There were two decks in the fore of the hull. There were also "proper beds, and proper sleeping births, and comfortable chairs that are adjustable to a nicety." The cabins were "beautifully lighted, carpeted, heated, ventilated, and decorated." It was like an ocean liner indeed: "the whole outfit speaks of comfort, indeed of luxury." The journalist classed passengers in the sky, and not those on the sea, "symbols of a new age of travel, argosies of the air, armadas of peace!"[26]

The story traveled. It went from a newspaper to the *Gazette*, where it was retold and renamed "Queen Marys of the Air."

The picture of all in the airline industry—from worker to flier—as doing their civic duty at the vanguard of change was in the image of the model passenger. A question was posed on a *Gazette* cover. It asked, "£3 12s 6d London-Paris or The Terrestrial Complex?" The question was paired with a piece about Britain in bad health. The country had caught the terrestrial complex, a virulent disease that caused people to act like cheap, irrational ground-worshippers, according to an unnamed leading newspaper. The airline had reduced the cost of flights to continental Europe and still, "a good many worthy citizens with a somewhat disturbing problem" refused to fly. The problem: citizens who preferred "rail and sea rates" could no longer use cost to justify their choice—the "excuse has perished." Now "we must ask ourselves if we are really 'air-minded,' or if a projected flight to the Continent is still fraught for us with the terrors of the unknown."[27]

It was coded language. A worthy citizen was someone who traveled. Citizens not flying ailed the nation. Air travel was the antidote, the airline the healer. Britain was sick because the public lacked sense. British people favored surface transport even when air transport cost the same. Technological backwardness scared them; meanwhile, they were terrified by technological innovation. Citizens of worth could heal the country by flying the national airline.

Imperial Airways built this image of the ideal airline passenger around upper middle-class notions of pleasure and opulence. Two of the first excursions it offered were tea flights over London and lunch flights between London and Paris. These were marketed as posh flights, not joyrides which the intended airline passenger considered cheap, vulgar, and common. Short Imperial Airways flights were promoted as chic, up-to-date. They were signs of class superiority and appreciation of technological change. The tea flight, which started in 1929, was a thirty-minute service. It cost £2 2s, which was more than double what a joyride cost. It epitomized modish frivolity. One ad announced a plan to offer tea flights at a "considerably reduced fare" during the London Season, a long-standing upper class social ritual. Much like balloon rides in the eighteenth and nineteenth centuries, tea flights were more about height than speed. They were for hosts to "give a novel party for friends who have already done all the usual things," and for boyfriends to impress their "fiancée up from the country." For £1 10s per ticket, Imperial Airways flew passengers over well-known sights like the Tower of London and Buckingham Palace. Passengers were sold privilege: a full tea service accompanied by the opportunity to look down and peep inside areas others could not.[28]

Airline travel was literally high society. Imperial Airways offered and operated a pleasure service from London to the Grand National in Liverpool. A ticket cost £8 8s. A company car drove passengers to and from the airport, and a *Heracles* class plane flew them to and from Liverpool. In-flight, they received a cold lunch on the way there, and a hot tea service on the way back. When they deplaned in Liverpool, passengers received entrance tickets to the famous steeplechase event. They sat in a special, reserved section.[29]

Imperial Airways sold segregation as one of its services.[30] The airline promoted it as one of the great benefits of traveling by air. A person could fly over and watch events such as the infamous annual Oxford versus Cambridge boat race from above. This sports-related service paired elevation with class advantage. (The flight cost £2 2s.) It was a high society flight that was quite different from the one to the Grand National. Airline travelers had an uninterrupted view of the race. Up in the sky, they were truly above the mass of spectators, separated from the crowd. They were actually untouchable, for a price.[31]

Height was used to sell domestic flights as leisurely and discriminatory. Speed-up was used to portray international and empire flights as unhurried and distinguished. Ads for the London to Paris lunchtime flight, for example, mixed relaxed efficiency with fastness and height. One of the first *Gazette* ads to show men and women traveling together boasted that round-trip airline passengers flew expeditiously to Paris: "To Paris while you read your paper and home again in time for dinner!"

The flight was plush and time efficient. Both women and men experienced the view from above ("for you the chops of the Channel look like ripples") and the advantage of the swift life ("you arrive in Paris fresh and unfatigued, having spent no more time in the air than it takes to run in your car from London to lunch with your cousins in the country"). This flight cost £7 12s.[32]

Mention of expense was telling. It is one thing to say how much something costs and another thing to describe it. The construction of the model airline passenger as lavish and economical was a call for the businessman and, to a lesser extent, the modern woman. Representations of airspace and airline travel were profoundly gendered. That the consummate passenger was the British man was hardly a shock; airspace and masculinity stayed knit together in the postwar public imagination.[33] (Those worthy citizens who rid Britain of its terrestrial complex were most likely men, in a Wellsian world.) That the archetype of this British man was the businessman was a bit more peculiar. The businessman who flew was ambitious and established and adventurous. He was also frugal. He valued speed-up: he valued time. The flying businessman was not an Edwardian dandy.

The magazine often depicted business travel as assurance, expediency, and productive rest. Imperial Airways promised reliance and gainful sleep. "Your mail may take wing and fly to the East, your goods may travel swiftly and safely over land and sea alike, you yourself may sleep a thousand miles distant from your morning's waking place." The businessman who flew slept. The airliner zipped him and his business around the world, safely and soundly.[34]

Business flights rewarded the traveler. Ads for them focused on the amount of time and money saved by flying, rather than on the amount of time and money spent. There was once a London businessman who took such a flight for the first time. His clients lived in ten places: Palestine, Iraq, Egypt, Anglo-Egyptian Sudan, Uganda, Kenya Colony, the Tanganyika Territory, Northern Rhodesia, Southern Rhodesia, and South Africa. Needing to travel over 20,000 miles to see them, he bought an airline ticket for £300, and went. He was gone for sixty days.

He returned to London. He wondered about airline travel and good business sense. He calculated, measured its value. Surface transport would have taken 180 days and cost £360 for a first-class ticket. He found that flying was slightly cheaper yet more exclusive. He had saved. He was pleased.

He could then make more money in the time that he saved. He noticed flight saved days, 120 of them for him. "Time is money," he interjected, and computed what each day was worth: "From my own viewpoint as a business man, I estimate the value of each of my working days at, say £3. Therefore the 120 days I saved by air represented to me a sum of approximately £360." He saved money because he saved time, and he was very pleased.

What made that happen gripped him: the direct, straight line. It made big places smaller, more manageable. Africa, for example, was inconvenient for him. Before, when he traveled the "big territory" by surface transport, he suffered "long detours and roundabout trips" and "heat, dust, fatigue," which zapped his energy. Direct and straight, airline travel made "all the difference." "The airways goes straight from one important point to another." It reduced layovers, which he found invaluable. Fewer, shorter stops did more than save him time. They cut back chances to buy trinkets, on impulse. Also, the businessman who flew didn't have to deal with Africans, in a snap, or as much, which was what he said.

He felt energized. Airline travel helped him "avoid fatigue." He found that flight was good for his "health and mental outlook." It shored up his power and strength. Invigorated, he did efficient and effective work because he was "fresh and vigorous, ready to plunge into the business on hand." "On all counts, I can say in conclusion the air tour scores. You save time. You save money," said the businessman to the airline during an interview.[35]

The absence of women from the image of the ideal airline traveler was conspicuous. The 1930s were years when women aviators were celebrated in Britain. Some like Amy Johnson were able to cultivate celebrity status by casting their daring flights abroad within the conventional narrative of risky travel as imperial adventure. They were seen as glamorous and feminine rather than risqué and lewd. Fashion designers made clothes to resemble the garments worn by women of the air and styled sharper, more streamlined cuts to invoke the sleekness of the airplane.[36]

When women as passengers were featured in the *Gazette*, they often appeared in pieces about flights to continental Europe, in strikingly different ways. In one scenario she was the flip side of the businessman.

She was timid, fragile. She was convinced flight was unsafe, unhealthy, too high, and too fast. One woman flew from London to Paris because she felt obligated; she had won the airline ticket at a charity event. (She wasn't a paying airline passenger.) She figured it was "Fate having decided that I must fly," and absolved herself of agency and responsibility. She considered herself to be like "many women," and swore, "I shall never fly; I would never think of flying." She, like others, had a "dislike of heights, a fear of air-sickness, a belief that height combined with great speed will affect heart or blood-pressure, lack of faith in the safety of air-travel, and lastly, a vague horror of an unknown element."

Then she flew. Airborne, her sentiments changed completely. "From the moment I set foot inside the machine every sense of fear vanished." Like men, she liked what she saw beneath her: "a rift," "the world like a pebble." She liked feeling "an extraordinary sense of detachment." Unlike men, she listed the daily tasks she was thankful to leave behind: "taxes, conferences, the stock market, work unfinished, worries unresolved." Later, she took four more flights and relished "heights varying from 50 to 8,000 feet."

Her story appeared in a *Gazette*, reprinted from the *Morning Post*. It was titled "Air Travel for Woman." It was an account, a lesson, and an endorsement. It educated through cautious adventure; explained why women should fly; told them how to act when airborne; and sold liberation from the mundane. Airline travel removed the typical woman from the monotony of everyday life and gave her new vistas. The woman who flew from London to Paris was reluctant at first. But she embraced her fate, overcame her fears, and her views and rhythms were transformed.[37]

Another kind of woman went farther. She flew from London to Zurich on a Thursday. She was Scottish and this was not her first flight. She preferred trips by plane: she needed to be efficient and effective, like a businessman. She had "less than three days at [her] disposal to go to Zurich, transact business, and return to London."

The woman arrived at the aerodrome in Croydon and learned there would be one woman onboard as a passenger: her. She was not taken aback. She went to "the revealing face" of the weighing machine and was pleased to find it turned toward the airline official and away from the crowd. The welcomed rotation of the scale accelerated the check-in process and hid her weight, which was, as H. Stuart Menzies remarked, "A neat idea that, especially for the women folk! and [sic] come to think of it, very tactful."[38] An agent hurried them along to the plane, just in case "there should be a latent craven who may elect to change her (or *his*—it has been known) mind."

She boarded the "floating hotel." Over the English Channel, she rejoiced, feeling "a glad exhilaration and warm rush of gratitude" because she "lived in this wonderful age of sky travel." "It is magic—white magic—the very soul of the poetry of motion—to be skimming up there on velvet air speeding so easily and lightly to foreign lands." For her, the airplane was an inherently good technology, and airline services were preferred. She was a woman who had business to do quickly, in foreign lands.[39]

White Flight

Three white men flew the empire routes in the 1930s. One flew to Iraq, one to India, and one to South Africa. They kept diaries and wrote letters while on their way. They described what they did and explained what those actions meant to them. Each one preferred something different: layovers, windows, and people. The objects themselves were not novel but the airborne experience of them was, which was what the men noted.

Sometimes the men described what it was like to see—and to be seen by—black and brown people on the ground. The men welcomed their actions, which they took as evidence of colonial envy of imperial flight. But what they understood as "a look of lust, a look of envy" might have been displays of antipathy and discontent.[40] Perhaps what seemed like friendly local responses were, in fact, flashes of colonial resistance. However short-lived or scarce in the archive, these scenes may well retrieve moments when racism was carried out and confronted on the fly.

The Layover

When Mr. W. D. H. McCullough, an Englishman, traveled from London to Baghdad on an Imperial Airways ticket in the early 1930s, he kept a travel diary. Sections were published in the *Gazette* as installments in a column called "Baghdad Bound." Subheadings like "From London" and "Over the Desert" mapped the route flown. They helped readers to travel the empire with McCullough.

Air travel along imperial routes took days. It was often intermodal and airplanes stopped frequently on the way. The layover was an important part of empire flights for reasons the previously mentioned businessman stated, and more. Speed-up deepened the compression of space by time; it reduced the number of stopovers and shortened the gap between multiple layovers. Airline passengers spent less time traveling between intermediary places, condensing and compacting the experiences they had in transit, which was what that businessman appreciated. Shortened gaps also meant that airplanes and their passengers ascended and descended rapidly and repeatedly between places. Quickly rising and falling, rising and falling, dramatized the differences between people above and people below. Many passengers cherished the experience, like McCullough. His itinerary: Fly London to Paris and then board an express train to Brindisi that same night. Spend two days on the train, passing through Switzerland and Milan, along the southeast coast of Italy to Brindisi. Then fly across the Mediterranean Sea to Piraeus, and spend the night. Then, fly to Rhodes and then to Cyprus. Refuel in Cyprus. Thereafter, fly over the Jordan River, land on the Sea of Galilee, take the ferry to Palestine, and spend the night. The next day, fly across the Syrian Desert, land at Rutbah Fort in Iraq, and then fly on to the aerodrome in Baghdad.

"This narrative starts a thousand feet above Limasol, in Cyprus," read the opening lines of his account. On a flying boat "climbing steadily and heading across the last strip of Mediterranean," McCullough recalled how his trip began. One Saturday afternoon he flew from Croydon to Paris on a *Hannibal* class craft, the first four-engine passenger biplane in the world. The plane was designed for people to travel in comfort. Before pressurized airplane cabins and 'above the weather' flights, passengers on other planes found it difficult, often sickening, to eat while flying. McCullough, however, enjoyed the airline's famed four-course lunch, carpeting, and soundproofing, and the full-service bar during the two hours and forty-five minute flight. In hindsight, he remembered this part of his trip as "pleasant" but "uneventful."[41]

McCullough felt imperious. He had a six-hour layover in Paris; Imperial Airways had booked him on the 9:30 p.m. express train to Brindisi.

He swam and ate at the airline's hotel while he waited and after dinner, he rested in the hotel lounge. Days later he decided that what had happened that night turned his pleasant and uneventful trip into a "magnificent" journey: "I had the rather exciting experience of having a uniformed official coming into the hotel lounge to ask for passengers on the Empire air route. I rose to my feet and strode pita-pat down the lounge, feeling every inch an Empire builder." McCullough often used the word 'magnificent' to describe his experiences after Paris; sometimes, like now, it was a stand-in for British progress and dominance. McCullough was proud and purposeful as the airline officer in regalia called, classified, and escorted passengers ceremoniously. He was embarking on what felt to him like an imperial project.

The observations that McCullough made while flying shed light on empire building, illuminating how imperialism and air travel coalesced on the cultural front in the decades between the First and Second World Wars. After Brindisi, McCullough reached Baghdad via Piraeus, Rhodes, Cyprus, Palestine, and Rutbah Fort at Rutbah Wells. En route, he described what he did, how he felt, and whom he saw during layovers. He evoked an orientalist language of otherness to do so. For example, in Rhodes he enjoyed bathing in "an Oriental version of the Brighton Metropole," while in Cyprus he shaded by the sea and "felt very pleased with life" when a "group of natives collected and stared," putting him on display. Before leaving Cyprus for Palestine, he observed, "We stared at the natives and the natives stared at us, and neither party seemed greatly impressed with the view." For McCullough, the ambivalence generated by gazing indifferently or derisively while pleasured, stemmed from the normalization of commercial flight. After all, the locals were looking at "what was no doubt their weekly exhibition of flying foreigners."

McCullough's plane trip to and overnight stay in Palestine exposed the discriminatory habits privileged white men in commercial flight reproduced from older ways of moving. Somewhere between Cyprus and Rutbah Fort, McCullough's traveling companions, who were "pretty tough old campaigners," schooled him on "the perils of the East." From instructions on how to shake tigers out of his trousers to tips on evading deadly mosquitoes, the other, more experienced men "spent a great deal of their time warning" him. Later, their exoticized cautions influenced McCullough's attitudes toward Palestine. When he was alone on the ground, he went for a walk, down to the sea, "gathering [his] first impressions of the East." He heard foreign music, which sounded to him like noise from "a hospital in which at least one of the patients is right at the top of the danger list." He "quickly came to the conclusion that there was a good deal to be said for the West," and went to bed. After some "occasional bursts of weird music and the howling of pi-dogs" broke the "silence of the night," McCullough was pleased when an "extremely fierce-looking young woman in a very original costume" woke him up at 3.30 a.m. She prepared him for his next flight.

In addition to the people and places encountered on the empire route, McCullough liked airline layovers. They underlined the literal and symbolic power of the airplane and its passengers in motion. Throughout his diary, references to leaving abruptly, ascending authoritatively, "climbing rapidly out," and landing "irreverently" revealed how the acceleration of taking off, the vertical trajectory of going airborne, and the deceleration of touching down taught some airline passengers how to detach themselves from seemingly intermediate places. McCullough observed: The "four engines thundered into life . . . the whole terrible force of our four engines let loose" after he alighted in Brindisi and "quickly" boarded a flying boat to Piraeus. "The effect is most inspiring," he declared, "rising rapidly into the air." After his half-hour in Rhodes, he delighted in the momentum of finishing leisurely drinks, returning swiftly "back to our machine," and flying away again.

The short duration and quick succession of layovers, as well as the flying that occurred in between them, prompted McCullough to describe himself in two ways. First, he characterized himself as forward-looking and progressive. Then, he thought about his national identity and asserted that he was metropolitan and British. As he flew into Rutbah Fort he saw, judged, and dreaded landing at "the most desolated and extraordinary hostelry in the world." It was "300 miles from any sign of civilisation . . . stuck right in the very centre of the Syrian desert." His attitude shifted from disdain to delight when he learned that the layover would last an hour and the station restaurant would serve those who "arrive out of the sky" an almost English breakfast during that time. Grounded in the desert, the fliers feasted on "bacon and eggs, coffee, iced drinks, toast and marmalade, and electric light."

McCullough listed electricity among the British products he con-
sumed in Iraq. He believed airline travel allowed him to see British industry from a new vantage point. Above the protectorate, ungrounded
altitude enabled him to watch the empire-state develop and modern-
ize the interior of a place he considered to be remote. As Priya Satia
reminds us, "It was in Iraq that the British first practiced, if never per-
fected, the technology of bombardment, there that they first attempted
to fully theorize the value of airpower as an independent arm of the
military"[42]

What McCullough noticed, thought, and wrote when he flew from
Palestine to Iraq exemplified these sentiments. Leaving Palestine, he felt
"something exceedingly thrilling" when he went from "the rather dirty
antiquity of the native village to the quiet efficiency of the British aerodrome." Airborne, he was "in complete comfort sipping iced drinks, far
above the hot and dusty earth" when a man from the military showed
him where a "famous British general" had fought during the First World
War. He peered through the window with reverence and watched as he
moved over where "our men" had fought "in a climate and surroundings
like these." His thought was fleeting; "in a very short time," McCullough's
impressions changed when the plane "flew very high—about 8,000 ft."
Up here, he found it "extremely interesting to see the plans that had been
made for laying the pipe line" in the desert. Then when landed, this aeri-
ally informed imperial outlook deepened during breakfast. McCullough
glanced at a lighting plant, which a British broadcasting company had
installed, and he "could not help feeling rather proud of the fact that this
British plant was carrying on so gallantly in such a forsaken part of the
globe." Less than an hour later, he was "soon several thousand feet up
feeling gloriously cool and comfortable again."[43]

The Window

Around the same time as McCullough flew, a Londoner named Mr. P. W.
Pitt declared, "I have had a great adventure." One autumn, he flew from
England to India, passing over and through France, "the length of Italy,"
Greece, "the Holy Land," the Arabian Desert, "the Persian Gulf from end
to end," and Balochistan. Forty-eight hours delayed, the flight, which
covered approximately five thousand miles, lasted nine days. During

that time, Pitt kept a diary and in June 1933, the *Gazette* published the first part of his travelogue: "The Magic Carpet—A Journey to India by Imperial Airways."

Pitt's travels began when a *Heracles* class plane brought him from an aerodrome in Croydon near London to Paris one morning. Pitt, like others at the time, was fascinated by the anatomy of the long-range biplane. Pitt, for example, counted forty-two seats and noticed four engines. He noted being aboard one of the "largest passenger carrying air liners in the world." He appreciated the comfort, smoothness, and quiet of a machine whose technological advance "does away with the tiresome necessity of having to plug ears with cotton wool." At 6,000 feet, *Heracles* was a "marvel of modern science."

References to 'the modern' appeared throughout the travelogue. For Pitt, they mostly materialized in combination with comments about speed-up. The nine-day duration of his flight, which he felt was "so short a time," offered panoramic views whose rapidly "changing scenes and all that they recalled had a strange effect upon my emotions." Through the airplane window, Pitt looked down, watched, and was transported. He felt present in a future, as "the whole history of the world had passed in review before [his] mind." From the locus of the plane, his "noisy modern spirit had been hushed by the associations of Palestine and the age-old unchanging mentality of the Arabs." History was outside the aircraft, below, inert, and beyond the rapidly moving payload without a past.

Cruising at altitude made passengers feel like they were in a different time and place. In the air, many of these incipient male travelers observed the affective effects of airborne flight. As the aforementioned reference to "changing scenes" revealed, Pitt sensed that passing comfortably, smoothly, quietly but quickly over the perceived past beneath him altered his emotions. He enjoyed being physically unable to touch what he was seeing. He enjoyed experiencing travel as contemplation. Aloft, moving east and south over western Europe, he "pondered," "wondered," "marveled," "dwelt upon the past glories of the Roman Empire," and was "saddened by the broken beauty of the Greeks." Leaving the debris behind, Pitt did something rare when, above the visual remnants of the wreckage below, he briefly considered contemporary European politics before moving on: "the seeming futility of . . . attempts to bolster up what may be a toppling civilisation."[44]

Alongside these somewhat maudlin sentiments, Pitt used language laden with a mix of racial and presentist overtones to describe his adventures above Palestine, "Arabia," and "the Arabs and the Turks." Compared to the imperial glories of Rome and ruined beauty of Greece, Pitt recalled "the old crusaders" when he encountered nonwestern people and places in-flight: a "profligate monster," "Sinbad the Sailor," and "the foundation of the famous fairy stories." On this section of the empire route, the Londoner likened himself to an early explorer who had "heard of [and possibly seen] an almost uncivilised race . . . whose existence is entirely unknown to most people." For Pitt, fast-paced flying to India was educational because it was emotional; it was a set of contained cultural and constructed historical experiences rooted in a newfangled form of detachment. As he put it, "All this and more I learnt" up in the air, in a new world, looking down at the old one through the window, as he passed it by.[45]

The People

Airline travel transformed the position and perspective of passengers from surface and horizontal to air and vertical. To explain to readers why this new way of moving was radical in its consequences, Imperial Airways and its clients used a range of images to turn going airborne into a colonial encounter. Among them were magic carpets, wings, and letters home.

When McCullough finished what he deemed and perhaps punned a "high-handed" mission, he called Imperial Airways a "magic carpet."[46] Similarly, when the *Gazette* published Pitt's travelogue it dubbed the airline thus, and when a journalist for *Modern Man* magazine described flying, he used the trope to explain his experience on Imperial Airways and the empire routes.[47] Why was flying on a plane like flying on a carpet? Why was flying magical?

Cultural references to airplanes as magic carpets existed before the empire-state and its airline forged routes in the 1920s. For example, four months after the First World War ended, an editor for the *Illustrated London News* used the image of the airplane as a magic carpet to describe his flight from London to Paris. For him the airplane was magical because it gave rise to a new class of mobility, reconfiguring the rift between the haves and the have-nots. As he put it, air travel "enabled its owners to be transported from one quarter of the globe to another at will . . . the rapid transition through space, the abolition of distance."[48]

By the time McCullough and Pitt flew the empire routes in the early 1930s, the association between airplanes and magic carpets registered differently. Alongside the above-mentioned associations with owner-ship, control, and instantaneous global passage, the meaning of airline travel expanded to include surveillance. As the adventures of Pitt and McCullough demonstrated, magic carpet references, with their long-standing orientalist affiliations, captured what it meant to fly over and watch rather than to pass through and touch the grounded lives of oth-ers; earlier remarks aligning airplanes with magic carpets seemed to as-sociate aerial movements more with transport than experience.[49]

This shift from prolonged horizontal to sustained vertical and horizontal travel reworked perceptions of colonial wildlife and race. Throughout the mid-1930s, the *Gazette* published a series of articles about what passengers flying over colonies saw. One article, "Wings over Africa" outlined how travel by air reoriented sight and prioritized distance. Prescriptively, it told readers that while flying from Alexan-dria to Johannesburg, they could swiftly "inspect quaint villages, note some of the curious customs of the little-known tribes, and catch fleet-ing glimpses of the continent's wildlife." It mentioned a male passenger who took pleasure in passing over and seeing the colonies: "elephants splashing about," "several groups of giraffe," "crocodiles and hippopot-ami were distinguishable," "great clouds of smoke from many bush fires," and "the best of the African natives." For him, this was "one of the most fascinating and thrilling of air journeys" because he "encountered"— without having to interact with—colonial life. For example, on his way to Uganda, he liked his look-down as he "passed over many native settle-ments, each surrounded by a wall of reeds and straw," and was extremely pleased when he could "detect black forms scattering from hut to hut, apparently calling to one another [to] come and see the white man rid-ing his 'strange bird.'"[50]

The airline traveler's reference to race is one of the few descriptions of how 'black' people in the colonies might have reacted to the metropoli-tan airline situating and moving privileged white men in and through the sky above them. On the one hand, the airborne man enjoyed the

double gaze of looking down at local inhabitants and having local inhabitants look up at him. He also liked how the vertical position of the
airplane distanced the watcher and the watched in a new way; he clearly
understood the power and privilege of his gendered, classed whiteness
in relation to it. On the other hand, his reference to the exaggerated gestures and wonderment of grounded subjects suggested that colonized
people might have found airline travel and the spectacle of colonizers
overhead absurd.

A newspaper article reprinted in the *Gazette* offers additional clues.
Three years before Imperial Airways winged that white man from northern to southern Africa, a journalist in Uganda observed, "The modern
Uganda native takes little notice of this new wonder which weekly appears over his head." Like the people McCullough met in Cyprus, the
local residents mentioned in this column found the "novelties of the
European" inconsequential. For the journalist, this indifference marked
ignorance: "So much that he cannot understand has been brought into
his surroundings and made part of daily life that further marvels per-
turb him very little." According to the author, the "modern efficiency"
and "amazement" of Imperial Airways profited European businessmen,
consumers, and other "us Colonials" while, for locals, air transport was
just another British technology. Like "the steam roller" or the "hot water
tap in his master's bedroom," the airline had "passed into his accepted
scheme of things. . . . It is enough for him that it has been brought by the
Europeans—all is thereby explained."⁵¹

To comprehend the significance of this observation of impassivity as
evidence of subaltern agency, it is important to note that the so-called
natives were colonial workers. With references to servants and market vendors pitted against comments about masters and patrons, the
journalist led readers to marvel at the moving plane by outlining how
an ascended airline descending affected the everyday life of labor on
the ground. When "the early activities of the day in the bazaar and the
market-day have subsided" and traders rest on verandahs while others
stroll around Entebbe, "the demeanour of them all clearly shows that for
them the chief business of the day is done." Then "suddenly, away in the
far distance, a speck appears in the sky. It rapidly approaches. . . . The
drone of the engines becomes louder and clearer and the huge 'plane is
quickly circling over the town," disrupting the pace of grounded work-

ers decelerating. For colonial workers and other oppressed people to disregard such efforts to establish Imperial Airways as a mighty and spectacular part of British imperial life—to ignore the constructed awesomeness of being airborne or to treat the technology of air transport as trivial—was likely a small but notable rebellious jab.[52]

Above and below, the experience of airline travel was about race. For some passengers, the physical gap between people in the air and on the ground repositioned racial hierarchies. During the summer of 1936, the *Gazette* published a series of letters that Harry, a man flying between Croydon and Johannesburg, wrote to his "Dearest Mother" in England. It was not the first or last time the magazine featured familial exchanges between male passengers and their kin.[53] However, Harry's letters were the only ones the *Gazette* deemed "good."[54]

What made Harry's letters so exceptional? At first glance, his missives were somewhat typical. Like other airline travelers, Harry wrote and sent his letters en route, and he described what it was like to inspect the below from the above, and to feel like he had conquered nature. He told "Dearest Mother" about seeing the sky change colors, as he reflected on how "the sun rose" like her son rose. He gawked at lives beneath him, acutely aware of the substantial somatic and technological distance that separated his existence from theirs: "we saw the Nile . . . a hive of activity, as wheels moved by donkeys, men in a line hoeing in unison certainly to a chant which we could not hear." Like other fliers, he also felt powerful when "we came down within 500 ft. of the ground" and the noise of the airplane spooked animals like the "four great herds of white elephant, which scattered as we flew over them." During layovers, he rather liked that "all was cool, clean and civilised and delightfully arranged" because it exhibited British betterment schemes, just as "the refreshments on a snow white table cloth showed that some Englishwoman (or at least British) was doing her bit to make the tropics better and brighter." Then, when his aerial escapades ended, he too concluded, "Imperial Airways put *up* the best show I've seen for efficiency and comfort of the passenger." Uplift, order, spectacle, and ease were all part of the performance.[55]

Unlike other airline travel writers, Harry explicitly linked speed-up to the formation of new racial differences and the obliteration of nuanced human diversity. On his way from Khartoum to Juba, he noticed how the landscape "changed gradually as we proceeded" south; "the trees got thicker" slowly down there. From the vantage point of speed-up Harry was able to survey and "see the hand of civilised man, as paths and roads went straight" across the territory's thickness. As Harry peered through the accentuated scope of his aircraft's quickened movement and suspended verticality, he deduced at a distance, "This is Africa now . . . from the air the villages look more like clumps of mushrooms than anything else. The natives are now just niggers the same as in Brazil."[56]

It is easy but amiss to suggest that affluent men alone helped build white flight, the move of white travelers from the below to the above. White women actively participated in the segregation practices that helped establish this new domain. In November 1937, the *Gazette* reprinted Genesta Long's empire air route story, which had first appeared in *Vogue*. (The writings of McCullough, Pitt, and Harry were previously unpublished.) Long was among the few women the magazine published. Her account was also one of the few that focused on women flying over the empire.[57]

Long flew Imperial Airways from England to South Africa. Like the male writers featured in the *Gazette*, she focused on what she saw when airborne in flight. She told her readers about "the full drama," "the kaleidoscopic changes of scenery," "the sudden arrivals in new worlds" that they would see if they took to the air. She talked about the magic carpet ride "over the hot Arabian deserts" and the "swoop over Africa," which she found to be the "most lovely and exciting flight of all." She also told women what to wear and when to wear what, when flying over the empire, which the men did not do for their gender. Long's instruction was a lesson the *Gazette* hoped women would want to learn: "We believe that it will be of particular interest to our women readers as it gives useful information on the type of clothes which should be worn."

Long included a meticulous shopping list. Women passengers en route to Africa must have "the right luggage and clothes." She had to be prepared. She needed two handbags and "a two-bottle, spill proof case for [her] day and evening scents, while [she] should have a special fitted travelling case for face lotions and all other liquid beauty things." She strongly advised, "For the first day's flight wear a light wool suit with a gay scarf and a reckless hat." Then, on the "next day wear a light linen frock and jacket, and have your dark glasses handy, for you will need them during the various stops." From remarks on how to wear an olive green "double felt hat" in Cairo to reminders to keep an "uncrushable lace dinner frock at hand, in case a party materialises" in Rome, Long told women how their bodies should look during flight.

Fashion advice was, and still is, more than advice about fashion. On those rare occasions when it was given in the *Gazette*, it was unabashedly about the intersectional construction of race, particularly whiteness, class, gender, and the aerial style. Long's directives chronicled, and thereby helped to create, the hazards and dangers women passengers faced while flying. Layovers, for example, were risky for white women, though not for men like McCullough. Long insisted that travel over Sudan had to be "a trouser day." "There are halts, at strange, desert places such as Malakal and Butiaba, where, leaning upon their spears, groups of apparently one-legged people stand staring; silent, stork-like Dinkas, coal-black." Women should be content to "watch carefully out of the window" and see the "savage red bluff of the Nandi Escarpment, a wild country and the home of a wild and difficult tribe," much as Pitt had done en route to India. That said, women must also prepare for and protect themselves from the black unknown of flight, according to Long and the two magazines that printed her work. Women need to keep wearing trousers when they fly over places "mysterious and pregnant with strange things, a bit of the primeval world lost in the heart of the dark continent." Only "after the many strange and primitive places you have seen from beneath the wings of your plane" should you put that "thin linen frock" back on.[58]

Skywriters

The air travel story is powerful. Sometimes people ask for it, sometimes people just give it, and sometimes people keep it to themselves. Not everyone has one because not everyone can.

The air travel story is never just a story. It has history. It was and remains a way people learned how to live—or live in relation to those who could be—in the air. One version encouraged people to use airmail. It taught them to trust, and now to expect, that their things would arrive quickly and safely on time. It was how some people unlearned how to wait.

Another kind of narrative explained how to be a passenger: how to move and occupy space; how to see and be seen; how to dress; to expect entertainment; to expect service; to expect to have an experience; to assume all onboard will be like you.

For the most part, the tales in this chapter were industry stories. They were part of how a culture of airline travel was made. For Imperial Airways, they helped to establish and sell British air travel. Other national airlines had their own stories to tell.

The colonial world was at the heart of how modern flight was fashioned. Airline passage altered how travelers understood themselves and felt about others. For first-generation passengers on the empire routes, the accelerated and sustained movement of the plane through vertical space reconfigured power. For some, the combination of hastening and hovering through the sky started to turn airspace into a dwelling place. Passengers like Pitt experienced the high speed of airborne mobility, the containment of the airliner cabin, and the airy gap between below and above as a transient yet inhabitable setting beyond historical time. Flying, the perceived seamlessness of being in the above led them to render the territories and folks being passed over as vestiges of an elsewhere and elsewhen.

For other airline travelers, the airplane journey was more than a mechanism of modernity. Going airborne generated feelings inextricably linked to furthering the enterprise of empire. Men like McCullough saw themselves as imperial agents, and they executed their Britishness accordingly. Long-haul layovers—the repeated act of rapidly ascending, descending, touching down, and abruptly taking off again—generated new geographies of selfhood. The heading-up, leveling, and coming-down of flight fashioned a very different way for these men on the go to imagine themselves inspecting metropolitan contrivances and instituting colonial order while dashing between places.

Flight was a colonial encounter. Passenger accounts illuminate how airline travel could vividly change a person's appreciation of cultural specificity and limit his, her, or their ability to empathize with others. Adventurers such as Harry enjoyed personal mobility in three-dimensional space largely because access to aerial surveillance facilitated a version of firsthand visual knowledge that made him feel racially superior. From his perspective, via the elevated vistas of the plane, all black people seemed the same.

Early airline travel enabled people to embody and experience the racial hierarchies of vertical power relations. The tales told about their experiences help us to understand the racialized practices, everyday oppressions, and dimensions of inequality that were—and still are—at work when people move overhead. Speed-up rearranged space, and the perceived miracle and magic of air transport was twofold for passengers: Its ability to reduce travel times shrank distances on the one hand and its ability to enlarge the span between sky and ground expanded distance on the other. On different planes, the inside and the outside seemed detached, never touching. For the grounded, however, this new form of movement might have meant something different. They are not dominant in the archive, but their momentary actions offer a slightly atypical way to make sense of air mobility during this period. Rather than imply that the onset of airline travel was profoundly remarkable, their gestures suggest that, though the geometry of empire was mounting upward and in the ordinary sky, there was a hint of familiarity about how to negotiate the arrival of this kind of power. Far from expressions of technological awe or evolution, pointing, disregarding, and gawking might also have been a way for people on the ground to uncover, then undercut, the racialist inflections embedded in the latest implement of imperial rule.

The Infrequent Flier

I return briefly to one of the earliest fragments in this book to highlight a few of the reasons why airline stories matter: Terminal, Fragment 2. The death of Jimmy Mubenga has received a lot of media coverage. It has appeared in this and other academic works, and nongovernmental organizations and activists have recounted it over and again. And thankfully so. The death of vulnerable people on commercial airlines, which includes people who are being deported, is not new. Many of the men and women who have died while escorted by private security corporations died in a manner similar to Mubenga. Those deaths are not as well known.

The passengers and crew members who were on board the British Airways flight with Mubenga have done a tremendous job of documenting and sharing their stories. Their detailed accounts have played important roles in the investigations and case studies of governmental and nongovernmental organizations. They have also helped to bring attention to one of the ways in which the commercial airline industry and the deportation industry support and profit from each other.

There are many reasons why the death of Mubenga is well known, but I want to draw attention to one in particular: the ground. Unlike most other cabin deaths, his came to pass on the ground; the plane had not taken off. Admittedly, as someone who studies cultural practices aboard airliners in flight, I am acutely aware of location. However, when one reads travel stories from that flight with location in mind, the significance of the sky starts to open up: "He'll be alright," a guard explained, "once we get him in the air."[59]

The airliner cabin is a place. This chapter has sought to show how air places were built through narrative, as well how those with access to airline travel learned to inhabit the airplane and live in the sky. In particular, it has drawn attention to the broader state projects that were involved in the construction of air places. Nowadays, occasional and frequent fliers tend not to think of the cabin as a place of humanity; from airmail to lessons about how to see the below from above, the normalization of air travel and the promotion of individualism were part of how the industry was made. The guard's statement points to how power, in particular state and corporate power, benefits from the idea of the cabin as a nonplace and flying as a liminal practice. 'Un-grounding' knowledge-making practices and critically sharing stories about the unremarkable—about *how* ordinary lives are lived in the everyday sky—is one way to struggle against the old flying lessons that have made the air, as the guard put it, seem like a place to "be alright."[60]

AIR CRAFT

Oversees

There are two white couples, man and woman, on a beach. They are standing in the water and sitting on the sand pointing at the airplane flying above and across them. The plane is high enough to fly; it is low enough to cast its shadow and to throw shade.

The scene is part of an advertisement. In 1937, Imperial Airways and Pan American Airways, the chief international air carrier for the United States, launched a new transatlantic service. The scene was designed to promote and sell it (see Figure 3).

BERMUDA . . . *IN 5 HOURS* is written across the top of the ad, in gold. Short, sharp white lines follow right behind the number "5" and the "H," signifying the fast pace and time of the new service. PAN AMERICAN AIRWAYS and IMPERIAL AIRWAYS are written in the left and right corners at the bottom of the ad, respectively. The letters of the names and the color of the plane's shadow appear to be made of the same shade of blue. The airplane itself is not shown. The route is difficult to discern. Conventional points of departure and arrival are not disclosed; the above and the below are shown.

The alliance is advertised. The scene is of two airlines, two countries, an up and down direction, one half of a route (Bermuda), fastness, one race, and three planes. The three planes are the airplane; the ocean, a much older plane; and the air plane, which the shadow helps illuminate. The other half of the route is New York.

For all of that to happen, an airline in the Caribbean had to end.

Figure 3. "Bermuda in 5 Hours," poster, 98–20257, NASM.

5

Routes

A route has roots.

At some point in the late 1930s, Imperial Airways mapped its international and empire routes—twice. One placed the world in the air. Land floated, above the clouds, in a dark blue sky, which could have also been the sea. The routes linked the continents. Speedbird, the airline's emblematic mark, was up there too (see Figure 4).

Three types of routes were shown on the map. There was a solid yellow route. Imperial Airways and its associated companies operated it. There was a broken yellow route. Each segment represented a service that was "projected or under investigation for operation." There was a solid green route. Other air transportation companies ran it.

An arrow on the left end of the green line said that the routes came from the right. At the center of the map was London. All routes seemed to start or bundle there. From the center, they spread across the world.

Figure 4. "Map of Empire," poster, 98–20236, NASM.

When the yellow routes touched spaces, those spaces turned into named places. Sometimes only a name appeared: Marseilles, Vienna, New York, Saigon. Sometimes territories lit up and were named: Dominions of Canada, Kenya, Lagos, and Sydney. Their regions, capitals, cities, and towns were named too. Their rivers and lakes were not. These places were pink, the cartographic color of the empire. The rest of the world was grey, blank space; the green route, which cut through, wrapped around, and touched spaces, did not transform those spaces into named places.

There were two spheres on the map. The smaller one, which explained what the three colored routes were, was the key. The larger one was a map of the routes operated by the airline and its affiliates; it was the unbroken yellow route, reconfigured. The map within a map had no land. Instead, it used miles to measure and state the air distance from London to some place. Shaped colors referenced "the daily and greater" frequency of flights.[1]

The second Imperial Airways map was called "The Link of Empire." It identified the routes the airline and its associated companies operated. Numbers on each route represented the frequency of services per week, in both directions (see Figure 5).

"The Link of Empire" did not show land, water, air, depth, distance, an above or below. The frequencies were the lone indications of time. There were no countries. There was no point of origin. There were cities and they were named. London was not one of them.

It was a map of movement. Each number represented two airplanes on the go.[2] There was no sense of when and where routes or times started and stopped; planes moved constantly through a continuous closed circuit system of straight lines and square switch points.

Both maps showed routes as networks. At first glance, each network seems closed. On the first map, routes linked and flowed in a seamless line across the world; however, the broken yellow route, which ran across the Atlantic, down the eastern United States, down the Caribbean sea, between London and Portugal, between Kano, Lagos, and Takoradi, and between eastern Australia and New Zealand, didn't actually exist. On the second map, all but one route twisted and branched through many places. They formed a single unbroken link through the empire. All of them existed and operated; however, the boxed route

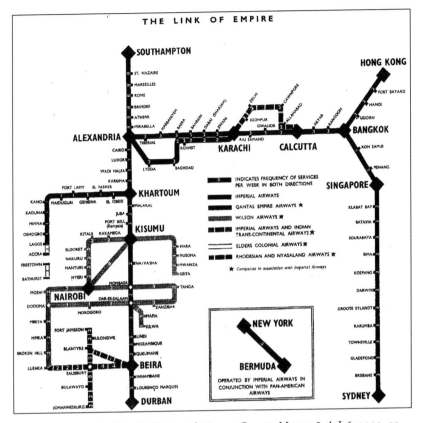

Figure 5. "The Link of Empire," *Imperial Airways Gazette*, May 1938, A1I-600000–05, NASM.

near the bottom did not bend. Imagined on the first map and realized on the second, the line between Bermuda and New York was set apart. It was not like the others.[3]

The Alliance

Bermuda–New York was the first transatlantic route of its kind between Britain and the United States, which may seem odd. We tend to use 'transatlantic' to denote bidirectional, left-to-right flows across the Atlantic Ocean (e.g., the transatlantic slave trade). This sense of the prefix trans- simply means across, to be on the other side of something. And an ocean has many sides.

In the summer of 1937, Imperial Airways and Pan American started a joint passenger service between a colony and a city. Each week, there were two return flights between Bermuda and New York. The frequency of scheduled passenger flights doubled within the year. Flying boats were used for the 5 hours and 30 minutes air journey. Imperial Airways flew the *Cavalier*, Pan American the *Bermuda Clipper*. The service was geared toward businessmen and vacationists.

The airlines promoted Bermuda–New York as a transatlantic route. Declarations such as "the first of trans-Atlantic air routes" and "the world's two greatest air transport systems" appeared together on materials such as timetables and brochures. Mention of "the first" implied that there were more transatlantic routes to come.[4]

The Bermuda–New York route was a feat. British and U.S. radio programs and newspapers praised the partnership and the new service. The National Broadcasting Corporation of America (NBC) and the British Broadcasting Corporation (BBC) aired the words of Captain W. N. Cumming on the same day. Cumming, a British pilot, was executing the final test flight before services began. During flight, he narrated what he could see from 3,000 feet in the air to listeners of the NBC and BBC programs. He described "the white roofs of Bermuda" as they quickly turned into "the dark buildings of New York," from the *Cavalier*. From the plane, which was named for the first British colonists of the Americas, he thanked the two countries for creating a single "remarkable flight." Newspapers also acknowledged the global power of the airline alliance. The route was the last link needed to "close the only gap in a system whereby the world will be girdled by air transport," according to the *New York Times*. In other papers it was called the "stepping stone."[5]

Bermuda–New York was the first step in the formation of an Anglo-American transatlantic airline system. The route opened up access to territories and financial markets. Imperial Airways obtained landing rights in the United States, and Pan American obtained them in the British Atlantic. The route also extended the global reach of Britain and the United States. As the publicity director of Pan American, William Van Dusen, put it, his airline had teamed up with "the big gun." Imperial Airways and Britain had "networks of routes spread across Europe, Africa, Asia, and India that already cover half the globe." Together, the two airlines and their countries were "moulding a new world force."[6]

Less than four weeks after the passenger service between Bermuda and New York had begun, the airlines started to survey other parts of the Atlantic.[7] The airlines each wanted to operate bidirectional, east-to-west routes across the northern and southern Atlantic. The northern passageway was well known for its geographic challenges. As the General Manager of Short Brothers, one of the first aircraft manufacturing companies, told the Institution for Mechanical Engineers, "The transatlantic route is the most difficult on which to establish regular services." A flight from England to Canada, by way of the Irish Free State and Newfoundland, spanned more than 2,000 miles of ocean, lasted approximately sixteen hours, and was restricted to the summer months. It was also known to be one of the most active oceanic trade routes in the world.[8]

The transatlantic was also a crucial part of the imperial air route scheme. Britain was eager to build along the southern corridor and desperate to create a commercial air bridge to Canada, its dominion in the north. And Pan American knew it. "They [Britain] must bridge the North Atlantic to complete the final link in an empire chain," Van Dusen sharply noted, so as "to hold every land under the British flag to the mother country." Bermuda–New York was "significant," as Van Dusen called it, because the route "bears an even greater importance."[9]

Meanwhile, down in Jamaica, a local colonial airline service was under way. For all kinds of reasons, which are about to unfold, its fate was tied to the future of Bermuda–New York. Transatlantic pathways between the United States and United Kingdom are some of the most significant commercial air corridors in the world. Their histories begin in the Caribbean.

The Recommendation

In 1926, the Secretary of State for Air, Sir Samuel Hoare, created the West Indian Air Transport Committee, which was a London-based group. He asked colleagues in the Colonial Office to help him assemble a committee to "consider generally what opportunities exist" for commercial aviation in the British Caribbean. They selected eight men from six organizations: the Air Ministry, Colonial Office, Department of Overseas Trade, General Post Office, West India Committee, and West Indian Aviation Committee. There was one delegate from each division, except for the Air Ministry, which had three. The committee gave Hoare its final report a year later. He reviewed the document and described it as a "valuable survey." It was twenty pages long.[10]

The committee found that several opportunities existed in the Caribbean and encouraged the development of a network of airline services throughout the region. It identified these advantages in the report. The reasons the report offered clarified what was considered an advantage: opportunities arose when their existence directly, not inadvertently, benefited Britain. The assumption was that anything that served Britain would by default serve the colonies. It was an old logic, long used to justify development initiatives in the Caribbean: if the master benefits so then does the slave.

Among the "many advantages" that "impressed" the delegates was an opportunity to master nature. Like Frederick Sykes at the first air conference, delegates imagined that commercial aviation would overcome what seemed to them to be obstacles. They measured the geographic span of the British Caribbean, which they estimated to be around 1,800 miles in length. They then contemplated the "considerable distances" between the islands, and from the chain of islands to British Guiana. Scheduled airline services would provide for the coveted "speeding-up" of communications and require the construction of "rapid transport facilities." Each feature would improve the flow of goods. It was a "maximum benefit" from the committee's point of view. Commercial air transportation promised to bridge distances faster than the maritime system already in place, which delegates assumed was a good thing. (The sea was central to Caribbean cultural life and livelihoods, to say nothing of its historical importance to the African diaspora and its significance to the growth of black radicalism during this period.)[11]

It was a judgment call steeped in the ideology of empire. The committee saw seagoing travel between islands as "non-existent or intermittent," which was part of the logic of speed-up. Delegates in London looked for movements that seemed fast, which was what they knew, valued, and wanted. They used their version of fastness to find and evaluate rate in the Caribbean with ease and without question. Britain required "regular and rapid transport" across a totally interconnected, though not necessarily integrated, Caribbean. The committee thought the current networks were shoddy because they didn't "draw closer the bonds of common interest." They were talking about imperial bonds. The goal was to move cargo faster between the Caribbean colonies, the dominion of Canada, and Europe, and to "facilitate administration of the islands of the Lesser Antilles." The objective resembled the racialized imperial air route scheme recommended to Churchill toward the end of October 1919, as the committee sought "to draw attention to the advantages which would accrue from the establishment of an air service between these two parts of the Empire [Canada and the West Indies]."[12]

The accelerated cargo was mainly mail and freight. The committee determined that they were the most "lucrative bulk for bulk," economically and culturally, given the promotional appeal of heaviness.[13] There were a few, sporadic references to passenger traffic in the report. Although West Indians were occasionally mentioned, for the most part they were present in their absence. The committee investigated "the prospects of future development of tourist traffic." In imperial cultures like London, the envisioned tourist, especially one headed for the tropics, was more often than not white.[14] As migrant workers moved back and forth between islands and the islands confronted extended population pressures, the writers of the report described fliers as "first class passengers." They delighted in the idea that these passengers would dart between islands in hours instead of days by boat. Island hopping by air would be a "saving in time." "The comparatively small size" of, and number of people on, each island were the reasons given for not picturing West Indians as airline passengers, despite population pressures widespread across the region.[15]

The committee entertained the possibility that foreign companies would help finance the development of commercial aviation in the British Caribbean. The airplane opened access to areas once difficult to reach. There was "valuable merchandise" there: timber, minerals, diamond and gold mining spots above rapids, and petroleum, which was of particular interest. The combination of petroleum and commercial aviation was full of "favourable opportunities" for the metropole. In one scenario, seaplanes would ferry full oil drums between Trinidad and Venezuela. The favorable opportunity was that foreign oil companies and other undertakings had already "expressed their willingness" to back a British air transport company in the Caribbean.[16]

It was a somewhat odd scenario. The growing presence of foreign operations in the area was one of the main arguments for the development of British air transport "as soon as reasonably possible." But it was pitted against concerns about "assuring adequate revenue." Fears about funds constrained the kind of commercial aviation delegates were willing to conjure up and carry out in the Caribbean. The report expressed an immediate desire to forge and fuse an empire route by establishing a comprehensive aviation system in the Americas. But the committee didn't think a "large subsidy from Imperial Funds" should be given. "A regular service throughout the West Indies cannot for the present be entertained."

There was another option. The committee recommended a more "practical solution" that involved the prevention of "foreign penetration," the protection of "British interests," and the development of "local services." The colonies could fund the imperial project. In short, the committee advocated for colonial airlines as a way to circumvent using imperial money to fund an imperial project.

The report advised Britain to encourage colonial governments to establish local airline services. It should start with places most likely to generate "early commercial success." These were the Bahamas, British Guiana, Trinidad, and the Windward and Leeward Islands. It advised "with some reluctance . . . that for purposes of trade alone they cannot at present recommend such a service for Jamaica." Ironically, Jamaica was where the feasibility of this proposal was tested.[17]

The Attempt

In June 1930, Archie de Pass launched one of the first local airlines in the British Caribbean: Caribbean Airways. A retired Royal Air Force captain from England, de Pass devised and registered his venture in colonial Jamaica. This meant that Caribbean Airways was a private British company. Its managing director and chairman was de Pass. Six other directors helped to administer the airline. Their professions, which included planter, merchant, and publisher, covered a wide range of areas and interests. All the directors resided in the Caribbean. Many of de Pass's Jamaican peers felt like he was one of them: "He was really practically a Jamaican; and they were pleased to have him as a Jamaican."[18]

When de Pass created Caribbean Airways, artificial flight was not unknown in the region. For more than a century, lighter-than-air craft such as sizable balloons hovered as scientific experiments over the islands. For decades, military fliers and other aviators maneuvered their heavier-than-air machines through the area. A few years before the airline began, Charles Lindbergh famously toured the territories, and the Trinidadian-born Hubert Fauntleroy Julian declared that he would be the first black aviator to fly solo across the Atlantic.[19]

By the 1930s, public interest in aviation was mounting in the Caribbean.[20] As part of this developing enterprise, Caribbean Airways survived the first year. Like airline executives in other parts of the world, its directors tried to secure the company's future by focusing primarily on the development of scheduled airfreight services. By the end of 1930, Caribbean Airways had flown an unknown amount of cargo from privately owned land in Kingston to nearby islands such as Cuba and Hispaniola with "great success" and had occasionally used a four-seater seaplane for local taxi and sightseeing work.[21]

Although Caribbean Airways endured its first year, it faced peculiar financial ruin in its second. In July 1931, de Pass wrote to the Secretary of State for the Colonies and declared that the company could not "run on private Capital."[22] To save the airline, de Pass and the other directors asked the Jamaican government to apply for an aviation advancement grant, which was a loan awarded and administered by the Colonial Development Fund in Britain. If granted, the imperial government in Britain would distribute funds directly to the colonial government in Jamaica, and Caribbean Airways would become a government-sponsored airline.

Support from the Jamaican government was not guaranteed. When twenty-six representatives from twelve Caribbean territories met in Barbados for "the contemplation of the idea of unified action" at the First West Indies Conference, the representative for Jamaica was most ambivalent about airlines. While some representatives thought a regional airline network was of "vital importance to the British Empire," he was fine with local services and lukewarm toward this "big project which was in the air."[23] Short remarks made in the popular press and archives alluded to the administration refusing to sponsor Atlantic Airways, a company that might have been proposed, rejected, and aborted around the same time that de Pass started his airline.[24] Likewise, records documenting the application process for Caribbean Airways revealed that the

Jamaican government had rebuffed aviation affairs for years. Minutes sent to the colonial secretary about the future of the airline indicated, "The attitude of the Government has always been that it would not get mixed up in running flying services."[25] The minutes also summarized the question foremost on the minds of decision makers amid a severe economic depression: "Why should the Government trouble about a concern such as this when we have excellent flying services at present at no cost to the Government?"[26]

In 1931, the somewhat apathetic stance of the Jamaican government shifted significantly. That year, officials decided that the administration would advocate on behalf of the airline. As a result, the government set out to secure imperial money from Britain. It submitted an application for an aviation advancement grant. In the supporting papers, the company's operational dreams curiously, and perhaps strategically, outweighed remarks about the airline's operational reality.[27]

Americanization

After years of relative indifference, what prompted the Jamaican government to support Caribbean Airways in the 1930s? When local entrepreneurs, colonial administrators, and imperial bureaucrats started to evaluate the utility of the airline, a series of debates and disputes arose about the United States and Pan American Airways. Attention to these conversations explains why the fate of Caribbean Airways was connected to concerns about the future of the British empire.

By the time de Pass asked for help and the Jamaican government asked for aid, Pan American—*the* international carrier for the United States—led commercial airline operations in the Caribbean. From its inception in 1927, Pan American focused on the development of aviation to and through the region. Its first flight and scheduled service operated between southwest Florida and northwest Cuba in the fall of that year. Shortly thereafter, the U.S. government asked Pan American to build "an American flag system of air transportation to Latin America."[28] The geography of the Caribbean was integral to the construction of this system; the United States and its carrier saw the archipelago and its ports as the perfect steppingstone for using limited-range flying boats between North and South America. As part of this imperial vision, Pan American started a scheduled service between Miami and the Bahamas in January 1929. The route, which was the company's foray into the British Caribbean, expanded, extended, and branched out quickly. Within two years, Pan American broadcast that it crisscrossed the Caribbean "more than 80,000 miles every week or 4,000,000 miles" annually.[29] Among the countries and islands included in this count were Haiti, the Dominican Republic, Trinidad, and Curaçao. Jamaica was not listed.[30]

Jamaica was strategically important to Pan American. As one of the southern- and westernmost islands in the Caribbean Sea, the airline considered Jamaica an ideal stopping point and refueling station en route to Central America.[31] In 1930, the company secured landing rights at Bumper Hall Airbase in Kingston and its operations underwent a dramatic transformation. In the winter of that year, approximately six months after Caribbean Airways began operating, Pan American introduced the first nonstop service between Jamaica and Panama. Before it had acquired landing rights at Bumper Hall, the airline flew from Florida to Panama by way of Cuba, British Honduras, and other places in Central America. Flying from Kingston enabled Pan American to cut the flying distance from 2,064 miles to 1,385 miles, compressing travel time from fifty-six to twenty-four hours, and offering "the longest nonstop over-water flight regularly operated at the time anywhere in the world."[32]

Across the Atlantic, officials in Britain were worried. Already apprehensive about the fact that British air transport lagged behind other countries, they feared Pan American's operations in the Caribbean would obstruct Hoare's "Empire Air Route" project.[33] The imperial government wanted to cultivate a sense of unity and cooperation among its territories by erecting a single unbroken air route across the entire empire, which was slightly different from what had been recommended to Churchill in 1919. As part of this project, it actively encouraged colonial governments to create local feeder lines to link with imperial air services. For the British Caribbean, the plan was clear. The imperial government wanted a network of regional airlines to reduce distances among the islands; to feed traffic into the major imperial air route and shrink travel times between the Caribbean and Britain; and to decrease distances between territories located north, south, east, and west of England, which was where the hub of the route was located.[34]

As Pan American's operations extended across the Caribbean and threatened the development of the empire air route, British bureaucrats wondered what to do. In the Air Ministry, an official mulled over the acquisition of landing rights at Bumper Hall and wrote to a colleague in the Colonial Office about "the danger of Pan American" in Jamaica. He explained that "an American monopoly of our operations combined with their occupation of the base would give the United States [*sic*] interests a stranglehold on any ultimate attempt to develop British Civil aviation in this area." Responding to the rising pressure, the Colonial Office decided to send Major R. H. Mayo to the Caribbean. As the technical adviser to Imperial Airways, he was asked to examine, evaluate, and expose prospects for British aviation over there. Before he left England, Mayo was given clear instructions: visit the colony of Bermuda and the Leeward Islands and discern how to implement the recommendations made by the West Indian Air Transport Committee.[35]

The Trip

Mayo left for the Caribbean four years after the West Indian Air Transport Committee disclosed its findings. He was charged with the task of surveying particular places; along the way, he changed his plans. In 1931, a combination of British ships and U.S. planes carried the technical adviser from England to Bermuda, south through the Leeward and Windward Islands to Trinidad.

In order to appreciate the long-term consequences of his altered plans, it is important to understand how Mayo and the airline he counseled felt about Pan American and the possibility of empire air routes in the western Atlantic. Like the government it served, Imperial Airways' initial operations from Britain to its overseas territories in the mid-1920s prioritized the development of British air services in Africa, Southeast Asia, and Australia, viewing collaboration with companies across the Atlantic as a way to establish commercial operations in the Americas.[36] With this approach in mind, Mayo, like members of the West Indian Air Transport Committee, believed that British-owned air services were lacking in the Caribbean. In his final report, he referred to certain "sources" that had severely constrained local aviation advances and marked Pan American as a "factor of outstanding importance." The overlap between the technical adviser and the committee ended there. Mayo commended the United States and condemned Britain for their respective aerial advances. In his opinion, the nation-state had done in the Caribbean what the empire-state had not been able to do for its colonies:

> This American organization has been able to do precisely what the West Indian Transportation Committee found to be commercially impracticable for British interests in 1926. It has introduced and maintained regular weekly services which not only link together the principal islands of the West Indies, but also provide through communication between these islands and North, South, and Central America. . . . [B]roadly speaking, the Pan American system provides a comprehensive main-line airways system for the whole of the West Indian Group.

According to Mayo, Pan American had pervaded, coalesced, and modernized areas of the British Caribbean. Such a claim played on the aforementioned fears about foreign companies impeding plans to advance British aviation in the Atlantic. It thwarted visions of forging imperial unity by air.

Mayo wanted Britain to inveigle Pan American. He believed that an alliance with Pan American would provide the infrastructure needed to operate adequate airline services in the Caribbean without further depleting an already exhausted imperial fund. There were two parts to his argument: money and politics. First, Mayo declared Pan American "a fait accompli" and implored the imperial government to foster aviation "in relation" to the existing carrier. To support this instruction, Mayo pointed out that the West Indian Air Transport Committee had already decided that a regional airline was "commercially impracticable" and concluded that the imperial government could avoid "subsidization on a very large scale" by joining forces with the U.S. airline.

Second, Mayo claimed that West Indian interests were ultimately expendable. He was "doubtful whether any political advantage which might be gained through such a service could be held to justify the inevitably high cost." Consequently, he concluded that Britain should cultivate regional airline services by backing foreign rather than colonial enterprises. Mayo believed this would allow Britain to get maximum gain for minimum money while advancing commerce and communication. The advantage was threefold. International collaboration would enhance exchanges among the islands, across the empire, and between Britain and the United States. As Mayo put it, "[T]he establishment of the main-line system of Pan American Airways may have made it more worthwhile for the Governments concerned to consider the possibilities of state-aided local services."

What might have motivated Mayo to pursue an alliance with a U.S. company? It was possible that his firm stance was tethered to an interest in generating a transatlantic airline service. During his tour, Mayo assessed options for the construction of a British flight path over and across the Atlantic. First, he considered fashioning a route between England, the Azores, and Bermuda. Mayo rejected this option because of weather patterns and infrastructural shortfalls, both which "were, from the aviation point of view, definitely bad."[37] Next, he offered some alternatives to this partially established route. Despite the fact that the North Atlantic was a notoriously dangerous course, Mayo argued that England–Newfoundland–New York–Bermuda should constitute the "inaugural stages of Atlantic air services." No companies were named and few reasons were given, yet Mayo envisioned a long-range service through the British territories and a "regular shuttle service" to cover the "trifling distance" between Bermuda and New York. A report on aviation for the Caribbean, which included remarks such as "good prospects that Imperial Airways and Pan American Airways would be able to co-operate" and the "desirability of co-operation between British and American interests," ended by deeming the route between Bermuda and New York the "almost inevitable . . . logical one."[38]

If Mayo imagined a transatlantic pathway that involved the United States, local aviation advances underway in Jamaica posed a significant threat. While in the Caribbean, Mayo felt that he should "pay a short visit" to the island, despite the fact that the West Indian Air Transport Committee had determined that Jamaica should not participate in an airline development scheme. He held that "developments which have been taking place" made it "desirable" for him to travel there. Later, he would claim that the "visit to this Colony assisted me in reviewing the prospects for British aviation in the West Indies generally." In other words, the future of British flight across the Atlantic rested on outcomes that were uncertain in Jamaica.

The developments Mayo mentioned referred to Caribbean Airways. During his time in the western Caribbean, Mayo learned that the company was operating interisland services to and from Kingston. This troubled him. Interested in using what he identified as "American taxpayer" funds to develop communication and transportation services for Britain, he was concerned that the operations of Caribbean Airways risked endangering the Pan American stronghold. After all, Kingston was a vital node in the intercontinental services of Pan American.

To a certain extent, it was peculiar that a struggling colonial carrier was considered a viable threat, in part because its competitor was an established company backed by the United States. Nonetheless, in his report Mayo went to great lengths to characterize the relatively new airline as a hindrance and liability. He was deeply concerned about the recently formed alliance between Caribbean Airways and the Jamaican government. He warned, "This company shall in future control all aviation operations at Jamaica on behalf of the Government. This appears to have given rise to a somewhat unfortunate situation in regard to Pan American."

Caribbean Airways had recently acquired the Bumper Hall airfield, which was the "somewhat unfortunate situation" mentioned by Mayo. Before he arrived on the island, the Jamaican government had decided to lease the air base to the local airline for "a nominal rent." According to the terms of the lease, Pan American had to pay all fees for landing rights and fuel taken aboard directly to the colonial carrier. Mayo feared that Pan American would relocate to Cuba, leaving Jamaica and therefore the British Caribbean because of "unduly high" charges.

Mayo knew that if he ultimately aimed to use U.S. money for British interests, he had to propose that Pan American maintain a monopoly in Jamaica. He advised the imperial government to oppose all domestic aviation projects in Jamaica; this was the only colony for which he argued this point. To support his claim and safeguard Pan American's stronghold, Mayo tried different tactics. For instance, he teetered toward environmental determinism and argued that the "geographic situation" of the island, which was "very mountainous and densely cultivated," did not easily lend itself to flying endeavors. He toyed with fears about financial ruin by claiming that a "substantial financial burden" would accrue for Britain if it allowed a colonial carrier to compete with a U.S. airline.

To convince state officials in London to intervene on behalf of a foreign company, Mayo ultimately used language that linked Caribbean Airways to the undoing of what he called "British prestige." First, he reminded readers of his report that "it is often stated that British prestige has suffered in the West Indies through the establishment of the Pan American Airways services and failure of British enterprise to compete in this field." Then, he drew on his firsthand knowledge and claimed that he "did not observe any signs that British prestige had suffered except at Jamaica." Next, he challenged the Britishness of the colonial company by arguing that "there is no British air service" in Jamaica. (The International Air Convention of 1919 held that all airlines registered in colonial territories must carry the nationality of their empire-states.)[39] Finally, he predicted that "a sound Anglo-American service on the Bermuda–United States route would do far more to enhance British prestige" than a colonial airline in the Caribbean. Deftly playing with the discord between Britain as an imperial state with unabashed global power strengthened by any means necessary and Britain as a colonial empire with maternal-like responsibilities toward dependent kith and kin, Mayo urged his audience to promote the prominence of the British nation, preserve the money of the imperial government, and obtain the dollars of American taxpayers by dissolving Caribbean Airways. It was, as he saw it, "a golden opportunity."[40]

The Choice

Whereas Mayo claimed that Caribbean Airways jeopardized chances for an international alliance with Pan American, Jamaican officials argued that their colonial airline could not compete with that foreign carrier. Attention to the strategies used by airline activists reveals that their fight for Caribbean Airways hinged on two vantage points: the political and the practical. While Mayo prepared his report, the Jamaican government applied for an aviation advancement grant. Success seemed likely for the pioneering carrier and colony. A few years earlier, the imperial government had started to thwart foreign efforts to advance air travel in or over British territories, using the language of prestige as justification. It pushed its counterparts in the dependencies to develop local air services and promulgated the Colonial Development Act. This legislation provided ample funds for different modernization projects. The "improvement of internal transport and communications" in crown territories was listed as an approved scheme.[41]

On Christmas Eve 1931, the colonial government and airline asked administrators of the Colonial Development Fund to grant them £100,000. The grant writers were intent on saving the company from insolvency so they wrote a document that focused on two facts: operations were well under way in Jamaica and the airline was British. For the first point, they underscored the fact that the company offered overseas flights to Haiti and Cuba, trained local pilots, helped inaugurate airmail services, and owned three amphibian aircraft: a Vickers Flying Boat, a Canadian Fairchild, and a de Havilland Moth. For the second point, they called attention to Jamaica's colonial status and emphasized that Caribbean Airways was the only British airline in the region. They stressed that the airline was cultivating air-mindedness and fostering "the flying spirit" among Britain's seafaring subjects.[42] They also toyed with imperial sympathies, noting plans to "form a nucleus of an all red North to South route."[43] Four months later, in April 1932, the advisory committee for the development fund met for the forty-seventh time in London. Consideration of the application written on behalf of Caribbean Airways was on the agenda. That day, when committee members rejected the request, neither the imagined kinship of empire nor the sense of duty fostered by it could convince the imperial government to support a British company in the colonies. Instead, the committee felt the Jamaican government "should be asked to state from a practical as apart from a political point" why it deserved the money.[44]

In Jamaica, the news was interpreted as rejection. Advocates for the airline were angry. Many of them felt that political concerns, such as defense against foreign enterprise, far outweighed practical matters, such as immediate effectiveness. For example, on May 2, 1932, W. D. B., who was a member of the Jamaican government and a determined campaigner for the local carrier, wrote to the Colonial Secretary and begged him to let Britain know that a subsidy would "avoid us being swamped by Pan American."[45] He believed it was "exceptionally galling" that a colonial enterprise was "done in the eye" by a foreign company and berated Imperial Airways for betting against another British company.[46] According to W. D. B., the Pan American stronghold shamed and degraded Jamaica and

Britain. In other letters, he admitted that from a "practical point of view" Pan American was "infinitely more efficient" than Caribbean Airways.[47] However, he strongly believed that from a "political point of view" it was "undesirable" to permit a company from the United States to "control flying services in a British Colony."[48] In a colony rocked by labor unrest and stirred by black nationalism, he worried about a total loss of local confidence not only in British industry, interest, and ingenuity but also in Britain's willingness to take care of its own.[49]

Stories about the struggle for Caribbean Airways rippled through the region. After the application for aid was submitted but before the rejection was rendered, airline directors corresponded with bureaucrats throughout the Americas. In their letters, they described the dire financial situation that Pan American had caused. Their letters did two things. First, they rallied support and demonstrated to the grant givers that other colonies and countries were interested in the airline. Second, they advertised that the denial and destruction of a colonial company endorsed and ensured the supremacy of a foreign venture. For instance, on February 17, 1932, when de Pass wrote to the British Legislation at San Salvador, he portrayed himself as a martyr whose "idea has been to foster British enterprise." He explained how there were "so many rotten eggs thrown at me for undertaking a purely patriotic work. . . . [M]y personal pride don't matter a damn! Let's get a British Base and British service going and let's get it going soon."[50]

For de Pass, the so-called rotten eggs came from the imperial government. In June 1932 he wrote to the Colonial Office in London and alerted officials to his predicament. According to de Pass, the rejection was a matter of "great potential Imperial importance." Citing a circular that the Secretary of State for the Colonies had sent in 1927, de Pass reminded bureaucrats in Britain that they had begged colonial governments to create local airlines. He cited the construction of the empire air route as evidence. Probing the limits of its imagination, he wondered if the Colonial Office considered "it important to have a British base here [in Jamaica] and a nucleus British Flying Service." Snidely, he questioned if "they desire to see the B. W. I. [British West Indies] and Bahamas entirely controlled as to Aviation Services by the United States."[51]

In other letters, de Pass questioned the meaning of empire. He believed the logic of empire obliged the imperial center to protect its colonies against foreign penetration. In June 1932, de Pass wrote to his father, who was connected to the imperial government in London. He begged him to tell his colleagues about the threat that Pan American posed to imperial unity. De Pass explained:

> It looks largely as though the whole world, bar the British Empire, were going bust. Although probably a most unideal practice, it is possible that, since most of the world refuses steadfastly to help itself, and thereby others to regain prosperity, the Empire may be forced to adopt a purely national programme, trading almost entirely within itself. . . . If a strictly national attitude is forced on the Empire, may it not be that a nucleus of Empire flying in a zone unfortunately entirely dominated by Yanks [may] prove very useful? I repeat there is no intention at all of playing David to P. A. A.'s [Pan American's] Goliath. It would need more than 100,000 stones to do that.[52]

For de Pass, colonial airlines were battling the might of a foreign power. From what officials in Britain called a "practical" standpoint, his reference to the fact that Caribbean Airways could not compete against Pan American without £100,000 was crucial because it explained exactly what the company needed to survive.[53] From a political standpoint, de Pass used religious language to summon the metropolitan fantasy of colonial airlines as vessels of empire. With imperial funds for stones and Caribbean Airways metonymically the empire, foreign giants would fall.

De Pass was not alone in his angered doubts and concerns about imperial fidelity and protection. In a series of exchanges with the colonial secretary, W. D. B. found himself asking severely critical questions of the imperial government, such as, "There is in reality only one clear cut issue in the whole of these protracted negotiations, namely, does the Imperial Government desire to see flying services in Jamaica in the hands of a foreign corporation, or does it not?" As he sought to rally both financial and symbolic support for the local colonial airline, which was providing "British services in a British colony," he turned to expressions of what he called "patriotism" and "reasons connected with the defense of the Empire."[54]

Less than a month after the advisory committee had made its decision the imperial government published Mayo's report. Fifteen months later, with the insolvency of Caribbean Airways secured, Imperial Airways and Pan American signed an agreement. Advised by Mayo, they agreed to operate all air routes in the British Caribbean in "joint-participation on a fifty-fifty basis."[55] A few years later, the two airlines launched the first transatlantic commercial air route and alliance between Britain and the United States: Bermuda–New York.[56]

For a while, references to the forced failure of Caribbean Airways appeared sporadically in Jamaican newspapers. Sometimes they emerged in columns about compensating the company for the early termination of the airmail contract and airbase lease.[57] Every so often they surfaced in a series of letters to the editor.[58] Briefly, they cropped up in the classifieds, as in a small box advertising "For Rent: Buildings at Bumper Hall."[59]

The Transatlantic

Two major points emerge from the attempt to understand how people in the British Caribbean thought about the onset of commercial aviation. First, people in the colonial Caribbean noticed a link between international airline travel and foreign domination. Entrepreneurs and other elites in the islands saw their version of flight as a form of resistance against changes occurring on the international front; they regarded locally owned airlines as a suitable defense mechanism against U.S. imperialism. Second, these agents envisioned their efforts to erect a viable colonial airline as part of a broader empire project. They strategically considered aviation companies registered in the colonies to be British and they believed it was the imperial government's duty to bail out businesses built at the behest of Britain.

The type of transatlantic flight that the forced failure of Caribbean Airways generated is very different from the kind of system that owners of the airline intended to build. Instead of giving rise to an intraempire service that might have accelerated transportation and communication between the Caribbean, Africa, India, and other places where many roots of the African diaspora rest, the shutdown induced international airline travel between Britain and the United States.

One advantage of reconstructing the history of Anglo-American flight from the vantage point of the colonies and the perspective of their present is that it reopens the broad spectrum of possibilities, and thus the futures, available to people at a time when they could not know what would flourish and what would falter. In moments of attempt, winners and losers do not yet exist, though the structural inequalities that will create them do.[60] This orientation allows us to illuminate innovators in the Caribbean building enduring global networks. Largely ignored by chroniclers of commercial aviation, these historical agents change the way we think about the formation of international alliances. Paying attention to them centers the powerful and enduring ways in which people in colonies helped create prevailing systems of mobility. It helps to turn the sky Caribbean.

Another advantage is that this outlook encourages us to reimagine the transatlantic. One of many geohistorical categories shaped by imperial expansion, the term 'transatlantic' is often used to refer to international exchanges taking place on an east-west axis across the ocean. With regard to transatlantic flight, this has tended to mean the movement of aircraft between continents such as North America and Europe, particularly the United States and Canada, and northwestern European countries. Familiarity with the Caribbean origins of pivotal routes such as Bermuda–New York challenges geographic determinism by interpreting the transatlantic in terms of geohistorical power relations; after all, a route between Bermuda and New York is also a route between Britain and the United States.[61]

People in the Caribbean seldom appear as instigators in the emergence of heavier-than-air commercial flight. For the former British Caribbean, this is understandable to a point. Around the Anglo-Atlantic world, repositories are riddled with documents about early aviation and subaltern innovation.[62] At first glance such advances might seem negligible. Amid a swell of documents dealing with airlines ascending in Latin America, North America, and Western Europe, they appear at best to be attempts, proposals, rumors, and brief mentions. Cast in the archives as trivial, ineffective, incomplete, or rejected, these ostensibly unproductive undertakings look like unimportant instances and nonevents.[63]

In retrospect, it is easy to see Caribbean Airways as a failure. After all, the airline only lasted a few years. Failures, however, are made through hindsight. As the controversies caused by the airline's existence remind us, advances under way on the margins do matter, regardless of how long they lasted. Ambassadors for the imperial government went to great lengths to terminate the pioneering enterprise and people in the colonies worked hard to show that the practical was political. Caribbean Airways might not have been a success, but in its insignificance, it was significant.

Lines

In 1949, the famous British graphic design artist, Abram Games, created a poster for the state-owned airline that succeeded Imperial Airways at the start of the decade: BOAC. The poster showcases the new Stratocruiser service between London and New York.

The design on the poster is of the horizon on the ocean, as seen from the sky. The central image is a four-page foldout map that is opening up and spreading out, or folding up and closing in. Three places are shown on the map. The United Kingdom is cut out of the center of the right-hand page, and the United States out of the left-hand one. The word "Atlantic Ocean" is spread across the middle pages, as are grid lines, a compass, and the Equator. There are no continents or islands. The right and left pages are red, blue, and white, which are the national colors of both countries. The middle pages are white and black, except for the Equator, which is notably a thin red and blue line.

Two Speedbirds fly in opposite directions over the Atlantic. One is en route to the United States and the other to the United Kingdom. A straight white line of dashes holds them together, across the Atlantic. Written across the top of the poster is the phrase "Fly the Atlantic by BOAC."

Certain things will happen if the map closes, and the United Kingdom and United States fold into one another. Distance will disappear, as an era of instantaneous travel opens up. Speedbirds will pass through, and keep going in unfettered flight. The black Atlantic will be pressed and gone (see Figure 6). If the map opens up, global power will spread in a different way. The white transatlantic line that binds the speedbirds together will ensure that the Anglo-American alliance remains intact. The black Atlantic will still be gone. It never was on the map to begin with.

Figure 6. "Fly the Atlantic," © Estate of Abram Games.

6

Descent

On August 4, 1939, members of parliament at Westminster promulgated the British Overseas Airways Act.[1] The law merged and dissolved Imperial Airways and British Airways, which was a four-year-old airline that served the European routes. (This British Airways and the British Airways of today are different airlines.) It established a new, state-owned airline: British Overseas Airways Corporation (BOAC). The Act laid out the rights, regulations, and responsibilities of the nationalized carrier. It laid bare concerns about the future of the nation, the empire, and the state.

The Act drew boundaries. It blurred the lines of demarcation between a foreign territory and an imperial domain. When the 'Airways' of the instrument of the state went from Imperial to British Overseas, it was more than a name change. The switch was a gentle nod to the tenuous, slowly shifting relationship between the nation-state and the colonial empire. The explanation of terms, which was a section of the Act, was another indication of this shift. The 'overseas' were "Erie" and "places outside of the British Islands." A 'country' was "a Dominion, British India, British Burma, a British colony, a British protectorate, any territory which is under His Majesty's protection or suzerainty, a foreign country," and a few other places. Both terms made a distinction between Britain and the rest of the world, as one might expect from such a document. But the last one did something else. It set Britain far apart from the empire. British colonies were lumped together with foreign territories, which matters in a document that outlined the initial terms for the state-owned airline.[2]

The arguments around the issue involved a rather counterintuitive point. For some lawmakers, the nightmarish upshot of empire was that the development of the British world had led to the underdevelopment of the British nation. In the undercurrents of the debates that surrounded the dissolution of Imperial Airways and the formation of

BOAC was the trace of an earlier vision: Britain as an empire without colonies.

Conflicting opinions and variant views abounded around transatlantic flight. There were concerns about the alliance between Imperial Airways and Pan American. Some of them were the very same ones advocates for Caribbean Airways had raised in their attempts to save the colonial airline; the imperial government found itself reflecting on a future that didn't happen, as it questioned if the alliance had undercut and degraded the international authority and reputation of Britain.

And there it was, the Caribbean, its imagination in their regret.

Laughter

On Wednesday, November 17, 1937, a fight erupted in the House of Commons when, at 3:48 p.m., Mr. Walter Robert Dempster Perkins demanded Viscount Swinton's head on a platter. Perkins, a Conservative member of parliament (MP) for Stroud and the vice president of the British Airline Pilots Association, was "thoroughly dissatisfied." The Secretary of State for Air had brought commercial aviation into "disrepute." Swinton had allowed Imperial Airways to make Britain a "second class" country. He asked the House to hold a general public inquiry. Maybe it would "shake the Air Ministry into a sense of their responsibilities, and into a realization of the seriousness of the present position."[3]

Three areas of the industry troubled Perkins: subsidies, aircraft, and aerodromes. For nearly two years, the government had backed two airlines: Imperial Airways and British Airways. Each subsidy funded different development projects. The larger of the two, which Imperial Airways had received, supported the advancement of the empire service. The other, which British Airways had obtained, encouraged the expansion of the European service.[4]

Perkins opposed dual spheres of operation, which the current scheme promoted. The state's inability to invest in one single airline had turned Britain into an international joke. "We know that all is not well," Perkins asserted, "We know that we are behind the Americans and the Germans, and we dislike being laughed at by the Americans and Germans, and even the Dutch."[5] Perkins insisted that split loyalties had marred Britain. The British commercial aviation industry was in a laughable state, and government attention unevenly divided between the continent and the empire was a big part of the problem.

Laughter was strange. The situation in Britain was hardly an anomaly. The U.S. government, for example, was backing several airlines. It turned out it was the aircraft and aerodromes of Britain that amused foreign states. Perkins told his colleagues that "several tales" were circulating about ramshackle British planes. One was about the time when Imperial Airways tried to run a scheduled night service to Berlin with a Royal Air Force castoff. The used equipment soon became "the object of a joke; German pilots actually tied a parrot's cage to its tail."[6] It was a disgrace for Britain. Perkins scolded the Air Ministry, again. The department oversaw both military and civil aviation, and those who "rule the roost" had treated the civil side like an "unwanted child." Perkins along with others wanted civil aviation out of there, "away from the militaristic outlook of the Air Ministry." He proposed that the Ministry of Transport serve as its new home. The division would force British aircraft manufacturers to make planes suitable for airline travel.[7]

This was about more than shoddy airliners. It was about sovereignty and the empire-state. First, there were fears in parliament about major economic decline. Some worried that Britain would no longer have access to the empire market because it couldn't make civil planes good enough to sell to dominions and colonies. "Wake up to the seriousness," Perkins bellowed. Britain was about to "lose for all time the whole of the Empire markets for British civil air power." In other words, Britain was on the brink of being edged out of its own empire. "It is true of our whole Empire," Perkins warned. "In the future a traveller wishing to fly around the world will fly by Imperial Airways over the Atlantic and also over the Pacific" on foreign-made planes.[8]

And then there were the aerodromes. What Perkins said about them and how people responded to him tells us what kind of 'Britain' they feared losing. Perkins said: "London, the heart of the world," had only one airdrome and "that one is only worthy of a second class Balkan State." The statement, which was soaked in ethnocentrism and laced with bigotry, pulled in two directions at once: Britain as empire ("heart of the world") and Britain as nation ("second class Balkan State"). The paltry state of the aerodrome was a sign of global power in decline. Perkins's unease about shabby facilities in the imperial center dovetailed with his concern for the country's aerial conduit to mainland Europe: London-Paris. Airline traffic on the route to neighboring countries was relatively weak. This was unacceptable to Perkins and others who felt that Imperial Airways, a public utility "heavily subsidised by the taxpayers of this country," had done more for the empire than it had for Britain.

Nationalism pervaded the claim. Perkins, in one of his more controversial statements, accused the airline of "not showing the flag in Europe." Imperial Airways had catered to "Empire traffic" and treated "European traffic" as "trivial." Perkins could not "help wondering whether nationalization of our internal air services and our external air services would not be preferable to the present position."[9] Total control meant Britain would no longer be the "laughing-stock of the world." It could be on top again.[10] Under the guise of innocence, Perkins assured the House he was "inspired simply and solely by a desire to see British civil aviation leading the world in just the same way as British shipping leads the world now."[11]

He didn't come right out and say it. But that doesn't mean it wasn't there. There was a racial subtext to all this agony over Britain losing its footing and being laughed at by other world powers. The grumble—the whole empire was better off than the entire nation—smacked of imperial, white spite. (Imperial: because Britain was set against the self-governing dominions. White: because Britain and the dominions, no matter the rank between them, were set against the colonies.) It was laden with insinuations about otherness: the governmental pecking order, racial hierarchy, white supremacy. The comparison drawn between empire and nation was a not so subtle version of them versus us: a hint of the racial slur—'how dare they?'—came with the mockery, as blame.

Members of the House reacted to the allegation that Imperial Airways had strengthened the empire but weakened Britain. Some applauded Perkins. Lieutenant-Colonel Moore-Brabazon, who had dreamed of imperial air routes when he served on Churchill's committee, appreciated the "sustained onslaught." He admired Perkins for having the "courage to criticize." Imperial Airways had "a mysterious connection with the State," which he minded. He didn't like that the airline was "always supposed to be the Government," and opposed monopolization. Moore-Brabazon had his eye on a "great Imperial job" and the "keenest" competition was needed to make it happen. The imperial air scheme envisioned years ago was back.

In theory, it was still a straightforward project: "encircle the globe" with British air lines. Britain had an empire air route and was focused on advancing it. The imperial air route scheme planned for a different kind of empire, racial supremacy in tow; the focus was on securing air pacts with the dominions, so as to ring the world with a new style of imperial rule (e.g., speed-up as access to air power and unfettered trade, for some people in certain places). In practice, it was, as Moore-Brabazon put it, "difficult." Britain had lost focus and sway. It was hung up on the idea (and reality) of a colonial empire; meanwhile, there were new techniques for and configurations of imperialism, and other states had started to take full advantage of them. The government had to "get back to a normal and sane outlook on life" and build the airline services Britain needed for that great imperial job.[12]

Others in the House rejected such claims outright. Geoffrey Mander, a Liberal MP, defended the reputation and record of Imperial Airways, "a great national institution." The airline had performed "national activities with great skill and resolution" and it had built an empire service that was "magnificent."[13] Colonel Sir Leonard Ropner, a Conservative MP with a shipping company, used similar language when he gave a forty-minute speech on "the magnificent organization of Imperial Airways." He latched onto high-speed and linked it to state power. The air services of Britain were "among the fastest in the world," Ropner asserted before he noted, "speed is one of the most expensive luxuries of modern times. You can have it if you are prepared to pay for it." Ropner was certain Britain would eventually reap rewards from this "colossal undertaking." Yes, continental service was "very slow" but it was also "extremely efficient." Moreover, the empire service "leads the world," which was a testament to British strength. He encouraged the House to settle down, realize what it already had, and be patient.[14]

Some officials wavered. A few thought the European services were mediocre, but they also thought it was unfair to fault just the airline or the empire; for them, problems with the country's world power status were systemic. Others, such as Sir Murray Sueter, wanted commercial aviation to return Britain to its glory days of global rule. Sueter, a pioneer in naval aviation, recounted the times when the country "mastered transport by sea" and talked about the opportunity to "lead the world in civil aviation." He acknowledged the groundbreaking work Imperial Airways had done to "blaze the trail," and having said that, stated that all was "backward."

Backwardness meant the usual: behind, unprogressive, underdeveloped, decline, reluctant, reversed. For Sueter, though, it was also tied to feelings of trepidation and ache. He found British air services in the South Atlantic and Caribbean disturbing and offered the Air Ministry "a little criticism": it was "so backward in finding a company to fly the Southern Atlantic." (The deal between Imperial Airways and Pan American should have taken care of this.) Britain lagged behind and its airline services needed to "speed up." Sueter noted that France and Germany had long since operated there: Britain was the slowness to their fastness.

Sueter shared a personal letter as evidence. A retired naval captain from Britain in Argentina was distraught. The "prestige" of his home country "suffers" in the Americas. For starters, Britain did not deliver its own airmail: "German machines carry our air mail." The captain saw this as a sign of great weakness. The airline and government had gone to great lengths to make airmail a decidedly British service, yet it paid other European countries to fly the mail for them; for example, in 1937, the postmaster-general paid French and German companies approximately £100,000 to fly British mails across the South Atlantic. The captain wanted British planes to transport British mail and freight across the region immediately. Doing so would boost and shore up British influence in the informal empire Europe was building in the Americas.[15]

For Sueter, this absence was about the formal empire too. He laid into the government for its mistreatment of the British Caribbean. He was upset that it had left the betterment of British people and places to the United States. He cautioned the government to stop its "dependence upon Pan American Airways to run our West Indies Service," and see "whether something can be done to hasten matters as much as possible" in the Atlantic. Bothered, he asked the House to ask the Air Ministry to "look into the whole question" of the goings-on over there.[16]

The debate ended at 7:30 p.m., nearly four hours after it began. To recap: The debate was about the effectiveness of the chosen instrument of the state, namely, had it advanced the empire but hurt the nation? The request was for a public inquiry, an investigation to review the choices Imperial Airways had made as well as the decisions it needed to make. The spread of issues included Britain as an international object of ridicule, especially in Europe and the United States; Britain as a global power in decline; Britain as a failure in the South Atlantic and Caribbean.

The Under-Secretary of State for Air, Lieutenant-Colonel Anthony John Muirhead, spoke last. He scrutinized the claims made by Perkins and sardonically assessed his performance: "He certainly executed a lively dance, though it was not in conventional costume." All the same, Muirhead agreed, "All is not perfect in the realm of civil aviation." He let them know that Swinton had given the go-ahead for an "inquiry into the charges of inefficiency," and agreed to publish "the findings, with reasons." Muirhead remarked, then adjourned: "If that is not actually the head . . . on a charger, I hope the hon. Member for Stroud will be satisfied that it is the scalp."[17]

Inquiry

Swinton put together a Committee of Inquiry into Civil Aviation. He appointed three men: Lord John Cadman, Sir Warren Fisher, and Sir William Brown. Cadman, the chair, was a professor of mining and the chairman of the Anglo-Persian Oil Company.[18] Fisher was Permanent Secretary of the Treasury as well as Head of the Civil Service. Brown was Permanent Secretary to the Board of Trade.

The composition of the committee was the subject of contentious debate. About a week after the first debate ended, Muirhead stood up in the House of Commons and announced the names of those on the committee. When he had finished the objections began. "Does the Minister realize that in every quarter of the House this is regarded as a trick on the part of the Ministry," Montague asked straightaway. Montague, an advocate of nationalization and monopolization, accused Swinton of chicanery and demanded to know if the men on the committee had any expertise. He questioned: "What qualifications have they? Who are they? Why should they be called upon to deal with questions of this character?" Montague continued and pointed out that Cadman could not be impartial given that his company supplied Imperial Airways with oil. He demanded the immediate removal and replacement of the current members.[19]

Clement Attlee chimed in. He backed Montague's request and noted several conflicts of interest, including the fact that Swinton had appointed a former secretary from his department to the committee. Attlee asked the prime minister, Neville Chamberlain, to review the appointments, which he did. Chamberlain sided with Montague and Attlee. The current committee was biased, he said. He asked Swinton to reconsider the appointments.

Six days later, Chamberlain had an answer, which he shared with the House. Swinton had agreed to reform the committee. He had removed Fisher and Brown, added three men with more neutral backgrounds, and appointed someone from his department as secretary. He had kept Cadman, which led Montague to complain. He asked Chamberlain if he realized how many MPs had previously objected to Cadman and requested that he find a chairman who was "less compromised politically." Chamberlain replied: "A singularly ungracious response."[20] That day, most people were okay with this version of the committee.

Swinton moved forward. He asked his reformed (and expanded) committee to look into several of the allegations made at the debate. The men were to review "charges of inefficiency" brought against Imperial Airways and the Air Ministry. Swinton told them to assess the existing British commercial aviation system, "particularly in Europe."[21]

Between December 1937 and February 1938, the committee met thirty times, heard testimony from sixty-eight different people, and read the written evidence of thirty-two more.[22] Four days after its last meeting, the committee sent a substantial report of findings and recommendations to Swinton. The report was controversial and divisive. Chamberlain's government decided to withhold it, even though it had promised to circulate the document once it was ready.[23] For nearly two months, his people stalled while they searched for explanations and solutions. During that time, members of the House of Commons, Perkins in particular, asked repeatedly to see the report, and the domestic and foreign press condemned—and remembered—the government for its untrustworthy behavior.[24]

In mid-March, the report was released, with two additional parts. There was a copy of the one-page "Terms of Reference" Swinton had given to the committee. There were thirteen pages of government observations on the report.[25]

The report blamed the government for failing to meet the needs of the British people in Britain. It declared that the Air Ministry was responsible, and held Imperial Airways accountable. The committee was convinced that "settlement" of the big problems would "automatically cure" the little ones. The obstructions, which "transcend in importance," were the policy and organization of the Air Ministry; the air services themselves; and the civil aircraft industry. Accordingly, it investigated the operation, organization, and administration of the chosen instrument of the state.[26]

The report concluded that the government had failed mainly in two areas: progress and nationhood. Like Perkins and to some extent Sueter, the committee had "a genuine apprehension" that commercial aviation in "this country is backward," while it thrived abroad in the empire. It was a situation of grave concern; according to the report, this was the first of the "main problems" to fix. That British air services flourished in the empire but fell apart on the international and domestic fronts, troubled the men on the committee. They were particularly anxious about the overall health of the nation; growing interest in autonomous and semiautonomous communities within the empire raised questions about Britain's place among them. "There is reason for more than apprehension," the committee warned as it underscored the pressing need for "this country" to take charge of British air travel.[27]

The sense of urgency was also related to the precarious state of scheduled British Air services in Europe. The committee found airline traffic between the country and continent wanting, and confirmed that such neglect had damaged "national prestige." If "our position is to be fully secured," then flights to all major European capitals had to happen immediately. It was "a matter of national importance." The committee advised that, to do this, commercial aviation in Britain would need to become more European. It encouraged the government not to take the military concern out of civil aviation. Airlines and air forces were "one—two sides of a single coin," and the "virility" and security of Britain depended on it staying that way. The committee used strong, gendered language. It likened air travel to a developing fetus, which hadn't "emerged from its present embryonic stage." It required wisdom and skill from military men to grow and take care of the nation, its figurative mother.[28]

The themes of motherhood, nurture, and protection also turned up in passages about the Caribbean and broader Atlantic. Concerns about the growth of British aviation in the colonies were largely economic.[29] The committee lamented the neglect of British interests in the Americas and wondered why so little had been done to protect and stimulate them. It drew attention to the colonies in the Caribbean and bemoaned the "severe foreign competition" that was "developing on the North Atlantic air route." It admonished the government for having allowed (and enabled) "the uncontested monopoly" of Pan American. This was a matter of "national prestige and trading considerations," which was slightly different from the combination of prestige and militarism it imagined for Europe. The recommendation: "expedite to the utmost" British air links and lines throughout the region. "Trade follows the flag," the committee reminded the government, as it encouraged it to remember the "older forms" of transport that had helped Britain prosper in the world, and trust air services to "hold good" and do the same." It expected air services in the Caribbean and Atlantic to thwart foreign influence and feed the financial interests of Britain, the imperial mother country.[30]

The government had a responsibility to protect and provide for Great and Greater Britain, and the chosen instrument of the state had a responsibility to the government. The committee was "profoundly dissatisfied" with Imperial Airways and ascribed Britain's "international and Imperial problems" to it. The committee recalled why the airline was created and why it had been heavily subsidized: "to secure the establishment and progressive development of British air services in Europe." With Air Ministry data, it showed how the airline had shirked its duties. Ultimately, Imperial Airways was liable for the "serious defects" in the country's European services, not the government.[31] The final recommendation: Imperial Airways needed to be reorganized and the Air Ministry restricted. A single, fully subsidized British airline should be established. As for the Air Ministry, it needed to work to prepare the country for its future, with "more vigor in initiating policy and foresight in planning."

The government, in its observations, tried to explain that the state had done its best over the years to serve "the common interest of all." The development of the empire air service was deliberate. The state thought the nation would indirectly benefit from a scheme that directly served the empire. The drawback was that such "concentration" left "relatively little money" to develop air services elsewhere (i.e., international ones to continental Europe and domestic ones within Britain itself). It was the "Speeding Up the Empire" campaign gone awry. In a roundabout way and for a short while, it seemed the empire had come out on top. It sped-up; Britain slowed-down.[32]

Motion

On March 16, 1938 at 4:10 p.m., Prime Minister Chamberlain asked parliament to approve the Cadman Report observations. He thanked and praised the committee for working "without fear or favour," and issued a few pointed comments about "some derogatory" remarks made by the opposition. He then explained the overarching and unifying goal of the committee, his government, and the two subsidized airlines: the rejuvenation of the "prestige of the country." They had done what they did for the "general advancement of British prestige throughout the world."[33]

A debate ensued for the next two days. Throughout, representatives talked a lot about prestige. For the most part, they used it to discuss influence as well as reputation. Often, it appeared in exchanges about speed-up, comfort, safety, completeness, and the modern character.

The officials had a row about the significance of the empire air service. They discussed a number of topics. One of them was the maintenance of routes. The prime minister, who supported the endeavor, used different tactics to explain why empire routes were important to Britain. He addressed their practical use and political value. Because of them Britain had "a network of air communications" spread around the world, which was "very valuable for social and commercial intercourse." He pointed to several instances of national advantage, one of which was airmail. The localized upkeep of the complex infrastructure of the routes made it possible to fly British mail cheaply. He firmly believed that sending mail quickly across the empire sustained imperial connections, constricted imperial bonds, and enable faster commercial transactions. "There are plans, as the House knows," he noted, "for bringing these services during the present year to Australia, Hong Kong, and New

Zealand, and at the same time preparations are being made to bridge the Atlantic through Canada and the United States." After envisioning ties with the United States and the dominions in the north Atlantic as well as with the dominions and colonies in Asia and the Pacific, he turned his attention to the colonies of the black Atlantic world: "Finally, steps are being taken to connect up the West African Colonies by a new air route down the West coast of Africa, which may subsequently be expected to cross the Atlantic to South America." He clarified why he thought tight, secure ties across the empire mattered to Britain; it was a discussion about British influence and political autonomy abroad.[34]

Chamberlain also addressed the symbolic importance of air routes. He used the rhetoric of kinship to discuss what the service meant to the empire as a whole. He told the House that it was "only fair" to honor those who have "given a great deal of their time and labor, and, indeed, in many cases, have risked their lives" to build and service the routes. They were reminded to remember that the project was an "achievement" for Britain; people elsewhere worked and sometimes died to build a globe-spanning British aviation industry.[35]

There was resentment toward the notion that the country had to experience the benefits of commercial aviation indirectly through the empire. Not surprisingly, one of the more steadfast speakers on this point was Attlee, a longtime advocate of progressive decolonization rather than passive self-government, and a future champion of the welfare state. He thanked the committee for not succumbing to the status of "Yes men." He also appreciated their report, which was of the "most scathing nature." It was "a vindication" of why they must "operate through inquiry." Attlee felt the prime minister had given "a most unBritish speech." He exclaimed: "I have never known such complacency." Attlee accused Chamberlain and his government of "Ministerial neglect," "flagrant neglect," "gross inefficiency," and "the state of inertia."

The reasons why the speech was un-British spoke to some of the versions of nationhood at stake in the debate. Attlee defined un-British in two ways. First, it was about unabashed boasting; here, being British meant modesty and reserve. Attlee faulted Chamberlain for his attention to "achievements" rather than "shortcomings." The latter left room for a discussion of improvement and progress, while the former was over and done with. Second, being un-British was about absolution and unaccountability; here, being British meant duty. Attlee maintained that commercial aviation's "evils are of long standing. They have not welled up in a moment." An abiding empire-oriented, capitalist state was the burdensome problem. Britain needed a "Government which will put national interests first and private profit after." Attlee hoped air transportation would be a "civilian industry, and eventually serve the cause of peace rather than to add to the causes of war."[36]

The relationship between military and civil aviation was a prickly topic. According to the third paragraph of the observations, the Air Ministry had to devote itself to the "military sphere," specifically the rearmament program, which explained why it had been unable to concentrate on civil concerns.[37] In other words, pressing military needs meant the government had to neglect civil affairs for the time being; it did not mean that military and civil aviation had to uncouple. Attlee agreed with one part of the argument. "Grave events are proceeding." Attlee concurred, Swinton was "obliged to give his whole attention" to military aviation. But that was all the more reason to not be "disingenuous" and admit that separate management was the "right way out of this muddle and mess."[38]

Others shared Attlee's opinion. For Mavis Constance Tate, the rearmament program was a "wholly false excuse." She reminded the House that Imperial Airways had flown old, obsolete airplanes long before the launch of the program in 1936. Tate, "very much disquieted" by the prime minister's comments, faulted the government for failing to put civil before military interests. This blunder explained why Britain trailed behind other countries: "I believe that to-day we should not have a quarter of the anxiety that we feel about our military aviation if we had developed civil aviation properly in the past." For her, civil aviation advanced military aviation, not the other way around.

Tate wanted an increase and acceleration of traffic on the empire routes. She addressed Chamberlain's explanations for the "concentration on Empire communications," and challenged, "[L]et them be in the vanguard of civil aviation, where they are by no means to-day." She implored the government to make use of "the speeded-up service." Imperial Airways flew "us to Calcutta in six days, Singapore in eight days, Brisbane in 12 days, and Sydney in 13 days." She urged the government to increase the speed of "the speeded-up service" and referenced the British straggling the Dutch as leverage. Their national carrier was flying to Calcutta in three and one-half days and Singapore in five.

Tate had certain things to say about the Caribbean, South America, and the Pacific. She didn't think the "expansion of civil aviation is merely a matter of prestige." She thought it was about trade too. She asked the prime minister point-blank if the empire was going to "receive any further attention and any speeding up," and when "the much too slow service which is promised" would arrive. She specifically wanted to know about a service to the Caribbean and South America and then across the Pacific. These are "essential if our prestige and trade interests are to be safeguarded."

At 7:30 p.m., nearly three and one-half hours after Chamberlain had presented the motion, the House decided to postpone the proceedings. That night, the final comments had to do with the transatlantic. Muirhead was talking about the departmental management of civil aviation when Tate interrupted. She demanded that he answer her earlier question about the South Atlantic, a service, she snarked, "which is specifically recommended in the Cadman Report."[39] Muirhead responded. He told her that the region was "one we wish to push on with as quickly as we can."[40] As he continued he uttered two sentences, each one a packed historical source:

> Trans-Atlantic services for example occupy the smallest paragraph in the report. It is quite easy in these days of publicity to get a headline but to get the Trans-Atlantic services reduced to the status of one small paragraph in this report is to my mind a triumph.[41]

Muirhead was talking about transatlantic services with territories in the southern Atlantic, not with the nations in the north. His comments about how this version of the transatlantic appeared in the report were correct. It was reduced to the smallest paragraph: and that is revealing of power. Yet the Caribbean still came into view, in spite of it being rendered minimal, fleeting, a glance. That speaks to power too.

Twelve days later, the debate resumed at 8:50 p.m. and lasted until 12:44 a.m. During those hours, one person raised the transatlantic, once. Sueter hoped the Air Ministry would "press on" with the northern and southern Atlantic. An all-British service across the North Atlantic could interrupt a "good deal of American competition in the near future." One in the South could show people in the region that Britain was not a "decadent nation." He also recapped his point about Britain flying its own mail; it could stop paying German and French companies £100,000 to carry its post.[42]

The construction of international lines was the focus of the resumed debate. For the most part, the exchanges were about Britain as a world power and at times, the deepening power of the United States. The House spoke of the magnitude of "the great Continent of America" and the possibility of Britain as one of the "most progressive countries in the world."[43] It also discussed the growth of the country's European routes, and continued to battle over "our problem," which was spending a "large amount of money" on the empire while needing to "show the flag on the Continent."[44] At times, it reviewed domestic services; "dissatisfied" representatives insisted that internal flights were required to "make our public air-minded."[45]

When the debate ended, the House voted on the observations: of the 196 members who voted, 129 said yes, while 67 chose no.

Result

The changes began. The government agreed to build more aerodromes in England. It grew the Air Ministry with three appointments. It doubled the annual subsidy set aside for air transport from £1,500,000 to £3,000,000. It decided to restructure Imperial Airways and British Airways. At first, Imperial Airways kept the empire service and British Airways got the bulk of the continental routes. Imperial Airways had to appoint a full-time chairman and one or two full-time directors. A few months later, the government resolved to merge the airlines and form BOAC, a public corporation.

Newspapers covered the committee, report, debates, and result. They described commercial aviation as weak and vulnerable in Britain. The *Times* explained its "deplorable inferiority," relayed that it was the "laughing-stock" of Europe, and dubbed it the "Cinderella of the Air Ministry." When it featured large sections of the report, it enlarged and bolded phrases like "Extreme Disquiet," "Nobody's Baby," "Defects of Policy," and "National Prestige." It encouraged the government to get going on the "restoration of British prestige." From time to time, the empire was mentioned and every so often, a few comments about the Atlantic were made. Next to nothing was said about the Caribbean. The small paragraph was now just a short phrase. A ravel of the race-based exclusion, then erasure, of the Caribbean from route development was part of reforming the British airline and its history.[46]

TRAILS

Wake

1

There are very few photographs of her from then. She grew up in a tiny place, not a small one like the others.[1] Her island is set apart, far from the mainland, which is an island too. In one of the photographs, she stands, young and still, hand on her hip, without a smile, in front of a commuter plane. It was there because it had crashed. She was there because it was something different: 3 x 3-inches, black and white.

It was the British Caribbean, 1950s or 1960s. She was from there, and the plane was from far away. She took a picture in front of the wreckage, like a tourist, with a rather defiant look on her face.

2

The British Airways Concorde G-BOAE is inside a white metal hangar, which is next to the Grantley Adams International Airport in Barbados. People are walking around Alpha Echo, which is the plane's more common name. Alpha Echo is part of the British Airways Concorde fleet; there are six other planes. The airline grounded the iconic jets after it terminated supersonic services in 2003. It sent the retired planes to countries that had had scheduled Concorde services. Six went to airports and museums in the United Kingdom and the United States, and one to Barbados. They are on display and preserved at airports and museums in each country. The airline retains ownership of them all.

The people are young and old. A few of them are from Barbados, but most of them are from abroad. They stop and photograph themselves standing in front of Alpha Echo: The sound of the active jets just outside is background noise. The people are smiling.

Conclusion

This book has argued that airline travel and empire had a complicated relationship in the early twentieth century, the formation of the former intertwined with the transformation of the latter. It has sought to bring race and racism sharply into focus, to understand them as more than secondary causes or side effects of that formidable union. Race and racism were there from the start, fueling the intertwinement that was remaking them.

One goal of this book has been to show the colonial origins of a seemingly national airline. Empire was central to the making of the airline that would become British Airways: Imperial Airways. The decision to create a government-backed airline was not a simple one in Britain. At state-funded conferences and in government-made committees, the press, and other places, bureaucrats, executives, government officials, and elites struggled to define the purpose, meaning, and advantage of commercial aviation for the nation and the empire. In their eagerness to figure out those things, they found themselves wrestling with and fighting over how, if at all, to prioritize the aerial development of one political entity over the other. Even though, in hindsight, the empire was arguably at its peak in the 1920s, decision makers were acutely aware of the precarious position of British global power as economic challenges, the proliferation of labor movements and nationalist protests, deepening U.S. imperialism, and other forces rattled the empire-state after the First World War. Some decision makers wanted to concentrate on erecting a robust web of routes between Britain and continental Europe while others felt commercial flights to and through the empire would serve the British world best. Ultimately, they opted for an airline that was ostensibly less international and more imperial, though the distinction between the two was hardly a neat one.

But what nation? Which empire? This book has sought to show that 'nation' and 'empire' were what Sonya Rose has called "ideological discourses."[1] Depending on the circumstances, the concepts stood in for what they helped to imagine and construct as concrete political units with real territorial boundaries (e.g., Great Britain; the British empire).[2] They were held together and teased apart too, cultivating a sense of oneness, belonging, and attachment; or otherness, exclusion, and alienation. In other words, nation and empire were more than political units: they were discursive practices. This matters when we try to understand how—and not just why—the decision to make an imperial airline was made. It illuminates how race and state power came together and helped to create ordinary air travel, a complex system of regulated mobility inclusive of racial subordination.[3]

Public and private stakeholders gathered as decision makers, well aware of the people and places that were part of the existing empire. Many of them desired to secure supremacy in and sovereignty of the air through commercial aviation. It was a wish caught up in dreams of a new global Britain. They envisioned principal air routes as imperial routes, a network of lines to link Britain to the dominions, Egypt, and India. They pictured secondary routes as colonial routes, local lines to connect the colonies to the dominions, not Britain. That is, systematically they imagined discriminatory pathways: the white and brown corridors of the empire, and the black ones that fed them. They saw a world with a racially hierarchical sky. And they set out to build it.

Those lines were not ordinary links. They were links *up*. We've seen in this book different examples of how aviation in general and airline travel in particular reconfigured the geometry of power.[4] The imperial work that gave rise to airborne mobility was partly about planes and planes: about altitude above ground level and the power of depth; about ensuring that some lives would be lived rather vertically (people with access to the air plane), and some more horizontally (people with access to only the flat, level surfaces of water and land). It also concerned the normalization of the insidious new pleasures and the promotion of rate and routinization: a state-sponsored airline, which operated a fleet of airplanes on a fixed schedule; its powered flying machines with fixed wings that displaced as they traversed the air element regularly; its commercial speed-up, certain people, things, and places lifted on time; its direct straight-line travels through the sky, which cut above those below, their movements grounded and slowed-down. Four expectations of air travel were taking shape. Three of them were found among other modes of transportation: convenience, comfort, and celerity. One of them not so much: ungrounded vertical separation.

The experience of being in the air fascinated early airline passengers, which confounded me when I first read their travel accounts. It wasn't simply the newness of it all then compared with the normality of it all now that struck me, though that was definitely part of it. Rather it was how aerial passage itself acutely shaped early air travelers' impressions of who they were and what was theirs in the world. Many of the passengers we met in this book had the resources—the money, the time—to *take* flight. For most, flying with privilege was the privilege of flying. It included laying claim to and inhabiting the sky, moving at altitude above ground level and feeling entitled to do so. It involved gathering speed. It allowed for overseeing, overviewing, and overlooking; a review, a survey, and a bird's-eye view.[5]

Writings by first fliers highlight the centrality of the overhead construction of race in the invention of the in-flight experience. Passengers relished soaring over while sweeping past what was beneath them. On board the state's chosen airline, winged along the empire route, they imagined, bought, and performed a kaleidoscope of power-laden identities: race, class, gender, metropolitanism. (Imperial Airways imagined, sold, and performed these identities too.) They flitted over colonies and looked down on wildlife, landscape, and people, fashioning whiteness on the move. The physical gap and pellucid air space between persons up in the sky and people down on the ground were key. As flying airline travelers gazed down upon people of color from a distance, they viewed them as racialized exotic others, less than and all the same. It was a colonial encounter, and it was almost but not quite like the ones had by water, road, and rail. That overhead position of the commercial plane traveling through the air was a phenomenon; it was not taken for granted; it was not underestimated. It was a purchase—something bought, a grip, and the advantage gained from both. There were those who could afford to *be* up there—a high society. Now, they were literally an upper class. Theirs was upward mobility in actuality. It was, to be precise, white flight—straight up, fast-moving segregation.[6]

For airline travelers, flying seemed just the ticket. For the chosen instrument of the state, it seemed just business. For the empire-state that chose to endow and use it, flying, the interconnectedness of airspace, airfare, airplanes, airtime, air routes, airports, and other air parts like air passengers, air cargo, air workers, airmail, air miles, and an airline, was nonmilitary airpower. These were messy, entangled, enduring consumer, business, and government affairs. The racial politics and practices that came out of, went into, and were changed by airline travel went beyond isolated acts of injustice and inhumanity. They were systemic. They were deeply entrenched in the imperialist setup of commercial aviation as well as the affective domain of volant colonization and white privilege. "Racism is so dangerous," Angela Davis has reminded us, "because it does not necessarily depend on individual actors, but rather is deeply embedded in the apparatus." "Racism underwrites" the modern air transport industry.[7]

Another goal of this book has been to call attention to the Caribbean. Its exclusion from the history of early air travel has gone on far too long. Ideas about the region and its relationship to imperial flight were there from the get-go. Futures were envisioned for it. From time to time, these thoughts and imaginings appeared in plans to establish, route, and recast Imperial Airways, if only in a word or two. The point here is not to advocate solely for the addition of the Caribbean to the existing literature. To do so would risk recalling an interpretive tradition that African diaspora and black Atlantic scholars have described as a form of disempowerment and have worked to deflate: thinking of places and people in the Caribbean as objects, not agents. Instead, I encourage a consideration of how love, as a diasporic approach, technique, and strategy, helps us to sense, gather, and study fragments and 'little somethings.' How it aids in our efforts to attend to allusions, snippets, attempts, traces, asides—no matter how long or how few; to find and experience affect in the archive; to compose, and to share vulnerable work.[8]

Insofar as the literature on British commercial aviation has taken empire into account, it has concentrated on early flights to, over, and within the Middle East, Africa, Oceania, Asia, and to a lesser extent, Canada. There is a certain logic to this kind of care. The areas were clear-cut parts of the empire air network, and Imperial Airways served all but Canada. Detailed records about them were kept, and the heftiness of those accounts is very much in evidence. The archive is awash in documentation on commercial air services in these locations. Newspapers, magazines, and other published materials are abundant in articles and images of Imperial Airways and its regional operations. Consequently, the history of empire airline travel has been told with them in mind.[9]

Traditionally, the sources have been used to write important, meticulous, descriptive works about British air transportation in those British overseas territories. Increasingly, they are being used to write vital, much-needed, critical works on the aerial domination of those places and the people in them. The problems associated with the first version of knowledge making are well known: history from above, history of the powerful, history from the center, history of the center, history by the winners, histories that silence, histories that exclude, histories that reproduce oppressive power, and so on. The second kind has its share of problems too. The shift away from descriptive explanation and toward critical interpretation has lessened but not eliminated the predilection for top-down positioning and perspective.[10] We see this tension in works that have skillfully exposed and critiqued airline services as state violence on the one hand and inadvertently followed and upheld the imperialistic logic of commercial aviation on the other.[11]

For example, the notion of mass air transit as a complex system of connection is a recurring theme in scholarship and the public imagination. There are extremely valuable articles and books about institutions as well as people forging, using, and experiencing air linkages for all sorts of reasons. This body of work has taken seriously the intricate bundle of ways in which air travel networks have been beneficial and injurious; profitable and exploitative; inconvenient, handy, and transformative.[12] The difficulty here is not with the study of connectivity itself; rather, it's with the study of it by itself. By focusing on air travel as a conduit of global connection we risk *setting* ourselves *up* to *overlook* those who are set apart. We risk going along with "imperial orders" and "imperial maps"—following their direction, arrangements, discipline, and directions, much like an empire airline and its passengers would do.[13]

We also risk muting, forgetting, or altogether erasing racial difference, which brings us back to the significant insignificance of the Caribbean.[14] When we explore the affairs of Imperial Airways south and east of London, exclude or bracket off the Caribbean but include Canada, a white dominion, and claim that British air networks were designed to unify the empire, we may find ourselves unwittingly engaged in and trapped by several matters at once: the reinscription of imperial knowledge and thus power; the deep-down racist assumption that the colonized are—*at some level*—the same; the devaluation of the Caribbean; and the twisted replication of "seeing like a state" while "smelling like a market"—in other words, ironically, doing what we are studying: violence.[15]

It is essential, then, that we struggle. If we want to create pieces that fathom out the world we have and account for the revolutionary potential of what Aimé Césaire called "extraordinary possibilities wiped out," it is important to bear down and strive to sense otherwise—to see and smell differently, if you will. To emancipate the imagination, we should seek "to know the unknowable," like Suzanne Césaire, "to think like poets," with Robin Kelley, and, like Fernando Coronil, to "wish to have a map . . . that would recognize the marks of human daring, a map that would dare our imagination, that would show new vistas and make us desire to mold the existing order into a different, dignified landscape for humankind." Because "the truth of a map," Coronil holds with clarity, love, and vision, "lies in its use. A map of history is not simply its model but its figuration. Our journey's desired destiny also defines the way we depict its trajectory."[16]

The history of Caribbean Airways offers such a map. It enables us to *see* and, I hope, experience the transatlantic differently. It slows down the quickened impulse to assume that transatlantic flight is solely the movement of aircraft over and across the ocean, along routes that connect physical geopolitical entities on the western and eastern sides of the Atlantic. The dominant vision is one of air links between ground locations on the North American and European continents, typically the United States and Britain.

The story of Caribbean Airways disrupts that view. It demands that we take prolonged notice of the affairs Imperial Airways had west of London, especially those it had with the airline whose route network would commandeer the Caribbean for much of the twentieth century: Pan American Airways. It compels us to reposition ourselves and look at the transatlantic from another angle. Like the traveler in Walcott's poem, it allows us to grow a Caribbean sky. The shutdown of the colonial airline was inextricably tethered to the opening up of transatlantic air services between Britain and the United States. Their histories are one and the same. After all, Caribbean Airways was a British airline—*in a sense*. The relationship between early British airline travel and empire has many sides and the colonial Caribbean is one of them. A part of Imperial Airways' story, the presence of Caribbean Airways, is a cartographic gift of redirection. To paraphrase Coronil and recall Baldwin's meditation on airspace, it dares us to envision the sky as territory, reconfigure routes, and see lines of disconnection in the air. From this vantage point, the transatlantic looks less like a *straight line* between east and west, less imperial and one-sided, and more like an *asymmetrical triangular-based pyramid*, a postcolonial invocation of diaspora: lines of power, north-south, apex aloft, for the airplane; lines of power, east-west, at the base, for the ships of Middle Passage; vertices of power, sharp nodal points where lines meet, broken pieces to struggle with.

Caribbean poets have been amassing and assembling broken pieces of triangular power relations for some time, undaunted by palpable incongruity. The poems explored and shared often as fragments throughout this book illuminate the disruptive energy and rebellious spirit of this approach: they teach us how to re-search, consider, and write—to toil, to grind, to think, heartened like Kelley, collectively on our own. When the image of overseas aircraft moving overhead appears in a poem, lines about violence and oppression usually follow. The lines are hard gifts. We can choose to follow and trace them, and to get up from under, so to speak, the crushing urge for connection—the 'where' in 'where are we going?'—and just go. The lines about the ordinary airplane, the airliner in particular, often point to, as they are infused by, the political present of the historical past.

Suzanne Césaire's radical poetic article "The Great Camouflage" illustrates this point. Published in 1945, the piece is an explosive commentary on how the beauty people ascribe to the nature of the Caribbean serves to "camouflage" slavery, capitalism, and imperialism in the colonies. At one point, the piece commands an air traveler to "look out the window of the aluminum clipper with its great banking turns" over the archipelago. They are told to see that "once again the sea of clouds is no longer virginal since the Pan American Airways System planes have been flying through." The passenger is instructed to notice "If there is a harvest maturing, now is the time to try to glimpse it, but in the prohibited military zones, the windows are closed." Afterwards, they are informed of the damaging effects of the Middle Passage, modernization, and "the degrading forms of the modern wage-system."

Césaire's lines are gifts. Each one contains 'pieces' to gather and care for, turning them over and over in order to *sense* a different way both to understand the complexities of a moment, and to reassemble the pieces. In Césaire's two lines, pieces such as "once again," "Pan American Airways System," "look out the window," and "the windows are closed" point to the indelible violence ensconced in airborne mobility. They offer different ways to approach researching and writing about that violence. And they open up different ways to *feel* that approach.[17] As scholars of postcolonial perspectives on imperial history have shown, working in archives outside and inside the metropole is about more than finding 'unknown' materials from the peripheries, and adding them to 'known' ones in the center. It is an occasion to hear and be touched by sources in a different way.[18] It is an opportunity to hold certainty lightly and critically at bay.

To work from love is slow and, at moments, vexing to the point of exasperating. These days, it is especially challenging to do so in the academy. There are many disobliging forces at work. Disciplines are closing ranks, funding is going away, tenure is under threat, bigotry is front and center, corporatism is all around, the neoliberal individual is promoted, and 'moreness' and 'nowness' are the orders of the day. The point here is not to lament, but to illuminate some of what makes it difficult to toil, grind, think, and read with love nowadays. There are worlds in a word. The work needed to reach them, from the researching to the reading, asks of us, with fading voice, to take (back) our time, lovingly.

NOTES

LIST OF ABBREVIATIONS OF SELECT PRIMARY SOURCES USED IN NOTES

CCDC: United Kingdom Air Ministry. *The Report of the Committee to Consider the Development of Civil Aviation in the United Kingdom.* Cmd. 5351

CICA: United Kingdom Air Ministry. *The Report of the Committee of Inquiry into Civil Aviation and the Observations of the H. M. Government Thereon.* Cmd. 5685

FWIC: *Report of the First West Indies Conference,* 1929. AVIA 2/299, NA

GAZETTE: *Imperial Airways Gazette*

GFAC: United Kingdom Air Ministry. *The Report on Government Financial Assistance to Civil Air Transport Companies.* Cmd. 1811

OCAT: West Indian Air Transport Committee. *Report on the Opportunities for Civil Air Transport in the West Indies,* Cmd. 2968. CO 318/386/7, NA

PARA: Major R. Mayo, *Report on the Prospects and Air-Port Requirements for British Aviation in the West Atlantic: Printed for the Use of the Colonial Office,* May 1932. 1B/5/79/606, JAR

PD: *Parliamentary Debates.* Commons, 5th series

TERMINAL

1 Lewis, "Jimmy Mubenga Death: Witness Accounts."

2 Taylor and Lewis, "Jimmy Mubenga Decision Prompts Fresh Questions over Investigations." Also Davis, *Freedom Is a Constant Struggle,* esp. 51–60; Inquest, *Updated Briefing on Death of Jimmy Mubenga.*

INTRODUCTION

1 For "spontaneous consent," see Gramsci in Forgacs, ed., *The Antonio Gramsci Reader.* The literature on power and consent is too long to reproduce here. For a provocative discussion, see Said, *Imperialism and Culture.* Rankine, *Citizen* offers a slightly different interpretation of race and exchange and has inspired my rereading of the saying.

2 See Zora Neale Hurston, "How It Feels to Be Colored Me" (1928), and "What White Publishers Won't Print" (1950), in Walker, ed., *I Love Myself When I Am Laughing,* 151–154, 168–172; hooks, "Zora Neale Hurston as Anthropologist and Writer," in *Yearning,* 135–144.

3 For comparative analysis of racialized technologies, see Sharma, "Beyond 'Driving While Black' and 'Flying While Brown.'"

4 For new literature on the history of black workers, segregation, and aviation, see Ortlepp, *Jim Crow Terminals*.

5 See Du Bois, *Souls of Black Folks*; Marshall, *Brown Girl, Brownstones*; Naipaul, *The Mimic Men*.

6 "After all, the history of black people has been a history of movement—real and imagined." Kelley, *Freedom Dreams*, 16.

7 Still, there were occasions when isolation occurred, exclusion was felt, and institutional hurt happened; for example, when the Caribbean was studied as part of World History but the 'World' was not studied as part of Caribbean History. Trouillot captures the pain and power of exclusive pasts in *Silencing the Past*. Chakrabarty connects curriculum politics, colonialism, and contemporary capitalism in *Provincializing Europe*.

8 On priority, privilege, and crossovers, see Cohen, "Unsettled Stories and Inadequate Metaphors."

9 On othering, see Cohn, "History and Anthropology."

10 The realms, though removed, were often relative. For the most part, the 'back then, when . . .' of history and the 'now, over there, where . . .' of anthropology were claims about circumstances in times and places different from yet connected to the 'right here, right now' of academic authors and their audiences. On distance and othering, see Darnton, *The Great Cat Massacre and Other Episodes in French Cultural History*.

11 'Survival strategy' is a nod to Herskovits on Africanisms and Mintz on creolization. As the infamous Herskovits-Frazier debate exposed, space-time in the African diaspora is distinctive. It is decidedly out of Middle Passage. Frazier, *The Negro Family in the United States*, esp. 3–16; Herskovits, *The Myth of the Negro Past*; Mintz, *Three Ancient Colonies*.

12 This particular idea follows Coronil's image of anthrohistory as a Borgesian "labyrinth whose exits become entrances into an expanding labyrinth, its arrivals are points of departure and its answers pose new questions." "Pieces for Anthrohistory," 302.

13 Cohen, "The Pursuits of Anthrohistory," 33.

14 Kelley, *Freedom Dreams*, 196. For the politics and economics of unsettling, see Murphy et al., *Anthrohistory*. For upsetting disciplines as a decolonizing project, see Dussel, "Beyond Eurocentrism."

CHAPTER 1. GROUNDWORK

1 Walcott, *The Prodigal*, 18.

2 But not their futures. Coronil's reading of Frantz Fanon's riff on revolution encourages "imagining a future that builds on the past but is not imprisoned by its horror." "Beyond Occidentalism," 51.

3 Among the Caribbean authors writing about position are Cliff, *The Land of Look Behind*; James, *Beyond a Boundary*; Lamming, *The Pleasures of Exile*.

4 Benjamin warns against safeguarding systems of knowledge and other forms of security that force us to forget that "the tradition of the oppressed teaches us that

the 'state of emergency' in which we live is not the exception but the rule. We must attain to a conception of history that is in keeping with this insight." "Theses on the Philosophy of History," in *Illuminations, 257.*

5 Kelley, *Freedom Dreams,* 170. For willingness and eroding Western dominance, see Mignolo, *Local Histories/Global Designs.*

6 Many scholars refer to ideas and practices in their definitions of empire, including Cooper, *Colonialism in Question,* esp. 154; Ho, "Empire through Diasporic Eyes"; Said, *Imperialism and Culture.*

7 For fieldwork about and in the imagination, see Appadurai, *Modernity at Large*; Rosemont and Kelley, eds., *Black, Brown, & Beige.* For an anthrohistorical understanding of future, past, and present, see Eiss, *In the Name of El Pueblo*; for locus, focus, and scope, see Pedersen, *American Value.*

8 I draw inspiration from Rediker on the "romance of the sea" in *Between the Devil and the Deep Blue Sea,* 3.

9 For notable examples, see Saint-Exupéry, *Airman's Odyssey*; "First Powered Flight Commemorative Panel" issued by the U.S. Postal Service, May 2003; Fitzgerald, "The Diamond as Big as the Ritz," in *The Diamond as Big as the Ritz and Other Short Stories,* 7–50; Hilton, *Lost Horizon*; Markham, *West with the Night.* For analysis of air accidents and allure, see Rieger, *Technology and the Culture of Modernity in Britain and Germany, 1890–1945.* For the airplane's image in popular culture, see Schwartz, *Flying Down to Rio*; Van Riper, *Imagining Flight.*

10 Bunch, "Museums and the Interpretation of African American History"; Hardesty, *Black Wings*; Moye, *Freedom Flyers.*

11 For memoirs: Bragg, *Soaring above Setbacks*; Broadnax, *Blue Skies, Black Wings*; Noble, *Jamaica Airman.* For biographical works: Bix, "Bessie Coleman: Race and Gender Realities behind Aviation Dreams"; Bourne, *The Motherland Calls*; Forsyth, *Black Flight.*

12 See Olaniyan and Sweet, eds., *The African Diaspora and the Disciplines*; Pirie, "Bibliographies."

13 Rucker observes, "Motion in our space has three degrees of freedom—no fewer and no more. . . . Normally, it is difficult for us to perform up/down motions; space is more three-dimensional for a bird or a fish than it is for us. . . . [S]pace is essentially one-dimensional for a car driving down a two-lane road [forward/backward], and essentially two-dimensional for a snowmobile or a car driving around an empty parking lot [forward/backward, left/right]." Space is three-dimensional for aircraft flying or submarines diving (forward/backward, left/right, up/down in depth). Along with three translational degrees of freedom, aircraft have three rotational degrees of freedom, namely, yaw, pitch, and roll. *Geometry, Relativity, and the Fourth Dimension,* 1. On dimensionality, society, and power, see Abbott, *Flatland*; Dewdney, Introduction to *Flatland.* On shape and the production of knowledge, see Sousanis, *Unflattening.*

14 On sky as frontier: Courtwright, *Sky as Frontier.*

15 For another take on deterritorialization and accountability, see Hardt and Negri, *Empire*. On intangible spaces, see Carroll, *An Empire of Air and Water*.

16 Baldwin, *Notes of a Native Son*, xiv.

17 See Barnes, *Journey from Jim Crow*; Bay, "Invisible Tethers"; Brown, *Dropping Anchor, Setting Sail*; Gilroy, *Darker than Blue*; Kelley, *Right to Ride*; Kelley, *Race Rebels*; Stein, *The World of Marcus Garvey*.

18 My thanks to Monica Eileen Patterson for this point.

19 Du Bois, "Of Our Spiritual Strivings," in *Souls of Black Folks*, 8; Morrison, *Song of Solomon*, 220. On Flying Africans, see Powell, "Summoning the Ancestors"; Snyder, "Suicide, Slavery, and Memory in North America." For illuminating verses about black women, imagination, and the sky, see Woodson, *Brown Girl Dreaming*.

20 It is beyond the scope of this book, but the bonds between people in Africa and the upper worlds are much older. See Kreamer, *African Cosmos*; Womack, *Afrofuturism*. For inspiring works on ethnography and outer space, see Messeri, *Placing Outer Space*; Valentine, Olsen, and Battaglia, "Extreme."

21 Here, 'ancient,' which comes from Mintz on the Caribbean in *Three Ancient Colonies*, helps to reimagine African diaspora and Atlantic world chronologies.

22 Bhimull, "Passages."

23 For Marx, "The important thing is not the market's distance in space, but the speed—the amount of time—with which it can be reached . . . while capital must on one side strive to tear down every spatial barrier to intercourse, i.e. to exchange, and conquer the whole earth for its market, it strives on the other side to annihilate this space with time, i.e. to reduce to a minimum the time spent in motion from one place to another." Marx, "The Chapter on Capital," in *Grundrisse*, 538.

24 Some early airlines, such as DELAG (1909), used lighter-than-air ships made by Zeppelin for passenger services.

25 The long list of scholarly works on civil aviation include Barry, *Femininity in Flight*; Corn, *The Winged Gospel*; Fritzsche, *A Nation of Fliers*; Palmer, *Dictatorship of the Air*; Tiemeyer, *Plane Queer*; Wohl, *The Spectacle of Flight*; Young, *Aerial Nationalism*.

26 See Dierikx, *Clipping the Clouds*; Pirie, *Air Empire*; Pirie, *Cultures and Caricatures of British Imperial Aviation*; Van Vleck, *Empire of the Air*. On militarized flight: Derby, "The Dictator's Seduction"; Omissi, *Air Power and Colonial Control*.

27 The critique of 'the gaze' is not new. Here, I use black/white to signify a power relationship that has other names (e.g., other/self, them/us, colonized/colonizer, colonial/imperial). See Baldwin, "On Being White . . . and Other Lies"; Fanon, *Black Skin, White Masks*; hooks, "Representations of Whiteness in the Black Imagination," in *Killing Rage*, 31–50.

28 Among them: Augé, *Non-Places*; Clifford, *The Predicament of Culture*; Griaule, "L'emploi de la Photographie Aerienne et la Recherche Scientifique"; Harris, *Cows, Pigs, Wars, and Witches*; Khosravi, *"Illegal" Traveller*. Notable exceptions: Batteau, "The Anthropology of Aviation and Flight Safety"; Gusterson, *Drone*; Nonini,

"Shifting Identities, Positioned Imaginaries"; Piot, *Nostalgia for the Future*; Raffles, *Insectopedia*; Redfield, *Space in the Tropics*; Vine, *Base Nation*; Yano, *Airborne Dreams*.

29 For example, Clifford, *Routes*; Ferguson, "Of Mimicry and Membership"; Gmelch, *Behind the Smile*; Lutz, ed., *The Bases of Empire*; Scheper-Hughes, "Kidney Kin."

30 For national identity and citizenship of artifacts, see Hecht, *The Radiance of France*; Mrázek, *Engineers of Happy Land*; Winner, "Do Artifacts Have Politics?"

31 Government official, discussion, January 2001.

32 Returned migrant, discussion, June 2001.

33 Airline executive, discussion, October 2000.

34 Return migrant, discussion, October 2000.

35 Nongovernmental organization director, discussion, April 2001.

36 Government official, discussion, January 2001.

37 On gaps, Patterson, "Childhood, Memory, and Gap." Also Davis, *Trickster Travels*.

38 For excellent overviews of routes, see Budd, "Global Networks before Globalization"; Higham, *Britain's Imperial Air Routes, 1918 to 1939*.

39 On slow analysis of scenes, see Stewart, *Ordinary Affects*.

40 Sebald, *On the Natural History of Destruction*, 4.

41 Walcott, "The Antilles: Fragments of Epic Memory," in *What the Twilight Says*, 69.

42 Walcott, "The Antilles," 69, emphasis mine.

43 Mintz, *Three Ancient Colonies*, 197–199.

44 Walcott, "The Antilles," 83–84. On lightness as value: Calvino, *Six Memos for the Next Millennium*. For other ways to approach love, see hooks, *All about Love*; Kelley's reading of James Baldwin on love in "Black Study, Black Struggle."

45 Wright argues in her groundbreaking work on diaspora that the idea of a multiverse aids in "conceiving of collective identities as dimensions" proliferating and having "endless valences." *The Physics of Blackness*, 110.

46 According to Wright, "Our *constructs* of Blackness are largely historical and more specifically based on a notion of spacetime that is commonly fitted into a linear progress narrative while our *phenomenological* manifestations of Blackness happen in what I term *Epiphenomenal* time, or the 'now,' through which the past, present, and future are always interpreted. . . . 'Epiphenomenal' time denotes the current moment, a moment that is *not* directly borne out of another (i.e., causally created)." Importantly, Wright pushes for a move away from, but not the total rejection of, the traditional notion of linear spacetime that has dominated African diaspora and black Atlantic studies. "Epiphenomenal time does not preclude any and all causality: only a *direct*, or *linear*, causality." *The Physics of Blackness*, 4, emphasis in original.

47 Gilroy, *The Black Atlantic*, 4. On futurity, see Mayer, "'Africa as an Alien Future.'"

48 On microhistory and attention, see Ginzburg, *The Cheese and the Worms*.

49 Here, "global white supremacy" references Mills on "racialized distributions" of power as remnants of "European domination." *Blackness Visible*, 98. For an excellent discussion of supremacy, see Pierre, *The Predicament of Blackness*.

LIMIT

1 Walcott, "The Schooner Flight," in *Collected Poems*, 355.

CHAPTER 2. ASCENT

1 See Christie, "Reflections on the Legend of Wayland the Smith"; Crouch, *Wings*, esp. 3–84; Fear, "Bladud"; Hagedorn, *Conquistadors of the Sky*; Hart, *The Dream of Flight*; Montagu, ed., *A Short History of Balloons and Flying Machines*, esp. 1–14; Parkinson, *This Gilded African*, 22; White, Jr., "Eilmer of Malmesbury, an Eleventh Century Aviator," 98.

2 For airplane as spectacle, see Corn, *The Winged Gospel*; Dixon, *Prosthetic Gods*; Wohl, *A Passion for Wings*.

3 On aerial warfare during the First World War, see Paris, *Winged Warfare*.

4 Davy, *Air Power and Civilization*, 110.

5 Davies, *A History of the World's Airlines*, 3. For a compelling analysis of identity politics and commercial aviation development in Europe, see Kranakis, "European Civil Aviation in an Era of Hegemonic Nationalism."

6 On popular postwar support for the airplane, see Edgerton, *England and the Aeroplane*; on ambivalence, see Davies, *A History of the World's Airlines*, esp. 30.

7 For endeavors, see Pirie, *Air Empire*.

8 For all quotes from the first conference, see Sir Frederick H. Sykes, "Civil Aviation and Air Services," in United Kingdom Air Ministry, *Air Conference*, 15–16.

9 For all quotes in the paragraph, see Lord Weir of Eastwood, "Speech to Delegates," in United Kingdom Air Ministry, *The 2nd Air Conference*, 81. For air service with France, see *GFAC*.

10 For all quotes in the paragraph, see Lord Gorell, "Civil Aviation," in United Kingdom Air Ministry, *The 2nd Air Conference*, 8–32.

11 'The same, changing' counterpoints "the changing same," a phrase LeRoi Jones (Amiri Baraka) used to describe creative forms of black agency. "The Changing Same (R & B and New Black Music)." On "the changing same" and diaspora, see Gilroy, "Sounds Authentic."

12 On distance and unease with proximity, see empire defined as "a large, diverse, geographically dispersed and expansionist political entity," in Hall and Rose, eds., "Introduction," 5. For separateness and incorporation across different types of empires (e.g., indirect rule and the British empire, assimilation and the French empire), see Burbank and Cooper, *Empires in World History*.

13 Gorell, "Civil Aviation," 9. On Northcliffe's statement, see Gollin, *No Longer an Island*.

14 See Hall, ed., *Cultures of Empire*.

15 The scene of address is from Butler, *Giving an Account of Oneself*. On scenes, addressability, and racism, see Rankine, *Citizen*, 49.

16 For all quotes in the paragraph, see Lt.-Col. Bristow, "Aerial Transport To-Day and To-Morrow," in United Kingdom Air Ministry, *The 2nd Air Conference*, 32–47.

For other examples, see comments by Colonel O. C. Armstrong (president of the Federation of British Industries) and Major-General Sir W. S. Brancker (Air League of the British Empire) in United Kingdom Air Ministry, *The 2ⁿᵈ Air Conference*, 83–88.

17 For all quotes in the paragraphs, see Sir Frederick H. Sykes, "Speech to Delegates," in United Kingdom Air Ministry, *The 2ⁿᵈ Air Conference*, 82–83.

18 Hardt and Negri's concept of empire is useful here, particularly in its attempts to decouple empire, "a *decentered* and *deterritorializing* apparatus of rule that progressively incorporates the entire global realm within its open, expanding frontiers," from imperialism, "an extension of the sovereignty of the European nation-states beyond their own boundaries." The empire that delegates discussed at the air conferences was imperial beyond doubt. But discussions like these and the airplane itself were key to the emergence of present-day empire, the "new global form of sovereignty" unaccompanied by imperialism. Attention to them makes room to explore how empire was becoming decentered and was deterritorializing in terms of land and water, but that doesn't mean a new kind of territorialization wasn't starting to *take place* in terms of air. Hardt and Negri, *Empire*, xii, emphasis in original.

19 For all quotes in the paragraph, see Sykes, "Civil Aviation and Air Services," in United Kingdom Air Ministry, *Air Conference*, 15.

20 For all quotes in the paragraph, see Gorell, "Civil Aviation," United Kingdom Air Ministry, *The 2ⁿᵈ Air Conference*, 24; Lord Gorell, "Speech to Delegates," in United Kingdom Air Ministry, *The 3ʳᵈ Air Conference*, 91.

21 Gorell, "Speech to Delegates," in United Kingdom Air Ministry, *The 3ʳᵈ Air Conference*, 92. For additional remarks, see those by Sir Sefton Brancker, Sir Samuel Hoare, Mr. F. Handley Page, Major H. Hemming, and Mr. Holt Thomas in United Kingdom Air Ministry, *The 3ʳᵈ Air Conference*.

22 *CICA*, 40.

23 "Terms of Reference," in *GFAC*, 16. Also see Staniland, *Government Birds*.

24 United Kingdom Air Ministry, *Agreement Made with the British, Foreign, and Colonial Corporation, Ltd., Providing for the Formation of a Heavier-than-Air Transport Company to Be Called the Imperial Air Transport Company, Ltd.*

SPEEDBIRD

1 British Airways Speedbird Centre, "The Speedbird," n.d. [probably late twentieth or early twenty-first century]. BASHC. Thank you to the press's anonymous reviewer for transformative remarks about skeuomorphic features.

CHAPTER 3. SPEED

1 F. H. Coventry, a British commercial artist known for his travel scenes, illustrated the brochure.

2 I draw inspiration from Hall's efforts to minimize sharp analytical distinctions between metropole and colony, reclaim the term 'Greater Britain' for 'other' Brit-

ish worlds (e.g., the colonies), and highlight how a Greater Britain shaped the development of the Great one. *Cultures of Empire,* 1.

3 Pieterse, *White on Black,* 172. Also see McClintock, *Imperial Leather;* Pinkus, *Bodily Regimes;* Richards, *The Commodity Culture of Victorian England.*

4 Auerbach, "Art, Advertising, and the Legacy of Empire," 2.

5 I use 'unfold' to capture the sense of developing and expanding, opening and spreading, and revealing through gradual exposure.

6 "Speeding Up the Empire," poster. 9A00689, NASM.

7 On idea, see Conrad's Marlow explaining, "What redeems it [colonial empire] is the idea only. An idea at the back of it; not a sentimental pretense but an idea; and an unselfish belief in the idea—something you can set up, and bow down before, and offer a sacrifice to." *Heart of Darkness,* 21.

8 Put differently: How could such a slogan not be nonsense? What did it mean, and to whom did it speak? See Iskin, "Father Time, Speed, and the Temporality of Posters around 1900"; Williams, "Advertising."

9 Honoré, *In Praise of Slowness,* 3.

10 For additional examples of speed defined as fastness, see Berman's reading of *Faust* in *All That Is Solid Melts into Air,* 49; Dixon, *Futurewise;* Gleick, *Faster;* Kingwell, "Fast Forward"; Millar and Schwarz, eds., *Speed—Visions of an Accelerated Age.*

11 Alonso, "Speed and the New World Religion," 365–373.

12 For all quotes, see Schwab, Interview, 41. Also, see Schwab in *In Praise of Slowness* saying, "We are moving from a world in which the big eat the small to one in which the fast eat the slow." Schwab quoted in Honoré, *In Praise of Slowness,* 4.

13 Virilio, *Speed and Politics,* 47. Also see Virilio, Interview, 82.

14 Calvino, *Six Memos for the Next Millennium,* 31–54.

15 Barthes, "The Jet-Man," in *Mythologies,* esp. 71–73; Kundera, *Slowness;* Schivelbusch, *The Railway Journey.*

16 Kundera, *Slowness,* 39.

17 Speed can also be constant (change in position without change in speed), instantaneous (speed of a moving object *at a particular moment* in time), and average (distance traveled divided by time traveled). Average speed is the focus of this chapter, unless otherwise mentioned. For the history of speed in physics, see March, *Physics for Poets.* My thanks to Frederick Becchetti for helping with kinematics and the physics of motion, and for inadvertently bringing me to Leibniz's works.

18 In considering "the awkwardness" of using 'discovery' or 'conquest' to describe Columbus in the Americas, Trouillot also illuminated the imperial politics of word choice. *Silencing the Past,* 115.

19 Harvey, *The Condition of Postmodernity,* 265–266; Lefebvre, *The Production of Space,* 25; Woolf, "Mr. Bennett and Mrs. Brown," 96.

20 To speak of a single futurist movement is difficult. There were different national camps, each with their own political agendas. A core network of beliefs about speed and simultaneity, however, cut across and connected them. See Hewitt, *Fascist Modernism;* Markov, *Russian Futurism;* Perloff, *The Futurist Moment.*

21 Marinetti, "Manifesto of Futurism," *Le Figaro*, February 20, 1909, front page.

22 For speed and other mediums, see works by Giacomo Balla, Umberto Boccioni, Angiolo Mazzoni, Gino Severini, and Antonio Sant'Elia.

23 For all quotes from the paper, see Marinetti, "The New Religion—Morality of Speed," *L'Italia Futurista* no. 1 (May 11, 1916), emphasis in original.

24 Boccioni, Carrà, Russolo, Balla, Severini, "Manifesto of the Futurist Painters," *Poesia* (February 11, 1910), 183.

25 Marinetti, "The Foundation and Manifesto of Futurism," 16.

26 For all passages from parable, see Marinetti, "Let's Murder the Moonshine."

27 Marinetti, "The New Religion—Morality of Speed," 103, emphasis in original.

28 Additional examples of aviation in Marinetti's work are in "Electrical War (a Futurist Vision—Hypothesis) (1911); "Technical Manifesto of Futurist Literature" (1912); "A Futurist Theater of the Skies Enhanced by Radio and Television" (1932). Examples from other futurists include Carrà, "Graphic Rhythm with Airplane— Homage to Blériot" (1914); Crane, "Cape Hatteras" (1930); Malevich, "Suprematist Composition: Airplane Flying" (1915). Notable works about futurism and flight include Benton, "Dreams of Machines"; Berghaus, ed., *Futurism and the Technological Imagination*; Bohn, "The Poetics of Flight"; Esposito, *Fascism, Aviation, and Mythical Modernity*; Piper, *Cartographic Fictions*.

29 "Why the First Manifesto should have impressed so many Continental and Russian writers and artists but have produced only one English Futurist, the painter C. R. W. Nevinson," R. W. Flint questioned in the Introduction to *Let's Now Murder the Moonshine*, 26.

30 Lewis, *Blasting and Bombardiering*, 34, emphasis in original. For an overview of Lewis's politics, see Foshay, *Lewis and the Avant-Garde*.

31 Lewis, *Blasting and Bombardiering*, 34–35, emphasis in original.

32 See Forster, "The Machine Stops"; Wells, "The Argonauts of the Air"; Wells, *The War Is in the Air and Particularly How Mr. Bert Smallways Fared*.

33 On the English countryside, see Matless, *Landscape and Englishness*; Rose, *Which People's War?*; Williams, *The Country and the City*. On the motorcar and postwar village life, see Lee's memoir, *Cider with Rosie*.

34 For all quotes from the story, see Buchan, *The Thirty-Nine Steps*, esp. 29–93.

35 Swift, *Gulliver's Travels*, 203. Among other early fliers are fairies, dragons, children, witches, and souls. Cressy, "Early Modern Space Travel and the English Man in the Moon"; Jankovic, "The Politics of Sky Battles in Early Hanoverian Britain."

36 Garnerin, *A Circumstantial Account of the Three Last Aerial Voyages Made by M. Garnerin*. On aviation law, see Banner, *Who Owns the Sky?*; Pascoe, *Aircraft*.

37 Glaisher's notes appeared in several nineteenth-century publications, including Marion, *Wonderful Balloon Ascents or The Conquest of the Skies*, 210.

38 Crouch, *Wings*; Holmes, *Falling Upwards*; Rolt, *The Aeronauts*.

39 Baden-Powell, "Aeronautics in the Twentieth Century." For public perceptions of airships, see Rieger, *Technology and the Culture of Modernity in Britain and Germany*, esp. 20–85.

40 The charge read in full: "The Committee have given very careful consideration to the question, 'How best to organise Imperial Air Routes,' which was the question specifically referred to them for consideration and advice when they were appointed." Advisory Committee on Civil Aviation to Winston Churchill (Secretary of State for Air), *Report on Imperial Air Routes*, 3.

41 For an elegant analysis of white empire, see Schwarz, *Memories of Empire, Volume I.*

42 Schivelbusch convincingly argues, "The annihilation of space and time was the early-nineteenth-century characterization of the effect of railroad travel." *The Railway Journey*, 33.

43 For all quotes in this section of the chapter, see Advisory Committee on Civil Aviation to Winston Churchill (Secretary of State for Air), *Report on Imperial Air Routes*, emphasis mine.

UPRISING

1 Beer, "The Island and the Aeroplane," 278–280.

2 Woolf, "Flying over London."

3 James, *The Case for West-Indian Self Government.* Pamphlet A, F2131.J25, WIC.

CHAPTER 4. PLANES

1 Woolf, "Flying over London," 167.

2 On black writers claiming what James Baldwin called "history as written by whites," see Baldwin, "James Baldwin."

3 Cole, "The Unquiet Sky," in *Known and Strange Things*, 207–211.

4 Fritzsche, *A Nation of Fliers*, esp. 191–199.

5 On postwar opinions: Biddle, *Rhetoric and Reality in Air Warfare*; Paris, *Winged Warfare*; GFAC.

6 Grey, "Joy-Riding and Commercial Aviation." Also *CCDC*, 8–9. On campaigns and propaganda: Paris, ed., *The First World War and Popular Cinema.* On films: Pirie, "Cinema and British Imperial Civil Aviation, 1919–1939."

7 Brian Riddle at the Royal Aeronautical Society graciously helped estimate when the last issue was released.

8 "The Importance of Imperial Airways Gazette," *Gazette*, 1.

9 On guidebooks, spectatorship, and governance, see Apter, "On Imperial Spectacle"; Grewal, *Home and Harem.*

10 "The Pageant of England," *Gazette*, 5. Also: "Fly to European Capitals," *Gazette*, 5; "Imperial Airways Gazette Makes Dentistry Pleasant," *Gazette*, 7; "India to South Africa by Imperial Airways," *Gazette*, 4.

11 The notion of scapes and their imagined worlds belongs to Appadurai, *Modernity at Large*, 30.

12 On colonial encounters and identity formation, see Gikandi, *Maps of Englishness*; Hall and Rose, "Introduction: Being at Home with the Empire."

13 A wonderful essay on airfreight and globalization is Lopez, "Flight," in *About This Life*, 73–109.

14 Sir Eric Geddes, "The Annual General Meeting of Imperial Airways," *Gazette*, 2; Imperial Airways, "Map of Empire and European Air Routes," 1936. A199006050000, ct. neg. 98–20236, NASM.

15 "Extension of the Empire Air Mail Programme," *Gazette*, 2.

16 On steamships: Coons and Varias, *Tourist Third Cabin*; Woollacott, *To Try Her Fortune in London*. On automobiles and trains: Divall, "Civilizing Velocity"; Walton, "Power, Speed, and Glamour."

17 *CCDC*, 26.

18 "Air Mail Traffic," *Gazette*, 2.

19 For weight in steamship culture, see Woollacott, *To Try Her Fortune in London*, 21.

20 There were other options. The airline used miles to measure distance; the Postmaster General used place to evoke an emotive sense of how far letters had flown. For example, when he wanted to say how far Christmas mail flew, he said 'from Britain to India' to indicate distance.

21 "Cross Channel Statistics," *Gazette*, 1. For numbers from the airline's first year, see Directorate of Civil Aviation, in United Kingdom Air Ministry, *Annual Report on the Progress of Civil Aviation*, 30.

22 For all quotes from the ad, see "The Advantages of Sending Your Letters and Freight by Air," *Gazette*, 8.

23 Geddes, "The Annual General Meeting of Imperial Airways," *Gazette*, 2.

24 For all quotes in the paragraph, see "The World Travels by Air," *Gazette*, 4.

25 "The Growth of Imperial Airways," *Gazette*, 8.

26 "Queen Marys of the Air," *Gazette*, 5.

27 Front Cover, *Gazette*, October 1930.

28 "Tea Flights," *Gazette*, 2.

29 "An Air Service to the Grand National," *Gazette*, 2.

30 For comparison, see aerial racial segregation in the United States in Woodward, *The Strange Career of Jim Crow*, esp. 117.

31 "See the Boat Race from the Air," *Gazette*, 2.

32 For all quotes in the paragraph, see "To Paris While You Read Your Paper," *Gazette*, 8.

33 Wohl, *A Passion for Wings*, 282. Also Millward, "The Embodied Aerial Subject"; Singer, *Like Sex with Gods*.

34 Front Cover, *Gazette*, January 1931.

35 "Flying 20,000 Miles on Business," *Gazette*, 2.

36 Burman, "Racing Bodies"; Rieger, "'Fast Couples.'"

37 "Air Travel for Women," *Gazette*, November 1933, 5.

38 Menzies, *All Ways by Airways*. TL 526.G7M55, NASM.

39 "In Swiss Cloudland," *Gazette*, 3, emphasis in original. My thanks to Mary Harris O'Reilly for pointing out that interwar references to 'white magic' were often about intentions that were good or bad, and were not necessarily about race. For a different approach to affect and air travel experiences, see Budd, "On Being Aeromobile."

40 Fanon, *The Wretched of the Earth*, 38. Also see Chow, "Where Have All the Natives Gone."

41 On in-flight experiences, see "Catering Up in the Air," *Gazette*, 6.

42 Satia, "The Defense of Inhumanity," 16.

43 Unless noted, for all quotes from McCullough, see "Baghdad Bound," *Gazette*, February 1934, 2; March 1934, 7; May 1934, 5.

44 On the complexities of empire and debris, see Stoler, ed., *Imperial Debris*.

45 Unless noted, for all quotes from Pitt, see "The Magic Carpet—A Journey to India by Imperial Airways," *Gazette*, 3.

46 McCullough, "Baghdad Bound," May 1934, 5.

47 "London to Baghdad in 3.5 Days," *Gazette*, 1.

48 Ingram, "To Paris in Two Hours and Twenty Minutes."

49 For surveillance technologies and their racial politics, see Browne, *Dark Matters*. For aerial surveillance before and during this period, see Omissi, *Air Power and Colonial Control*; Satia, *Spies in Arabia*.

50 For all quotes in the paragraph, see "Wings over Africa," *Gazette*, 1. For another example, see "What Air Passengers See While Flying from Brisbane to Singapore," *Gazette*, 2.

51 As an example of flight serving metropolitans abroad, he noted, "Urgent merchandise is hurried to us with astonishing rapidity." For all quotes in the paragraph and this footnote, see L., "Our Air Link with Home," *Gazette*, 1.

52 For all quotes in the paragraph, see L., "Our Air Link with Home," *Gazette*, 1. On interpreting daily acts of resistance, see Kelley, *Race Rebels*.

53 See "Letters from an Air Traveller to His Son," *Gazette*.

54 Harry, "A Good Letter," *Gazette*.

55 Emphasis mine. For all quotes in the paragraph, see Harry, "A Good Letter," *Gazette*.

56 For all quotes in the paragraph, see Harry, "A Good Letter," *Gazette*.

57 Long later became the well-known writer Genesta Hamilton. For a woman airline passenger writing prescriptively about flying the empire route to Australia, see "Flying in Comfort," *Gazette*, 6–7. For gender and imperial aerial subjectivity, see Millward, *Women in British Imperial Airspace, 1922–1937*.

58 Unless noted, for all quotes from Long, see "South Africa by the *Empire* Flying Boat," *Gazette*, 2–4.

59 Taylor and Lewis, "Jimmy Mubenga Decision Prompts Fresh Questions over Investigations."

60 On whiteness and flight, see Back, "Falling from the Sky."

CHAPTER 5. ROUTES

1 "Map of Empire," poster. 98–20236, NASM.

2 For example, the map showed one "4" on the Nairobi-Kisumu route. Imperial Airways offered four one-way flights each week, in each direction; eight flights moved weekly on this route. On other routes, places listed between 'anchor cities'

might have been stopovers. For example, Penang and Koh Samui might have been stopovers on the Singapore-Bangkok route, which would change the number of circulating airplanes.

3 On maps: Harley, "Deconstructing the Map"; Tufte, *Visual Explanations.*

4 "New York–Bermuda in 5 Hours," Timetable and Tariff Brochure, April 6, 1938. R. E. G. Davies Files, NASM.

5 Cumming, "Bermuda to New York," *Gazette,* 4; "Atlantic Air Service," *Times* (New York). LH 15/3/120, LHCMA; "Bermuda at the End of Plane Route," July 16, 1937. F2–788040–25, NASM; "Ocean Flying," *Times* (London). LH 15/3/120, LHCMA. Also Allen, "Want to Fly the Atlantic," n.d. F2–788040–25, NASM; "Wings Roar Over Seas Skyways," *Times* (New York). F2–788040–25 NASM.

6 William Van Dusen to Señor, June 21, 1937. Box 208, UM.

7 Imperial Airways, "First Experimental Trans-Atlantic Flight West and East-bound," July 1937. AW/1/7271, BASHC.

8 Gouge, "Transatlantic Air Transport with Particular Reference to Flying Boats." F2–788040–25, NASM. Also, "Atlantic Mails by Air," March 1935. F2–788040–25, NASM; "Atlantic Air Navigation," *Times* (New York). F2–788040–20, NASM. On trade: "Atlantic Air Service Soon to Be Reality," June 10, 1936. F2–788040–25, NASM; "Ocean Air Transport," January 1937. F2–788040–25, NASM; "North Atlantic Air Service: Germany's Preliminary Work—Plans of the U.S.A.," n.d. F2–788040–25, NASM. On scholarship: Davies, *A History of the World's Airlines*; Graham, *Geography and Air Transport*; Sealy, *The Geography of Air Transport.*

9 William Van Dusen to Señor, 21 June 1937. Box 208, UM. For Pan American in the Atlantic, see Van Vleck, *Empire of the Air.*

10 "Terms of Reference"; "Introduction," *OCAT,* A2.

11 "Introduction," *OCAT,* 5. For Sykes, see "Civil Aviation and Air Services," in United Kingdom Air Ministry, *Air Conference,* 15. On mobility and black nationalism in the 1920s and 1930s, see Putnam, *Radical Moves.*

12 "West Indies Service"; "Canada and the West Indies," *OCAT,* 7, 17.

13 "Trinidad–British Guiana Route," *OCAT,* 11.

14 Sheller, *Consuming the Caribbean.*

15 "West Indies Service"; "Summary"; "Trinidad–British Guiana Route," *OCAT,* 8, 17, 11. For escalating population pressures, see Wallace, *The British Caribbean.*

16 "Trinidad-Curaçao-Maracaibo," *OCAT,* 11–12.

17 For all quotes in this and previous paragraphs, see "Trinidad-Curaçao-Maracaibo"; "West Indies Service"; "Local Opportunities"; "Introduction," *OCAT,* 11–12, 8, 9, 5.

18 "Meeting Called Yesterday to Secure Practical Interest in Caribbean Airways," *Daily Gleaner* (Kingston).

19 For eighteenth-century lighter-than-air craft in the Americas, see Dubois, *Avengers of the New World*; for military fliers in Haiti and the Dominican Republic, see Roorda, "The Cult of the Airplane among U.S. Military Men and Dominicans during the U.S. Occupation and the Trujillo Regime."

20 Hanna, "Early Days of Commercial Aviation in Jamaica," 11.

21 "The Activities of Caribbean Airways," *Daily Gleaner* (Kingston).

22 Archie de Pass to Secretary of State for the Colonies, July 21, 1931. 1B/5/77/1931/76, JAR.

23 For all quotes in the paragraph, see A. E. V. Barton, "Civil Aviation," and Sir Edward Davson, "Civil Aviation," in *FWIC*.

24 For examples, see "West Indies Airways Plan Is Official: Jamaica Likely to Have Service Shortly," *Daily Gleaner* (Kingston); "The Aircraft Services in West Indies," *Daily Gleaner* (Kingston).

25 W. D. B. [full name unknown] to Colonial Secretary (Jamaica), April 26, 1933. 1B/5/79/576, JAR.

26 W. D. B. to Colonial Secretary (Jamaica), May 8, 1933. 1B/5/79/576, JAR.

27 References to the airline's operational history are limited; remarks about staff numbers, fares, and finances are notably vague, if not veiled. For example, see "New Air Service between City and Santiago," *Daily Gleaner* (Kingston).

28 Pan American Airways, "Outline of the History of Latin American Services," n.d. [probably 1945–46]. Box 372/1517.6, UM.

29 Pan American Airways, "Our Air Mail Service with Latin America: To Promote the Wider Use of Inter-American Air Communication," August 1931. Box 20/10.06.0, UM.

30 On U.S. foreign policy and Pan American: Smith, *Airways Abroad*; Van Vleck, "The 'Logic of the Air.'" On Pan American, U.S.-American empire building, and Caribbean geography: Davies, *A History of the World's Airlines*; Oldenziel, "Islands."

31 "Meeting Called Yesterday to Secure Practical Interest in Caribbean Airways," *Daily Gleaner* (Kingston).

32 Pan American Airways, "Outline of the History of Latin American Services," n.d. [probably 1945–46]. Box 372/1517.6, UM.

33 Sir Samuel Hoare, "Appendices to the Summary of Proceedings," in United Kingdom Air Ministry, *Imperial Conference*, 192–201.

34 For overviews, see Edgerton, *England and the Aeroplane*.

35 For all quotes in the paragraph, see C. le Bullock (Air Ministry) to Under Secretary of State (Colonial Office), October 27, 1931. 1B/5/77/1931/76, JAR.

36 United Kingdom Air Ministry, *Report of the American Aviation Mission*; W. Churchill in United Kingdom Air Ministry, *Report on Imperial Air Routes*; Clipping from *Flight*, "The First Imperial Air Route," December 30, 1926. F11-600000.03, NASM. For techno-political constraints influencing route development, see McCormack, "Airlines and Empires."

37 For limitations, see *PARA*, esp. 82.

38 For desire and cooperation, see *PARA*, esp. 87.

39 United Kingdom Air Ministry, *Convention Relating to International Air Navigation*, article 5. Also Amendment, "The Air Navigation Act (Colonies, Protectorate, Mandated Territories)," Order No. 346 (1929) to United Kingdom Bill, *Air Navigation Act*, 1920. 1B/5/77/122, JAR.

40 Unless noted, for quotes in this section, see *PARA*. On mother country mentality, see Rose, *Which People's War?*

41 Colonial Development Act, 1929, 20 Geo. 5, c.5 (U.K.). Also Dierikx, "Struggle for Prominence," esp. 340–346; Lyth, "The Empire's Airway's," 877–878.

42 In addition to Edgerton and Fritzsche on air-mindedness and empire/nation building, see Palmer, "Peasants into Pilots"; Pirie, "British Air Shows in South Africa, 1932/33."

43 For all quotes in the paragraph, see Summary of Answers to the Scheduled Questions, December 24, 1931. 1B/5/77/76, JAR. For Caribbean Airways' contributions, see "The Activities of Caribbean Airways," *Daily Gleaner* (Kingston); "Meeting Called Yesterday to Secure Practical Interest in Caribbean Airways," *Daily Gleaner* (Kingston); and other papers in 1B/5/77/7, JAR.

44 Forty-Seventh Meeting of Colonial Development Advisory Committee (London), April 20, 1932. 1B/5/79/557, JAR. Also Colonial Development Fund (London), March 7, 1932. CO 137/795/18, NA.

45 W. D. B. to Colonial Secretary (Jamaica), May 2, 1932. 1B/5/79/557, JAR.

46 W. D. B. to Colonial Secretary (Jamaica), May 2,1932. 1B/5/79/557, JAR. For intimations of a "close working agreement" between Imperial Airways and Pan American, see W. D. B. to Colonial Secretary (Jamaica), May 28, 1932. 1B/5/79/557, JAR. Also Jackson, *Imperial Airways and the First British Airlines, 1919–40*, esp. 38–42.

47 W. D. B. to Colonial Secretary (Jamaica), May 28,1932. 1B/5/79/557, JAR.

48 W. D. B. to Colonial Secretary (Jamaica), May 28, 1932. 1B/5/79/557, JAR. For additional examples of political and practical concerns, see Mr. Battershill (Jamaica) to Secretary of State for the Colonies (London), October 30, 1932. 1B/5/79/606, JAR.

49 W. D. B., memorandum, June 26, 1933. 1B/5/79/642, JAR.

50 For all quotes in the paragraph, see Captain Archie de Pass (Jamaica) to D. (British Legislation, San Salvador), February 19, 1932. 1B/5/79/557, JAR.

51 For all quotes in the paragraph, see Captain Archie de Pass (Jamaica) to Under Secretary of State for the Colonies (London), June 8, 1932. 1B/5/79/576, JAR.

52 Captain A. de Pass (Jamaica) to Sir E. de Pass (London), June 8, 1932. 1B/5/79/557, JAR. Also Sir E. de Pass (London) to Under Secretary of State for the Colonies (London), January 21, 1932. CO 137/795/18, NA.

53 Forty-Seventh Meeting of Colonial Development Advisory Committee (London), April 20, 1932. 1B/5/79/557, JAR.

54 W. D. B. to Colonial Secretary (Jamaica), April 26, 1933. 1B/5/79/576, JAR; W. D. B. to Colonial Secretary (Jamaica), May 8,1933. 1B/5/79/576, JAR.

55 Note of a meeting held in the Colonial Office (London), July 24, 1933. DO 35/267/2, NA.

56 For aviation and U.K.-U.S. international relations: Engel, *Cold War at 30,000 Feet*; Sampson, *Empires of the Sky*. For the air alliance's global implications: Dobson, *Peaceful Air Warfare*; Lyth, "The Empire's Airways," esp. 878–879; H. Smith, *Airways Abroad*, esp. 38–53.

57 For example, "£1,600 Compensation to Be Paid to Caribbean Airways," *Daily Gleaner* (Kingston).

58 See passages about patriotism in city merchant's letter to the editor of *Daily Gleaner* (Kingston), October 24, 1934; and questions about "the spirit of British civilization" in another city merchant's letter to the editor of *Daily Gleaner* (Kingston), October 26, 1934.

59 "For Rent," *Daily Gleaner* (Kingston).

60 A. Césaire, *Discourse on Colonialism*; Hacking, *The Taming of Chance*; Latour, *Aramis or the Love of Technology*; Sandage, *Born Losers*.

61 Coronil, "Beyond Occidentalism," influences my point about transatlantic exchanges taking place on a north-south axis.

62 For subalternity and place, see Mignolo, *Local Histories/Global Designs*.

63 On archives, knowledge, and the Caribbean, see Trouillot, *Silencing the Past*.

CHAPTER 6. DESCENT

1 Royal Assent, August 4, 1939, Commons, 5th ser., vol. 350 (1938–39), col. 2852.

2 British Overseas Airways Act, 1939, 2 & 3 Geo. 6, c. 45 (U.K.).

3 Walter Robert Dempster Perkins, *PD*, vol. 329, November 17, 1937, cols. 417–418, 421, 434.

4 For British Airways Ltd. subsidy, see United Kingdom Air Ministry, *England-Scandinavia Civil Air Transport Services*.

5 Perkins, *PD*, vol. 329, November 17, 1937, col. 417.

6 Perkins, *PD*, vol. 329, November 17, 1937, col. 417.

7 Perkins, *PD*, vol. 329, November 17, 1937, col. 423; also Lieutenant-Colonel John Moore-Brabazon, *PD*, vol. 329, November 17, 1937, cols. 438–439.

8 Perkins, *PD*, vol. 329, November 17, 1937, cols. 417–418, 431.

9 Perkins, *PD*, vol. 329, November 17, 1937, cols. 426, 429, 431.

10 Perkins, *PD*, vol. 329, November 17, 1937, col. 431.

11 Perkins, *PD*, vol. 329, November 17, 1937, col. 418.

12 For all quotes in this and the previous paragraph, see Lieutenant-Colonel John Moore-Brabazon, *PD*, vol. 329, November 17, 1937, cols. 434–440.

13 Geoffrey Mander, *PD*, vol. 329, November 17, 1937, col. 460.

14 For all Colonel Sir Leonard Ropner's quotes, see *PD*, vol. 329, November 17, 1937, cols. 449–458.

15 For estimates, see "Other Services," in *CICA*, 7. CO 323/1563/9, NA. For an analysis that pays close attention to the political geography, see Dodds, *Pink Ice*. For informal empire in the South Atlantic, see Miller, "Informal Empire in Latin America."

16 For all Sir Murray Sueter's quotes, see *PD*, vol. 329, November 17, 1937, cols. 444–449.

17 For all quotes in the paragraph, see Lieutenant-Colonel Anthony John Muirhead, *PD*, vol. 329, November 17, 1937, cols. 472–479.

18 F. Smith, "John Cadman, Baron Cadman, 1877–1941."

19 Montague, *PD*, vol. 329, November 24, 1937, cols. 1219, 1247.

20 Montague, *PD*, vol. 329, November 30, 1937, col. 1880; Prime Minister Neville Chamberlain, *PD*, vol. 329, November 30, 1937, col. 1880.

21 "The Report," in *CICA*, 5. CO 323/1563/9, NA.

22 See "List of Witnesses," in *CICA*, 36–38. CO 323/1563/9, NA.

23 On promise, see Muirhead, *PD*, vol. 329, November 17, 1937, col. 479; Chamberlain, *PD*, vol. 329, November 30, 1937, col. 1880.

24 See Perkins, *PD*, vol. 331, February 16, 1938, col. 1873; Perkins, *PD*, vol. 332, February 24, 1938, col. 532; *Time*, "Cadman Castigation"; "The Cadman Report," *Times* (London).

25 *CICA*.

26 For all quotes in the paragraph, see "Introduction," in *CICA*, 6. CO 323/1563/9, NA.

27 For all quotes in the paragraph, see "The Position To-Day," in *CICA*, 6. CO 323/1563/9, NA.

28 For all quotes in the paragraph, see "Air Services"; "Air Services and Operating Companies"; "Air Ministry Organisation," in *CICA*, 13, 32, 9–12. CO 323/1563/9, NA.

29 Cadman, chairman of an oil company and the committee, had long been interested in the Caribbean, particularly in Trinidad and its petroleum. Perhaps his business interests in the region prompted the committee to focus on aviation there.

30 For all quotes in the paragraph, see "Other Services"; "Air Services," in *CICA*, 7, 13. CO 323/1563/9, NA.

31 On duty and culpability, see "Imperial Airways, Ltd.'s Management"; "Past Policy," in *CICA*, 14–15, 7–8. CO 323/1563/9, NA.

32 For all quotes in this and the previous paragraphs, see "Imperial Airways, Ltd.'s Management"; "Past Policy"; "Summary of Main Recommendations," in *CICA*, 14–15, 7–8, 31–33. CO 323/1563/9, NA.

33 For all quotes in the paragraph, see Prime Minister Neville Chamberlain, *PD*, vol. 333, March 16, 1938, cols. 433–441.

34 For all quotes in the paragraph, see Chamberlain, *PD*, vol. 333, March 16, 1938, cols. 437–439. For Chamberlain's views on empire, see *The Neville Chamberlain Diary Letters*, esp. 164; Self, *Neville Chamberlain*, esp. 138–151.

35 For all quotes in the paragraph, see Chamberlain, *PD*, vol. 333, March 16, 1938, col. 439.

36 For all quotes in this and the previous paragraph, see Clement Richard Attlee, *PD*, vol. 333, March 16, 1938, cols. 441–449.

37 "Observations of His Majesty's Government on the Report of the Committee of Inquiry into Civil Aviation," in *CICA*, i. CO 323/1563/9, NA. For rearmament program and Chamberlain on empire's longevity, see Ruggiero, *Neville Chamberlain and British Rearmament*.

38 For all quotes from Attlee, see *PD*, vol. 333, March 16, 1938, cols. 442–448.

39 For all quotes from Mavis Constance Tate, see *PD*, vol. 333, March 16, 1938, cols. 464–485.

40 Lieutenant-Colonel Anthony John Muirhead, *PD*, vol. 333, March 16, 1938, col. 485.

41 Muirhead, *PD*, vol. 333, March 16, 1938, col. 485.

42 For all quotes in the paragraph, see Sir Murray Sueter, *PD*, vol. 333, March 28, 1938, cols. 1796–1797.

43 Morgan Jones, *PD*, vol. 333, March 28, 1938, col. 1761.

44 W. L. Everard, *PD*, vol. 333, March 28, 1938, cols. 1730–1731.

45 J. R. Robinson, *PD*, vol. 333, March 28, 1938, col. 1777. See also N. J. Hulbert, *PD*, vol. 333, March 16, 1938, col. 463.

46 "The Cadman Report," *Times* (London); "The Committee's Report," *Times* (London). LH 15/3/120, LHCMA. For additional examples, see "Big Changes in Civil Aviation," *Telegraph* (London). LH 15/3/120, LHCMA; Goodfellow, letter to the editor; Straight, letter to the editor. For frequency and size, see "Division of the Subsidy," *Times* (London). For race-based exclusionary practices in the colonial Caribbean, see Putnam's discussion of "mobility control" in *Radical Moves*, 82–122.

WAKE

1 On the Caribbean as a small place, see Kincaid, *A Small Place*.

CONCLUSION

1 Rose, *Which People's War?* 10.

2 As many scholars have discussed, naming political entities is complicated, tricky, and sometimes rather messy when it comes to the British Isles. A provocative overview of the debate is found in Rose, *Which People's War?* See especially chapter 7, which explains, "As a nation state Great Britain, geographically and politically speaking, was as much an empire as it was a nation for it had been formed by England's incorporation of Wales, Scotland, and Ireland." Also see Colley, *Britons*.

3 For regulated mobility, security, and freedom, see Bigo, "Freedom and Speed in Enlarged Borderzones."

4 My 'geometries of power' is similar to but not the same as Doreen Massey's path-breaking work on "power-geometry." For Massey, "the term power-geometry does not imply any specific form (any specific geometry). It is a *concept* through which to analyze the world, in order perhaps to highlight inequalities, or deficiencies in democracy." See "Concepts of Space and Power in Theory and in Political Practice," 19, emphasis mine.

5 Le Corbusier famously wrote about aerial vision and spectacle in *Aircraft*, at BL.

6 For an excellent analysis of white flight and racial violence, albeit on the ground, see Connolly, *A World More Concrete*.

7 Davis said: "We need to popularize understandings of how racism underwrites the death penalty, and so many other institutions." Commercial aviation is one of those institutions. *Freedom Is a Constant Struggle*, 17, 30.

8 Among works on ethnography in the archive I found particularly helpful are those by Paul K. Eiss, Ann Laura Stoler, and Katherine Verdery. The same goes for Kathleen Stewart's ethnographic work on scenes and the something. Eiss, *In*

the Name of El Pueblo; Stewart, *Ordinary Affects*; Stoler, *Along the Archival Grain*; Verdery, *Secrets and Truths*.

9 Among works on archival power, silences, and mentions, and bulky evidence shaping my thinking are Amin, *Event, Metaphor, Memory*; Cohen, *The Combing of History*; Fuentes, *Dispossessed Lives*; Trouillot, *Silencing the Past*.

10 Dubois, "Atlantic Freedoms."

11 For a different take on empire making and the logic of airline travel, see Van Vleck, *Empire of the Air*.

12 A sampling of those not mentioned earlier include essays in Cwerner, Kesselring, and Urry, eds., *Aeromobilities*; Dienel and Lyth, eds., *Flying the Flag*. Also Pirie, "Passenger Traffic in the 1930s on British Imperial Air Routes." For works helping illuminate this point, though with different sources, positions, and perspectives, see Raboteau, *Searching for Zion*; Sheller, "Air Mobilities on the U.S.-Caribbean Border."

13 Coronil, "Beyond Occidentalism," 52. Also Coronil, "Towards a Critique of Globalcentrism."

14 My reference to forgetting and erasing racial difference builds on bell hooks's work on a world without racism, especially her point about "the flaw" in Martin Luther King, Jr.'s notion of beloved community: "It was the insistence that such a community could exist only if we erased and forgot racial difference." "Beloved Community," in *Killing Rage*, 31–50, 263. I find Henrietta Moore's critique of Edwin Ardener's theory of muteness useful for thinking about dominance, difference, and anthropological knowledge. *Feminism and Anthropology*.

15 The last point is found in Fernando Coronil's sharp review of James Scott's *Seeing Like a State*, in which he exposes the possibility of this double-edged sword, namely, reinscribing while studying how the state and the capitalist market generate violent authoritative power through technologies of modernization. "Smelling Like a Market." Also see Scott, *Seeing Like a State*, esp. his discussion of the airplane and what he calls "authoritarian high modernism."

16 A. Césaire, *Discourse on Colonialism*, 43; S. Césaire, "Alain and Esthetics," 18; Coronil, "Smelling Like a Market," 129; Kelley, *Freedom Dreams*, 196. The recent debates on struggle, especially those dealing with intellectual work, reinscription, resistance, and transformation, have helped me clarify this point. There are many, including Alexander, "Ta-Nehisi Coates's 'Between the World and Me'"; Coates, *Between the World and Me*; Davis, *Freedom Is a Constant Struggle*; Kelley, "Black Study, Black Struggle"; Taylor, *From #BlackLivesMatter to Black Liberation*.

17 For all passages from S. Césaire's essay, see "The Great Camouflage," 40.

18 Moraña, Dussel, and Jáuregui, eds., *Coloniality at Large*.

BIBLIOGRAPHY

LIST OF ABBREVIATIONS OF MAJOR ARCHIVES

BASHC: British Airways Speedbird Heritage Centre, Harmondsworth
BL: British Library, London
BNA: Barbados National Archive, Black Rock
JAR: Jamaica Archives and Records Department, Spanish Town
LHCMA: Liddell Hart Centre for Military Archives, King's College, London
NA: National Archives, Kew
NASM: National Air and Space Museum, Smithsonian Institution, Washington, D.C.
UM: University of Miami, Richter Library, Special Collections Division, Coral Gables
WIC: West Indies Collection, University of the West Indies, Cave Hill

SOURCES

Abbott, Edwin. *Flatland: A Romance of Many Dimensions*. 1884. Reprint, New York: Signet Classic, 1984.

Advisory Committee on Civil Aviation to Winston Churchill. *Report on Imperial Air Routes*. Cmd. 449. London: His Majesty's Stationary Office, October 30, 1919.

Alexander, Michelle. "Ta-Nehisi Coates's 'Between the World and Me.'" *New York Times*, August 17, 2015, www.nytimes.com

Alonso, Juan. "Speed and the New World Religion." *Queen's Quarterly* 108, no. 3 (Fall 2001): 365–373.

Amin, Shahid. *Event, Metaphor, Memory: Chauri Chaura, 1922–1992*. Berkeley: University of California Press, 1995.

Appadurai, Arjun. *Modernity at Large: Cultural Dimensions of Globalization*. Minneapolis: University of Minnesota Press, 1996.

Apter, Andrew. "On Imperial Spectacle: The Dialectics of Seeing in Colonial Nigeria." *Comparative Studies in Society and History* 44, no. 3 (July 2002): 564–596.

Auerbach, Jeffrey. "Art, Advertising, and the Legacy of Empire." *Journal of Popular Culture* 35, no. 4 (2002): 1–23.

Augé, Marc. *Non-Places: Introduction to an Anthropology of Supermodernity*. Translated by John Howe. New York: Verso, 1992.

Back, Les. "Falling from the Sky." *Patterns of Prejudice* 37, no. 3 (2003): 341–353.

Baden-Powell, Major Baden. "Aeronautics in the Twentieth Century." In *A Short History of Balloons and Flying Machines*, edited by Lord Montagu, 89–94. London: Car Illustrated, 1907.

Baldwin, James. "James Baldwin: The Art of Fiction No. 78." Interview by Jordon Elgra-
bly. *Paris Review* 91 (Spring 1984). www.theparisreview.org.
———. *Notes of a Native Son*. 1955. Reprint, Boston: Beacon Press, 2012.
———. "On Being White . . . and Other Lies." In *The Cross of Redemption: Uncollected
Writings*, edited by Randall Kenan, 166–170. 1984. Reprint, New York: Vintage, 2010.
Banner, Stuart. *Who Owns the Sky? The Struggle to Control Airspace from the Wright
Brothers On*. Cambridge: Harvard University Press, 2008.
Barnes, Catherine A. *Journey from Jim Crow: The Desegregation of Southern Transit*.
New York: Columbia University Press, 1983.
Barry, Kathleen M. *Femininity in Flight: A History of Flight Attendants*. Durham: Duke
University Press, 2007.
Barthes, Roland. *Mythologies*. Translated by Annette Lavers. 1957. Reprint, New York:
Hill and Wang, 1972.
Batteau, Allen W. "The Anthropology of Aviation and Flight Safety." *Human Organiza-
tion* 60, no. 3 (2001): 201–211.
Bay, Mia. "Invisible Tethers: Transportation and Discrimination in the Age of Katrina."
In *Katrina's Imprint: Race and Vulnerability in America*, edited by Keith Wailoo,
Karen M. O'Neill, Jeffrey Dowd, and Roland Anglin, 21–33. New Brunswick: Rut-
gers University Press, 2010.
Beer, Gillian. "The Island and the Aeroplane: The Case of Virginia Woolf." In *Nation
and Narration*, edited by Homi Bhabha, 265–290. New York: Routledge, 1990.
Benjamin, Walter. "Theses on the Philosophy of History." In *Illuminations: Essays and
Reflections*, translated by Harry Zohn, 253–264. 1950. Reprint, New York: Schocken
Books, 1968.
Benton, Tim. "Dreams of Machines: Futurism and l'Esprit Nouveau." *Journal of Design
History* 3, no 1 (1990): 19–34.
Berghaus, Günter, ed. *Futurism and the Technological Imagination*. New York: Rodopi,
2009.
Berman, Marshall. *All That's Solid Melts into Air: The Experience of Modernity*. New
York: Penguin, 1988.
Bhimull, Chandra D. "Passages: Airborne in an African Diaspora." *Anthropology and
Humanism* 29, no. 2 (December 2014): 129–144.
Biddle, Tami Davis. *Rhetoric and Reality in Air Warfare: The Evolution of British and
American Ideas about Strategic Bombing, 1914–1945*. Princeton: Princeton University
Press, 2002.
Bigo, Didier. "Freedom and Speed in Enlarged Borderzones." In *The Contested Politics
of Mobility*, edited by Vicki Squire, 31–50. New York: Routledge, 2011.
Bix, Amy. "Bessie Coleman: Race and Gender Realities behind Aviation Dreams." In
Realizing the Dream of Flight, edited by Virginia P. Dawson and Mark D. Bowles,
1–27. Washington, D.C.: National Aeronautics and Space Administration, 2005.
Boccioni, Umberto, Carlo Carrà, Luigi Russolo, Giacomo Balla, and Gino Severini.
"Manifesto of the Futurist Painters." In *Manifesto: A Century of Isms*, edited by
Mary Ann Caws, 182–184. 1910. Reprint, Lincoln: University of Lincoln Press, 2001.

Bohn, Willard. "The Poetics of Flight: Futurist 'Aeropoesia.'" *MLN* 121, no. 1 (2006): 207–224.

Bourne, Stephen. *The Motherland Calls: Britain's Black Servicemen & Women*. Gloucestershire: History Press, 2012.

Bragg, Janet Harmon. *Soaring above Setbacks*. Washington, D.C.: Smithsonian Institution Press, 1996.

British Overseas Airways Act, 1939, 2 & 3 Geo. 6, c. 45 (U.K.).

Broadnax, Samuel L. *Blue Skies, Black Wings: African American Pioneers of Aviation*. Lincoln: University of Nebraska Press, 2008.

Brown, Jacqueline Nassy. *Dropping Anchor, Setting Sail: Geographies of Race in Black Liverpool*. Princeton: Princeton University Press, 2005.

Browne, Simone. *Dark Matters: On the Surveillance of Blackness*. Durham: Duke University Press, 2015.

Buchan, John. *The Thirty-Nine Steps*. 1915. Reprint, London: Aeonian Press, 1965.

Budd, Lucy. "Global Networks before Globalization: Imperial Airways and the Development of Long-Haul Air Routes." *GaWC Research Bulletin* 253 (December 5, 2007). www.lboro.ac.uk.

———. "On Being Aeromobile: Airline Passengers and the Affective Experiences of Flight." *Journal of Transport Geography* 19, no. 5 (September 2011): 1010–1016.

Bunch, Lonnie. "Museums and the Interpretation of African American History." In *Technology and the African-American Experience: Needs and Opportunities for Study*, edited by Bruce Sinclair, 187–196. Cambridge: MIT Press, 2004.

Burbank, Jane, and Frederick Cooper. *Empires in World History: Power and the Politics of Difference*. Princeton: Princeton University Press, 2010.

Burman, Barbara. "Racing Bodies: Dress and Pioneer Women Aviators and Racing Drivers." *Women's History Review* 9, no. 2 (2000): 299–326.

Butler, Judith. *Giving an Account of Oneself*. New York: Fordham University Press, 2005.

Calvino, Italo. *Six Memos for the Next Millennium*. Translated by Patrick Creagh. New York: Vintage Books, 1988.

Carrà, Carlo. *Graphic Rhythm with Airplane—Homage to Blériot*. 1914. Pen and ink with graphite and collage on graph paper. 15 9/16 in. x 10 7/8 in. National Gallery of Art, Washington, D.C.

Carroll, Siobhan. *An Empire of Air and Water: Uncolonizable Space in the British Imagination, 1750–1850*. Philadelphia: University of Pennsylvania Press, 2015.

Césaire, Aimé. *Discourse on Colonialism*. Translated by Joan Pinkham. 1955. Reprint, New York: Monthly Review Press, 2000.

Césaire, Suzanne. "Alain and Esthetics." In *The Great Camouflage: Writings of Dissent (1941–1945)*, edited by Daniel Maximin and translated by Keith L. Walker, 11–18. 1941. Reprint, Middletown: Wesleyan University Press, 2009.

———. "The Great Camouflage." In *The Great Camouflage: Writings of Dissent (1941–1945)*, edited by Daniel Maximin and translated by Keith L. Walker, 11–18. 1945. Reprint, Middletown: Wesleyan University Press, 2009.

Chakrabarty, Dipesh. *Provincializing Europe: Postcolonial Thought and Historical Difference*. Princeton: Princeton University Press, 2000.

Chamberlain, Neville. *The Neville Chamberlain Diary Letters: The Heir Apparent, 1928–1933*. Vol. 3, edited by Robert Self. Aldershot: Ashgate, 2002.

Chow, Rey. "Where Have All the Natives Gone." In *Displacements: Cultural Identities in Question*, edited by A. Bammer, 125–151. Durham: Duke University Press, 1994.

Christie, Janet B. T. "Reflections on the Legend of Wayland the Smith." *Folklore* 8, no. 4 (Winter 1969): 286–294.

City Merchant. Letter to the Editor. *Daily Gleaner* (Kingston), October 26, 1934.

Cliff, Michelle. *The Land of Look Behind: Prose and Poetry*. Ithaca: Firebrand Books, 1985.

Clifford, James. *The Predicament of Culture: Twentieth-Century Ethnography, Literature, and Art*. Cambridge: Cambridge University Press, 1988.

———. *Routes: Travel and Translation in the Late Twentieth Century*. Cambridge: Harvard University Press, 1997.

Coates, Ta-Nehisi. *Between the World and Me*. New York: Spiegel & Grau, 2015.

Cohen, David William. *The Combing of History*. Chicago: Chicago University Press, 1994.

———. "The Pursuits of Anthrohistory: Formation against Formation." In *Anthrohistory: Unsettling Knowledge, Questioning Discipline*, edited by Edward L. Murphy, David William Cohen, Chandra D. Bhimull, Fernando Coronil, Monica Eileen Patterson, and Julie Skurski, 11–36. Ann Arbor: University of Michigan Press, 2011.

———. "Unsettled Stories and Inadequate Metaphors: The Movement to Historical Anthropology." In *CLIO/ANTHROPOS: Exploring the Boundaries between History and Anthropology*, edited by Eric Tagliacozzo and Andrew Wilford, 273–294. Stanford: Stanford University Press, 2009.

Cohn, Bernard S. "History and Anthropology: The State of Play." *Comparative Studies in Society and History* 22, no. 2 (April 1980): 198–221.

Cole, Teju. *Known and Strange Things: Essays*. New York: Vintage, 2016.

Colley, Linda. *Britons: Forging the Nation, 1707–1837*. New Haven: Yale University Press, 1992.

Colonial Development Act, 1929, 20 Geo. 5, c. 5 (U.K.).

Connolly, N. D. B. *A World More Concrete: Real Estate and the Remaking of Jim Crow South Florida*. Chicago: University of Chicago Press, 2014.

Conrad, Joseph. *Heart of Darkness*. 1902. Reprint, Boston: Bedford Books, 1996.

Coons, Lorraine, and Alexander Varias. *Tourist Third Cabin: Steamship Travel in the Interwar Years*. New York: Palgrave Macmillan, 2003.

Cooper, Frederick. *Colonialism in Question: Theory, Knowledge, History*. Berkeley: University of California Press, 2005.

Cooper, Frederick, and Ann Laura Stoler, eds. "Between Metropole and Colony: Rethinking a Research Agenda." In *Tensions of Empire: Colonial Cultures in a Bourgeois World*, 1–56. Berkeley: University of California Press, 1997.

Corn, Joseph J. *The Winged Gospel: America's Romance with Aviation, 1900–1950*. New York: Oxford University Press, 1983.

Coronil, Fernando. "After Empire: Reflection on Imperialism in the Americas." In *Imperial Formations*, edited by Ann L. Stoler, Carole McGranahan, and Peter Perdue, 241–274. Santa Fe: School for Advanced Research Press, 2007.

———. "Beyond Occidentalism: Towards Nonimperial Geohistorical Categories." *Cultural Anthropology* 11, no. 1 (February 1996): 51–87.

———. "Pieces for Anthrohistory: A Puzzle to Be Assembled Together." In *Anthrohistory: Unsettling Knowledge, Questioning Discipline*, edited by Edward L. Murphy, David William Cohen, Chandra D. Bhimull, Fernando Coronil, Monica Eileen Patterson, and Julie Skurski, 301–316. Ann Arbor: University of Michigan Press, 2011.

———. "Smelling Like a Market." *American History Review* 106, no. 1 (February 2001): 119–129.

———. "Towards a Critique of Globalcentrism: Speculations on Capitalism's Nature." *Public Culture* 12, no. 2 (2000): 351–374.

Courtwright, David T. *Sky as Frontier: Adventure, Aviation, and Empire*. College Station: Texas A&M University Press, 2005.

Crane, Hart. "Cape Hatteras." In *The Bridge: A Poem*, 37–48. 1930. Reprint, New York: Liveright, 1992.

Cressy, David. "Early Modern Space Travel and the English Man in the Moon." *American Historical Review* 111, no. 4 (October 2006): 961–982.

Crouch, Tom D. *Wings: A History of Aviation from Kites to the Space Age*. New York: W. W. Norton, 2003.

Cumming, Captain W. N. "Bermuda to New York." *Imperial Airways Gazette*, July 1937.

Cwerner, Saulo, Sven Kesselring, and John Urry, eds. *Aeromobilities*. New York: Routledge, 2009.

Daily Gleaner (Kingston). "The Activities of Caribbean Airways." May 6, 1931.

———. "The Aircraft Services in West Indies." August 24, 1933. CO 323/1096/11, NA.

———. "For Rent." June 22, 1935.

———. "Meeting Called Yesterday to Secure Practical Interest in Caribbean Airways." September 25, 1931.

———. "New Air Service between City and Santiago." June 7, 1931.

———. "£1,600 Compensation to Be Paid to Caribbean Airways." November 6, 1934.

———. "West Indies Airways Plan Is Official: Jamaica Likely to Have Service Shortly." August 28, 1929.

Darnton, Robert. *The Great Cat Massacre and Other Episodes in French Cultural History*. New York: Basic Books, 1984.

Davies, R. E. G. *A History of the World's Airlines*. London: Oxford University Press, 1964.

Davis, Angela Y. *Freedom Is a Constant Struggle: Ferguson, Palestine, and the Foundations of a Movement*. Chicago: Haymarket Books, 2016.

Davis, Natalie Zemon. *Trickster Travels: A Sixteenth Century Muslim between Worlds*. New York: Hill and Wang, 2006.

Davy, Maurice John Bernard. *Air Power and Civilization*. London: George Allen & Unwin, 1941.

Derby, Lauren. "The Dictator's Seduction: Gender and State Spectacle during the Trujillo Regime." *Callaloo* 23, no. 3 (Summer 2000): 1112–1146.

Dewdney, A. K. Introduction to *Flatland: A Romance of Many Dimensions*, by Edwin A. Abbott, 7–23. New York: Signet Classic, 1984.

Dienel, Hans-Liudger, and Peter Lyth, eds. *Flying the Flag: European Commercial Air Transport since 1945.* New York: St. Martin's Press, 1998.

Dierikx, Marc. *Clipping the Clouds: How Air Travel Changed the World.* Westport: Praeger Publishers, 2008.

———. "Struggle for Prominence: Clashing Dutch and British Interests on the Colonial Air Routes, 1918–42." *Journal of Contemporary History* 26, no. 2 (1991): 333–351.

Divall, Colin. "Civilizing Velocity: Masculinity and the Marketing of Britain's Passenger Trains, 1921–1939." *Journal of Transport History* 32, no. 2 (December 2011): 164–191.

Dixon, Patrick. *Futurewise: The Six Faces of Global Change.* 3rd edition. London: Profile Books, 2004.

Dixon, Robert. *Prosthetic Gods: Travel, Representation, and Colonial Governance.* St. Lucia: University of Queensland Press, 2001.

Dobson, A. P. *Peaceful Air Warfare: The United States, Britain, and the Politics of International Aviation.* Oxford: Oxford University Press, 1991.

Dodds, Klaus. *Pink Ice: Britain and the South Atlantic Empire.* New York: Palgrave, 2000.

Du Bois, W. E. B. *Souls of Black Folks.* 1903. Reprint, New York: Bantam Classic, 1989.

Dubois, Laurent. "Atlantic Freedoms." *Aeon*, November 7, 2016, aeon.co.

———. *Avengers of the New World: The Story of the Haitian Revolution.* Cambridge: Harvard University Press, 2004.

Dussel, Enrique. "Beyond Eurocentrism: The World System and the Limits of Modernity." In *The Cultures of Globalization*, edited by Frederic Jameson and Masao Miyoshi, 8–31. Durham: Duke University Press, 1998.

Edgerton, David. *England and the Aeroplane: An Essay on a Militant and Technological Nation.* Manchester: University of Manchester Press, 1991.

Eiss, Paul K. *In the Name of El Pueblo: Place, Community, and the Politics of History in Yucatán.* Durham: Duke University Press, 2010.

Engel, Jeffery A. *Cold War at 30,000 Feet: The Anglo-American Fight for Aviation Supremacy.* Cambridge: Harvard University Press, 2007.

Esposito, Fernando. *Fascism, Aviation, and Mythical Modernity.* New York: Palgrave Macmillan, 2015.

Fanon, Frantz. *Black Skin, White Masks.* Translated by Charles Lam Markmann. 1952. Reprint, New York: Grove Press, 1967.

———. *The Wretched of the Earth.* Translated by Constance Farrington. 1961. Reprint, New York: Grove Press, 1963.

Fear, A. T. "Bladud: The Flying King of Bath." *Folklore* 103, no. 2 (1992): 222–224.

Ferguson, James G. "Of Mimicry and Membership: Africans and the 'New World Society.'" *Cultural Anthropology* 17, no. 4 (November 2002): 551–569.

Fitzgerald, F. Scott. *The Diamond as Big as the Ritz and Other Short Stories.* 1922. Reprint, New York: Penguin Books, 1996.

Flight. "The First Imperial Air Route." December 30, 1926. F1i-600000.03, NASM.

Flint, R. W. Introduction to *Let's Murder the Moonshine: Selected Writings.* 1972. Reprint, Los Angeles: Sun & Moon Press, 1991.

Forgacs, David, ed. *The Antonio Gramsci Reader.* New York: NYU Press, 2000.

Forster, E. M. "The Machine Stops." In *The Eternal Moment and Other Stories,* 13–85. 1909. Reprint, New York: Harcourt, Brace & Company, 1928.

Forsyth, Roger Albert. *Black Flight: Breaking Barriers to Blacks in Aviation.* Los Angeles: AllCourt Publishing, 2002.

Foshay, Toby Avard. *Lewis and the Avant-Garde: The Politics of the Intellect.* Montréal: McGill-Queen's University Press, 1992.

Frazier, Franklin E. *The Negro Family in the United States.* 1939. Reprint, New York: Dryden Press, 1951.

Fritzsche, Peter. *A Nation of Fliers: German Aviation and the Popular Imagination.* Cambridge: Harvard University Press, 1992.

Fuentes, Marisa J. *Dispossessed Lives: Enslaved Women, Violence, and the Archive.* Philadelphia: University of Pennsylvania Press, 2016.

Garnerin, André-Jacques. *A Circumstantial Account of the Three Last Aerial Voyages Made by M. Garnerin, viz. from Vauxhall Gardens, Accompanied by Madame Garnerin and Mr. Glassford, on Tuesday, August 5, 1802.* London: A. Neil, 1802.

Geddes, Sir Eric. "The Annual General Meeting of Imperial Airways." *Imperial Airways Gazette,* November 1933.

Gikandi, Simon. *Maps of Englishness: Writing Identity in the Culture of Colonialism.* New York: Columbia University Press, 1996.

Gilroy, Paul. *The Black Atlantic: Modernity and Double Consciousness.* Cambridge: Harvard University Press, 1993.

———. *Darker than Blue: On the Moral Economies of Black Atlantic Culture.* Cambridge: Harvard University Press, 2011.

———. "Sounds Authentic: Black Music, Ethnicity, and the Challenge of a 'Changing' Same." *Black Music Research Journal* 11, no. 2 (Autumn 1991): 111–136.

Ginzburg, Carlo. *The Cheese and the Worms: The Cosmos of a Sixteenth-Century Miller.* Translated by J. and A. Tedeschi. 1976. Reprint, Baltimore: Johns Hopkins University Press, 1992.

Gleick, James. *Faster: The Acceleration of Just about Everything.* New York: Pantheon Books, 1999.

Gmelch, George. *Behind the Smile: The Working Lives of Caribbean Tourism.* Bloomington: Indiana University Press, 2003.

Gollin, Alfred. *No Longer an Island: Britain and the Wright Brothers.* Stanford: Stanford University Press, 1984.

Goodfellow, Alan. Letter to the Editor. *Times* (London), March 16, 1938.

Gouge, A. "Transatlantic Air Transport with Particular Reference to Flying Boats." In *The Institution of Mechanical Engineers.* London: Institution of Mechanical Engineers, 1939. F2–788040–25, NASM.

Graham, Brian. *Geography and Air Transport.* Chichester: John Wiley and Sons, 1995.

Grewal, Inderpal. *Home and Harem: Nation, Gender, Empire, and the Cultures of Travel.* Durham: Duke University Press, 1996.

Grey, C. G. "Joy-Riding and Commercial Aviation." *Illustrated London News*, September 9, 1919.

Griaule, Marcel. "L'emploi de la Photographie Aerienne et la Recherche Scientifique." *L'anthropologie* 47 (1937): 469–471.

Gusterson, Hugh. *Drone: Remote Control Warfare.* Cambridge: MIT Press, 2016.

Hacking, Ian. *The Taming of Chance.* Cambridge: Cambridge University Press, 1990.

Hagedorn, Dan. *Conquistadors of the Sky: A History of Aviation in Latin America.* Gainesville: University of Florida Press, 2008.

Hall, Catherine, ed. *Cultures of Empire: Colonizers in Britain and the Empire in the Nineteenth and Twentieth Centuries.* New York: Routledge, 2000.

Hall, Catherine, and Sonya O. Rose, eds. "Introduction: Being at Home with the Empire." In *At Home with the Empire: Metropolitan Culture and the Imperial World*, 1–31. Cambridge: Cambridge University Press, 2006.

Hanna, W. J. "Early Days of Commercial Aviation in Jamaica." *Jamaica Journal* 24, No. 2 (March 1992): 11–18.

Hardesty, Von. *Black Wings: Courageous Stories of African Americans in Aviation and Space History.* Washington, D.C.: Smithsonian Institution Press, 2008.

Hardt, Michael, and Antonio Negri. *Empire.* Cambridge: Harvard University Press, 2000.

Harley, J. B. "Deconstructing the Map." *Cartographica* 26, no. 2 (Spring 1989): 1–20.

Harris, Marvin. *Cows, Pigs, Wars, and Witches: The Riddles of Culture.* New York: Random House, 1974.

Harry. "A Good Letter." *Imperial Airways Gazette*, May–September 1936.

Hart, Clive. *The Dream of Flight: Aeronautics from Classical Times to the Renaissance.* London: Faber, 1972.

Harvey, David. *The Condition of Postmodernity: An Enquiry into the Origins of Cultural Change.* Oxford: Blackwell, 1989.

Hecht, Gabrielle. *The Radiance of France: Nuclear Power and National Identity after World War II.* Cambridge: MIT Press, 1998.

Herskovits, Melville J. *The Myth of the Negro Past.* 1941. Reprint, Boston: Beacon Press, 1958.

Hewitt, Andrew. *Fascist Modernism: Aesthetics, Politics, and the Avant-Garde.* Stanford: Stanford University Press, 1993.

Higham, Robin. *Britain's Imperial Air Routes, 1918 to 1939.* London: Foulis & Co., 1960.

Hilton, James. *Lost Horizon.* 1933. Reprint, New York: Pocket Books, 1969.

Ho, Engseng. "Empire through Diasporic Eyes: A View from the Other Boat." *Society for the Comparative Study of Society and History* 46, no. 2 (April 2004): 210–246.

Holmes, Richard. *Falling Upwards: How We Took to the Air.* New York: Pantheon, 2013.

Honoré, Carl. *In Praise of Slowness: How a Worldwide Movement Is Challenging the Cult of Speed.* San Francisco: HarperCollins, 2004.

hooks, bell. *All about Love: New Visions.* New York: William Morrow, 2000.

———. *Killing Rage: Ending Racism.* New York: Holt, 1995.

————. *Yearning: Race, Gender, and Cultural Politics.* Cambridge: South End Press, 1990.

Imperial Airways Gazette. "The Advantages of Sending Your Letters and Freight by Air." July 1934.

————. "Air Mail Traffic." February 1933.

————. "An Air Service to the Grand National." March 1933.

————. "Air Travel for Women." November 1933.

————. "Catering Up in the Air." September 1937.

————. "Cross Channel Statistics." July 1928.

————. "Extension of the Empire Air Mail Programme." August 1938.

————. "Fly to European Capitals." September 1937.

————. "Flying in Comfort." July 1938.

————. "Flying 20,000 Miles on Business." March 1933.

————. Front Cover. October 1930.

————. Front Cover. January 1931.

————. "The Growth of Imperial Airways." September 1934.

————. "Imperial Airways Gazette Makes Dentistry Pleasant." December 1935.

————. "The Importance of Imperial Airways Gazette." April 1933.

————. "In Swiss Cloudland: A Scotswoman's Voyage." July 1933.

————. "India to South Africa by Imperial Airways." April 1935.

————. "Letters from an Air Traveller to His Son." October 1936–May 1937.

————. "London to Baghdad in 3.5 Days." June 1933.

————. "The Pageant of England." April 1935.

————. "To Paris While You Read Your Paper." August 1934.

————. "Queen Marys of the Air." July 1936.

————. "See the Boat Race from the Air." March 1933.

————. "Tea Flights." February 1931.

————. "What Air Passengers See While Flying from Brisbane to Singapore." November 1936.

————. "Wings over Africa." May 1936.

————. "The World Travels by Air." February 1937.

Ingram, B. S. "To Paris in Two Hours and Twenty Minutes." *Illustrated London News,* September 6, 1919.

Inquest. *Updated Briefing on Death of Jimmy Mubenga.* London, May 2013. www.inquest.org.uk.

Iskin, Ruth E. "Father Time, Speed, and the Temporality of Posters around 1900." *Kronoscope* 3, no. 1 (2003): 27–50.

Jackson, A. S. *Imperial Airways and the First British Airlines, 1919–40.* Lavenham: Terence Dalton Ltd., 1995.

James, C. L. R. *Beyond a Boundary.* 1963. Reprint, Durham: Duke University Press, 1993.

————. *The Black Jacobins: Toussaint L'Ouverture and the San Domingo Revolution.* 1938. 2nd edition. Reprint, New York: Vintage Books, 1963.

———. *The Case for West-Indian Self Government*. London: Hogarth Press, 1933. Pamphlet A, F2131.J25, WIC.

Jankovic, Vladimir. "The Politics of Sky Battles in Early Hanoverian Britain." *Journal of British Studies* 41, no. 4 (October 2002): 429–459.

Jones, LeRoi. "The Changing Same (R & B and New Black Music)." In *Black Music*, 205–241. 1968. Reprint, New York: Akashic Books, 2010.

Kelley, Blair L. M. *Right to Ride: Streetcar Boycotts and African American Citizenship in the Era of Plessy v. Ferguson*. Durham: University of North Carolina Press, 2010.

Kelley, Robin D. G. "Black Study, Black Struggle." *Boston Review*, March 2016, bostonreview.net.

———. *Freedom Dreams: The Black Radical Imagination*. Boston: Beacon Press, 2002.

———. *Race Rebels: Culture, Politics, and the Black Working Class*. New York: Free Press, 1994.

Khosravi, Shahram. *"Illegal" Traveller: An Auto-Ethnography of Borders*. New York: Palgrave Macmillan, 2010.

Kincaid, Jamaica. *A Small Place*. New York: Farrar, Straus, and Giroux, 1988.

Kingwell, Mark. "Fast Forward: Our High-Speed Chase to Nowhere." *Harper's Magazine*, May 1998.

Kranakis, Eda. "European Civil Aviation in an Era of Hegemonic Nationalism: Infrastructure, Air Mobility, and European Identity Formation, 1919–1933." In *Materializing Europe: Transnational Infrastructures and the Project of Europe*, edited by Alexander Badenoch and Andreas Fickers, 290–326. London: Palgrave McMillan, 2012.

Kreamer, Christine Mullen. *African Cosmos: Stellar Arts*. New York: Monacelli Press, 2012.

Kundera, Milan. *Slowness*. Translated by Linda Asher. New York: HarperCollins, 1996.

L., F. J. "Our Air Link with Home." *Imperial Airways Gazette*, December 1933.

Lamming, George. *The Pleasures of Exile*. 1960. Reprint, Ann Arbor: University of Michigan Press, 1992.

Latour, Bruno. *Aramis or the Love of Technology*. Cambridge: Harvard University Press, 1996.

Le Corbusier. *Aircraft: The New Vision*. London: Studio, 1935.

Lee, Laurie. *Cider with Rosie*. 1959. Reprint, New York: Vintage, 2002.

Lefebvre, Henri. *The Production of Space*. Translated by Donald Nicholson-Smith. 1974. Reprint, Oxford: Blackwell, 1998.

Lewis, Paul. "Jimmy Mubenga Death: Witness Accounts." *Guardian*, October 15, 2010, www.guardian.co.uk.

Lewis, Wyndham. *Blasting and Bombardiering*. 1937. Reprint, Berkeley: University of California Press, 1967.

Long, Genesta. "South Africa by the *Empire* Flying Boat." *Imperial Airways Gazette*, November 1937.

Lopez, Barry. *About This Life: Journeys of the Threshold of Memory*. New York: Alfred A. Knopf, 1998.

Lutz, Catherine. "Empire Is in the Details." *American Ethnologist* 22, no. 4 (November 2006): 593–611.

Lutz, Catherine, ed. *The Bases of Empire: The Global Struggle against U.S. Military Posts*. New York: NYU Press, 2009.

Lyth, Peter. "The Empire's Airways: British Civil Aviation from 1919–1939." *Revue Belge de Philologie et d'Histoire*, no. 78 (2000): 865–887.

Malevich, Kazimir. *Suprematist Composition: Airplane Flying*. 1915. Oil on canvas. 22 7/8 in. x 19 in. Museum of Modern Art, New York.

March, Robert H. *Physics for Poets*. 4th edition. New York: McGraw-Hill, 1996.

Marinetti, F. T. "Electrical War (a Futurist Vision-Hypothesis)." In *Let's Murder the Moonshine: Selected Writings*, edited by R. W. Flint, 112–116. Translated by R. W. Flint and Arthur A. Coppotelli. 1911. Reprint, Los Angeles: Sun & Moon Press, 1991.

———. "The Foundation and Manifesto of Futurism." In *F. T. Marinetti: Critical Writings*, edited by Günter Berghaus, 11–17. Translated by Doug Thompson. 1909. Reprint, New York: Farrar, Straus, and Giroux, 2006.

———. "A Futurist Theater of the Skies Enhanced by Radio and Television." In *F. T. Marinetti: Critical Writings*, edited by Günter Berghaus, 408–409. Translated by Doug Thompson. 1932. Reprint, New York: Farrar, Straus, and Giroux, 2006.

———. "Let's Murder the Moonshine." In *Let's Murder the Moonshine: Selected Writings*, edited by R. W. Flint, 53–62. Translated by R. W. Flint and Arthur A. Coppotelli. 1909. Reprint, Los Angeles: Sun & Moon Press, 1991.

———. "Manifesto of Futurism." In *Let's Murder the Moonshine: Selected Writings*, edited by R. W. Flint, 47–52. Translated by R. W. Flint and Arthur A. Coppotelli. 1909. Reprint, Los Angeles: Sun & Moon Press, 1991.

———. "The New Religion—Morality of Speed." In *Let's Murder the Moonshine: Selected Writings*, edited by R. W. Flint, 102–104. Translated by R. W. Flint and Arthur A. Coppotelli. 1916. Reprint, Los Angeles: Sun & Moon Press, 1991.

———. "Technical Manifesto of Futurist Literature." In *F. T. Marinetti: Critical Writings*, edited by Günter Berghaus, 107–119. Translated by Doug Thompson. 1912. Reprint, New York: Farrar, Straus, and Giroux, 2006.

Marion, F. *Wonderful Balloon Ascents or The Conquest of the Skies: A History of Balloons and Balloon Voyages*. New York: Charles Scribner, 1871.

Markham, Beryl. *West with the Night*. 1942. Reprint, Berkeley: North Point Press, 1983.

Markov, Vladimir. *Russian Futurism: A History*. Berkeley: University of California Press, 1968.

Marshall, Paule. *Brown Girl, Brownstones*. New York: Random House, 1959.

Marx, Karl. *Grundrisse: Foundations of the Critique of Political Economy*. Translated by Martin Nicolaus. 1858. Reprint, New York: Penguin Books, 1973.

Massey, Doreen. "Concepts of Space and Power in Theory and in Political Practice." *Doc. Anàl. Geogr.* 55 (2009): 15–26.

Matless, David. *Landscape and Englishness*. London: Reaktion Books, 1998.

Mayer, Ruth. "'Africa as an Alien Future': The Middle Passage, Afrofuturism, and Postcolonial Waterworlds." *Amerikastudien/American Studies* 45, no. 4 (2000): 555–566.

McClintock, Anne. *Imperial Leather: Race, Gender, and Sexuality in the Colonial Context*. New York: Routledge, 1995.

McCormack, R. "Airlines and Empires: Great Britain and the 'Scramble for Africa,' 1919–1939." *Canadian Journal of African Studies* 10, no. 1 (1976): 87–105.

McCullough, W. D. H. "Baghdad Bound." *Imperial Airways Gazette*, February 1934.

———. "Baghdad Bound." *Imperial Airways Gazette*, March 1934.

———. "Baghdad Bound." *Imperial Airways Gazette*, May 1934.

Menzies, H. Stuart. *All Ways by Airways*. London: Imperial Airways, 1932. TL 526. G7M55, NASM.

Messeri, Lisa. *Placing Outer Space: An Earthly Ethnography of Other Worlds*. Durham: Duke University Press, 2016.

Mignolo, Walter. *Local Histories/Global Designs: Coloniality, Subaltern Knowledges, and Border Thinking*. Princeton: Princeton University Press, 2000.

Millar, Jeremy, and Michiel Schwarz, eds. *Speed—Visions of an Accelerated Age*. London: Photographers' Gallery, 1998.

Miller, Rory. "Informal Empire in Latin America." In Vol. 5, *The Oxford History of the British Empire: Historiography*, edited by Wm. Roger Louis, 437–449. Oxford: Oxford University Press, 1999.

Mills, Charles W. *Blackness Visible: Essays on Philosophy and Race*. Ithaca: Cornell University Press, 1998.

Millward, Liz. "The Embodied Aerial Subject: Gendered Mobility in British Inter-War Air Tours." *Journal of Transport History* 29, no. 1 (March 2008): 5–22.

———. *Women in British Imperial Airspace, 1922–1937*. Montreal: McGill-Queen's University Press, 2008.

Mintz, Sidney W. *Three Ancient Colonies: Caribbean Themes and Variations*. Cambridge: Harvard University Press, 2010.

Montagu, Lord, ed. *A Short History of Balloons and Flying Machines*. London: Car Illustrated, 1907.

Moore, Henrietta. *Feminism and Anthropology*. Minneapolis: University of Minnesota Press, 1988.

Moraña, Mabel, Enrique Dussel, and Carlos A. Jáuregui, eds. *Coloniality at Large: Latin America and the Postcolonial Debate*. Durham: Duke University Press, 2008.

Morrison, Toni. *Song of Solomon*. New York: Penguin Books, 1977.

Moye, Todd J. *Freedom Flyers: The Tuskegee Airmen of World War II*. Oxford: Oxford University Press, 2010.

Mrázek, Rudolf. *Engineers of Happy Land: Technology and Nationalism in a Colony*. Princeton: Princeton University Press, 2002.

Murphy, Edward L., David William Cohen, Chandra D. Bhimull, Fernando Coronil, Monica Eileen Patterson, and Julie Skurski, eds. *Anthrohistory: Unsettling Knowledge, Questioning Discipline*. Ann Arbor: University of Michigan Press, 2011.

Naipaul, V. S. *The Mimic Men*. New York: Macmillan, 1967.

Noble, E. Martin. *Jamaica Airman: A Black Man in Britain, 1943 and After*. London: New Beacon, 1984.

Nonini, Donald M. "Shifting Identities, Positioned Imaginaries: Transnational Traversals and Reversals by Malaysian Chinese." In *The Cultural Politics of Modern Chinese Nationalism*, edited by Aihwa Ong and Donald M. Nonini, 203–227. New York: Routledge 1997.

Olaniyan, Tejumola, and James H. Sweet, eds. *The African Diaspora and the Disciplines.* Bloomington: Indiana University Press, 2010.

Oldenziel, Ruth. "Islands: The United States as a Networked Empire." In *Entangled Geographies: Empire and Technopolitics in the Global Cold War*, edited by Gabrielle Hecht, 13–41. Cambridge: MIT Press, 2011.

Omissi, David E. *Air Power and Colonial Control: The Royal Air Force, 1919–1939.* Manchester: Manchester University Press, 1990.

Ortlepp, Anke. *Jim Crow Terminals: The Desegregation of American Airports.* Athens: University of Georgia Press, 2017.

Palmer, Scott W. *Dictatorship of the Air: Aviation Culture and the Fate of Modern Russia.* Cambridge: Cambridge University Press, 2006.

———. "Peasants into Pilots: Soviet Air-Mindedness as an Ideology of Dominance." *Technology and Culture* 41:1 (2000): 1–26.

Paris, Michael. *Winged Warfare: The Literature and Theory of Aerial Warfare in Britain, 1859–1917.* Manchester: Manchester University Press, 1992.

Paris, Michael, ed. *The First World War and Popular Cinema: 1914 to the Present.* New Brunswick: Rutgers University Press, 2000.

Parkinson, Wenda. *This Gilded African.* London: Quartet, 1978.

Parliamentary Debates. Commons. 5th series. Vol. 329. 1937–38.

———. Commons. 5th series. Vol. 331. 1937–38.

———. Commons. 5th series. Vol. 332. 1937–38.

———. Commons. 5th series. Vol. 333. 1938.

———. Commons. 5th series. Vol. 350. 1938–39.

Pascoe, David. *Aircraft.* London: Reaktion Books, 2003.

Patterson, Monica Eileen. "Childhood, Memory, and Gap: Reflections from an Anthrohistorian on Georges Perec's *W or the Memory of Childhood*." In *Anthrohistory: Unsettling Knowledge, Questioning Discipline*, edited by Edward L. Murphy, David William Cohen, Chandra D. Bhimull, Fernando Coronil, Monica Eileen Patterson, and Julie Skurski, 81–96. Ann Arbor: University of Michigan Press, 2011.

Pedersen, David. *American Value: Migrants, Money, and Meaning in El Salvador and the United States.* Chicago: University of Chicago Press, 2013.

Perloff, Marjorie. *The Futurist Moment: Avant-Garde, Avant Guerre, and the Language of Rupture.* Chicago: University of Chicago Press, 2003.

Pierre, Jemima. *The Predicament of Blackness: Postcolonial Ghana and the Politics of Race.* Chicago: University of Chicago Press, 2013.

Pieterse, Jan Nederveen. *White on Black: Images of Africa and Blacks in Western Popular Culture.* New Haven: Yale University Press, 1992.

Pinkus, Karen. *Bodily Regimes: Italian Advertising under Fascism.* Minneapolis: University of Minnesota Press, 1995.

Piot, Charles. *Nostalgia for the Future: West Africa after the Cold War.* Chicago: University of Chicago Press, 2010.

Piper, Karen. *Cartographic Fictions: Maps, Race, and Identity.* New Brunswick: Rutgers University Press, 2002.

Pirie, Gordon. *Air Empire: British Imperial Civil Aviation, 1919–39.* Manchester: Manchester University Press, 2009.

———. "Bibliographies." uct.academia.edu.

———. "British Air Shows in South Africa, 1932/33: 'Airmindedness,' Ambition and Anxiety." *Kronos: Southern African Histories,* 35 (2009): 48–70.

———. "Cinema and British Imperial Civil Aviation, 1919–1939." *Historical Journal of Film, Radio, and Television* 23, no. 2 (2003): 117–131.

———. *Cultures and Caricatures of British Imperial Aviation.* Manchester: Manchester University Press, 2012.

———. "Passenger Traffic in the 1930s on British Imperial Air Routes: Refinement and Revision." *Journal of Transport History* 25, no. 1 (March 2004): 63–83.

Pitt, P. W. "The Magic Carpet—A Journey to India by Imperial Airways." *Imperial Airways Gazette,* June 1933.

Powell, Timothy B. "Summoning the Ancestors: The Flying Africans' Story and Its Enduring Legacy." In *African American Life in Georgia Lowcountry: The Atlantic World and the Gullah Geechee,* edited by Philip Morgan, 253–280. Athens: University of Georgia Press, 2010.

Putnam, Lara. *Radical Moves: Caribbean Migrants and the Politics of Race in the Jazz Age.* Chapel Hill: University of North Carolina Press, 2013.

Raboteau, Emily. *Searching for Zion: The Quest for Home in the African Diaspora.* New York: Atlantic Monthly Press, 2013.

Raffles, Hugh. *Insectopedia.* New York: Vintage, 2010.

Rankine, Claudia. *Citizen: An American Lyric.* Minneapolis: Graywolf Press, 2014.

Redfield, Peter. *Space in the Tropics: From Convicts to Rockets in French Guiana.* Berkeley: University of California Press, 2000.

Rediker, Marcus. *Between the Devil and the Deep Blue Sea: Merchant Seamen, Pirates, and the Anglo-American Maritime World.* Cambridge: Cambridge University Press, 1987.

Richards, Thomas. *The Commodity Culture of Victorian England: Advertising and Spectacle, 1851–1914.* Stanford: Stanford University Press, 1990.

Rieger, Bernhard. "'Fast Couples': Technology, Gender, and Modernity in Britain and Germany during the Nineteen-Thirties." *Historical Research* 76, no. 193 (August 2003): 364–388.

———. *Technology and the Culture of Modernity in Britain and Germany, 1890–1945.* Cambridge: Cambridge University Press, 2005.

Rolt, L. T. C. *The Aeronauts: A History of Ballooning, 1783–1903.* London: Longmans, 1966.

Roorda, Eric Paul. "The Cult of the Airplane among U.S. Military Men and Dominicans during the U.S. Occupation and the Trujillo Regime." In *Close Encounters of*

Empire: Writing the Cultural History of U.S.–Latin American Relations, edited by G. M. Joseph, C. C. LeGrand, and R. D. Salvatore, 269–310. Durham: Duke University Press, 1998.

Rose, Sonya O. *Which People's War? National Identity and Citizenship in Britain, 1939–1945*. Oxford: Oxford University Press, 2003.

Rosemont, Franklin, and Robin D. G. Kelley, eds. *Black, Brown, & Beige: Surrealist Writings from Africa and the Diaspora*. Austin: University of Texas Press, 2009.

Rucker, Rudolf. *Geometry, Relativity, and the Fourth Dimension*. New York: Dover Publications, 1977.

Ruggiero, John. *Neville Chamberlain and British Rearmament: Pride, Prejudice, and Politics*. Westport: Greenwood Press, 1999.

Said, Edward. *Imperialism and Culture*. New York: Knopf, 1993.

Saint-Exupéry, Antoine de. *Airman's Odyssey*. 1939. Translated by Stuart Gilbert and Lewis Galantière. Reprint, New York: Harcourt Brace and Company, 1984.

Sampson, A. *Empires of the Sky: The Politics, Contests, and Cartels of World Airlines*. New York: Random House, 1984.

Sandage, Scott. *Born Losers: A History of Failure in America*. Cambridge: Harvard University Press, 2005.

Satia, Priya. "The Defense of Inhumanity: Air Control and the British Idea of Arabia." *American Historical Review* 111, no. 1 (February 2006): 16–51.

———. *Spies in Arabia: The Great War and the Cultural Foundations of Britain's Covert Empire in the Middle East*. New York: Oxford University Press, 2008.

Scheper-Hughes, Nancy. "Kidney Kin: Inside the Transatlantic Kidney Trade." *Harvard International Review* 27, no. 2 (Winter 2006): 62–65.

Schivelbusch, Wolfgang. *The Railway Journey: The Industrialization of Time and Space in the 19th Century*. 1977. Reprint, Berkeley: University of California Press, 1986.

Schwab, Klaus. "A Fragile Time for Globalism." Interview by David R. Gergen. *U.S. News and World Report*, February 11, 2002.

Schwartz, Rosalie. *Flying Down to Rio: Hollywood, Tourists, and Yankee Clippers*. College Station: Texas A&M University Press, 2004.

Schwarz, Bill. *Memories of Empire, Volume I: The White Man's World*. Oxford: Oxford University Press, 2011.

Scott, James. *Seeing Like a State: How Certain Schemes to Improve the Human Condition Have Failed*. New Haven: Yale University Press, 1999.

Sealy, Kenneth. *The Geography of Air Transport*. Chicago: Aldine Publishing, 1957.

Sebald, W. G. *On the Natural History of Destruction*. Translated by Anthea Bell. New York: Random House, 2003.

Self, Robert. *Neville Chamberlain*. Aldershot: Ashgate, 2006.

Sharma, Sherri. "Beyond 'Driving While Black' and 'Flying While Brown': Using Intersectionality to Uncover the Gendered Aspects of Racial Profiling." *Columbia Journal of Gender and Law* 12, no. 2 (2003): 275–309.

Sheller, Mimi. "Air Mobilities on the U.S.-Caribbean Border: Open Skies and Closed Gates." *Communication Review* 13, no. 4 (2010): 269–288.

———. *Consuming the Caribbean: From Arawaks to Zombies*. New York: Routledge, 2003.

Singer, Bayla. *Like Sex with Gods: An Unorthodox History of Flying*. College Station: Texas A&M University Press, 2003.

Smith, F. E. "John Cadman, Baron Cadman, 1877–1941." *Obituary Notices of Fellows of the Royal Society* 3, no. 1 (December 1941): 915–928.

Smith, Henry Laad. *Airways Abroad: The Story of American World Air Routes*. Madison: University of Wisconsin Press, 1950.

Snyder, Terri L. "Suicide, Slavery, and Memory in North America." *Journal of American History* 97, no 1 (June 2010): 39–62.

Sousanis, Nick. *Unflattening*. Cambridge: Harvard University Press, 2015.

Staniland, Martin. *Government Birds: Air Transport and the State in Western Europe*. Lanham: Rowman & Littlefield, 2003.

Stein, Judith. *The World of Marcus Garvey: Race and Class in Modern Society*. Baton Rouge: Louisiana University Press, 1991.

Stewart, Kathleen. *Ordinary Affects*. Durham: Duke University Press, 2007.

Stoler, Ann Laura. *Along the Archival Grain: Epistemic Anxieties and Colonial Common Sense*. Princeton: Princeton University Press, 2010.

———. *Imperial Debris: On Ruins and Ruination*. Durham: Duke University Press, 2013.

Straight, Whitney. Letter to the Editor. *Times* (London), March 21, 1938.

Swift, Jonathan. *Gulliver's Travels*. 1726. Reprint, Oxford: Oxford University Press, 1919.

Taylor, Keeanga-Yamahtta. *From #BlackLivesMatter to Black Liberation*. Chicago: Haymarket Books, 2016.

Taylor, Matthew, and Paul Lewis. "Jimmy Mubenga Decision Prompts Fresh Questions over Investigations." *Guardian*, July 17, 2012, www.guardian.co.uk.

Telegraph (London). "Big Changes in Civil Aviation." March 9, 1938. LH 15/3/120, LHCMA.

Tiemeyer, Phil. *Plane Queer: Labor, Sexuality, and AIDS in the History of Male Flight Attendants*. Berkeley: University of California Press, 2013.

Time. "Cadman Castigation." March 21, 1938.

Times (London). "The Cadman Report." March 9, 1938.

———. "The Committee's Report." March 9, 1938. LH 15/3/120, LHCMA.

———. "Division of the Subsidy." May 19, 1938.

———. "Ocean Flying: Five Air-Minded Nations." October 3, 1935. LH 15/3/120, LHCMA.

Times (New York). "Atlantic Air Navigation." May 16, 1929. F2–788040–20, NASM.

———. "Atlantic Air Service: Agreement with U.S." December 13, 1935. LH 15/3/120, LHCMA.

———. "Wings Roar over Seas Skyways." December 17, 1939. F2–788040–25, NASM.

Trouillot, Michel-Rolph. *Silencing the Past: Power and the Production of History*. Boston: Beacon Press, 1995.

Tufte, Edward R. *Visual Explanations: Images and Quantities, Evidence and Narratives*. Cheshire: Graphic Press, 1997.

United Kingdom Air Ministry. *Agreement Made with the British, Foreign, and Colonial Corporation, Ltd., Providing for the Formation of a Heavier-than-Air Transport Company to Be Called the Imperial Air Transport Company, Ltd.* Cmd. 2010. London: His Majesty's Stationery Office, 1923.

——. *Air Conference.* Cmd. 1157. London: His Majesty's Stationery Office, October 12–14, 1920.

——. *Annual Report on the Progress of Civil Aviation.* Cmd. 2489. London: His Majesty's Stationery Office, April 1924–March 1925.

——. *Convention Relating to International Air Navigation.* Cmd. 226. London: His Majesty's Stationery Office, 1919.

——. *England-Scandinavia Civil Air Transport Services.* Cmd. 5203. London: His Majesty's Stationery Office, June 1936.

——. *Imperial Conference.* Cmd. 2769. London: His Majesty's Stationery Office, October 28, 1926.

——. *The Report of the American Aviation Mission.* Cmd. 384. London: His Majesty's Stationery Office, July 19, 1919.

——. *The Report of the Committee to Consider the Development of Civil Aviation in the United Kingdom.* Cmd. 5351. London: His Majesty's Stationery Office, January 1937.

——. *The Report of the Committee of Inquiry into Civil Aviation and the Observations of the H. M. Government Thereon.* Cmd. 5685. London: His Majesty's Stationery Office, March 1938.

——. *The Report on Government Financial Assistance to Civil Air Transport Companies.* Cmd. 1811. London: His Majesty's Stationery Office, February 15, 1923.

——. *Report on Imperial Air Routes.* Cmd. 449. His Majesty's Stationery Office, October 30, 1919.

——. *The 2ⁿᵈ Air Conference.* Cmd. 1619. London: His Majesty's Stationery Office, February 7–8, 1922.

——. *The 3ʳᵈ Air Conference.* Cmd. 2599. London: His Majesty's Stationery Office, February 6–7, 1923.

Valentine, David, Valerie A. Olsen, and Debbora Battaglia. "Extreme: Limits and Horizons in the Once and Future Cosmos." *Anthropological Quarterly* 85, no. 4 (2012): 1007–1026.

Van Riper, A. Bowdoin. *Imagining Flight: Aviation and Popular Culture.* College Station: Texas A&M University Press, 2003.

Van Vleck, Jenifer. *Empire of the Air: Aviation and the American Ascendancy.* Cambridge: Harvard University Press, 2013.

——. "The 'Logic of the Air': Aviation and the Globalism of the 'American Century.'" *New Global Studies* 1, no. 1 (October 2007).

Verdery, Katherine. *Secrets and Truths: Ethnography in the Archive of Romania's Secret Police.* Budapest: Central European University Press, 2014.

Vine, David. *Base Nation: How U.S. Military Bases Abroad Harm America and the World.* New York: Metropolitan Books, 2015.

Virilio, Paul. "Perception, Politics, and the Intellectual." Interview by Niels Brügger. *Slagmark* 18 (1991): 145–160. In *Virilio Live: Selected Interviews*, edited by John Armitage and translated by Stacey Cozart, 82–96. London: Sage Publications, 2001.

———. *Speed and Politics: An Essay on Dromology*. Translated by Mark Polizzotti. 1977. Reprint, New York: Semiotext(e), 1986.

Walcott, Derek. *Collected Poems: 1948–1984*. New York: Farrar, Straus, and Giroux, 1986.

———. *The Prodigal: A Poem*. New York: Farrar, Straus, and Giroux, 2004.

———. *What the Twilight Says*. 1992. Reprint, London: Faber and Faber, 1998.

Walker, Alice, ed. *I Love Myself When I Am Laughing: A Zora Neale Hurston Reader*. New York: Feminist Press, 2011.

Wallace, Elisabeth. *The British Caribbean: From the Decline of Colonialism to the End of Federation*. Toronto: University of Toronto Press, 1977.

Walton, John K. "Power, Speed, and Glamour: The Naming of Express Steam Locomotives in Inter-War Britain." *Journal of Transport History* 26, no. 2 (September 2005): 1–19.

Wells, H. G. "The Argonauts of the Air." In *The Short Stories of H. G. Wells*, 391–405. 1895. Reprint, London: Benn, 1927.

———. *The War Is in the Air and Particularly How Mr. Bert Smallways Fared*. 1908. Reprint, Lincoln: University of Nebraska Press, 2005.

West Indian Air Transport Committee. *Report on the Opportunities for Civil Air Transport in the West Indies*. Cmd. 2968. London: His Majesty's Stationery Office, September 1927. CO 318/386/7, NA.

White, Lynn, Jr. "Eilmer of Malmesbury, an Eleventh Century Aviator: A Case Study of Technological Innovation, Its Context, and Tradition." *Technology and Culture* 2, no. 2 (Spring 1961): 97–111.

Williams, Raymond. "Advertising: The Magic System." In *Problems in Materialism and Culture: Selected Essays*, 170–193. London: NLB, 1980.

———. *The Country and the City*. 1973. Reprint, Oxford: Oxford University Press, 1975.

Winner, Langdon. "Do Artifacts Have Politics?" In *The Social Shaping of Technology: How the Refrigerator Got Its Hum*, edited by Donald MacKenzie and Judy Wajcman, 26–38. Milton Keynes: Open University Press, 1985.

Wohl, Robert. *A Passion for Wings: Aviation and the Western Imagination, 1908–1918*. New Haven: Yale University, 1994.

———. *The Spectacle of Flight: Aviation and the Western Imagination, 1920–1950*. New Haven: Yale University Press, 2005.

Womack, Ytasha L. *Afrofuturism: The World of Black Sci-Fi and Fantasy Culture*. Chicago: Chicago Review Press, 2013.

Woodson, Jacqueline. *Brown Girl Dreaming*. New York: Nancy Paulsen Books, 2014.

Woodward, C. Vann. *The Strange Career of Jim Crow*. 3rd edition. 1955. Reprint, New York: Oxford University Press, 1974.

Woolf, Virginia. "Flying over London." In Vol. 4, *Collected Essays*, 167–192. London: Hogarth Press, 1967.

―――. "Mr. Bennett and Mrs. Brown." In *Captain's Death Bed and Other Essays*, 94–119. 1924. Reprint, Harcourt Brace, 1950.

Woollacott, Angela. *To Try Her Fortune in London: Australian Women, Colonialism, and Modernity*. Oxford: Oxford University Press, 2001.

Wright, Michelle M. *The Physics of Blackness: Beyond the Middle Passage Epistemology*. Minneapolis: University of Minnesota Press, 2015.

Yano, Christine R. *Airborne Dreams: "Nisei" Stewardesses and Pan American World Airways*. Durham: Duke University Press, 2011.

Young, Edward M. *Aerial Nationalism: A History of Aviation in Thailand*. Washington, D.C.: Smithsonian Institution Press, 1995.

INDEX

above: black Atlantic and, 27; as place, 20, 23, 64, 83, 91–92, 94, 99, 102; as position, 18, 35, 54, 57–59, 63, 78–79, 87, 96. *See also* altitude; below; direction; ground

advertising: airmail, 74; business flights, 79–80; imperialism in, *45*, 45–48, 64. *See also* posters

Advisory Committee on Civil Aviation, 60

Aerial Nationalism (Young), 156n25

aerodromes, 81, 126, 127–28, 139

Aeroplane, 69

aerostats, 20

Africa: with colonialism, 89–90; culture, 156n20; as inconvenient, 80. *See also* South Africa

African diaspora: Black Star Line and, 64; with imagination transcending domination, 19–20; love and, 25–27; scholarship on aviation, 17; sensing of, 15; slavery and, 19

air, as commercial space and territory, 19, 61

aircraft, types, 20. *See also* airplanes; balloons

Aircraft Transport and Travel, 32

airliner cabins, as places for whites, 6

airline travel: in context, 5–6; gender and, 79; origins of, 16, 18; skywriters and, 93–95

airmail: internationalism and imperial unity with, 74; role of, 71, *73*, 75, 130, 139, 163n20; weight of, 72

air plane, 99, 146

airplanes, 6; Concorde G-BOAE or Alpha Echo, 143; in First World War, 31–32, 55; *Heracles* class, 87; obsolete, 126–27, 130, 137; with speed direction, change in, 53–55

airports, as places for whites, 6

air routes, 71, 136; Bermuda—New York, 103–5, 114, 116; colonialism and, 23, 61–62, 80; in context, 27–28, 101–3; England to India, 86–88; England to South Africa, 92–93; Jamaica—Panama, 111; London to Baghdad, 82–86; Miami—Bahamas, 111–12; transatlantic, 103–5. *See also* empire routes; imperial routes

airships, 59–60

air shows, 31–32

air space, 6, 19, 147

airspace: as dwelling place, 94; gender and, 79; imaginings, 58, 151; role of, 59, 70, 148; speed and access to, 20

Alonso, Juan, 48

Alpha Echo (Concorde G-BOAE), 143

altitude, 55, 59–60, 86–87, 146–47. *See also* above; below

Americanization of colonies, 24, 110–12

anthrohistory, 9, 16, 24, 154n12

anthropology, 8, 21

"The Antilles: Fragments of Epic Memory" (Walcott), 25–26

Appadurai, Arjun, 162n11

archetypes, speed with gendered, 50–51

archive, 9, 82, 95, 121, 148, 152, 168n63

Ardener, Edwin, 171n14

artificial flight, 18, 31, 108

ABOUT THE AUTHOR

Chandra D. Bhimull is Associate Professor at Colby College, where she teaches in the Department of Anthropology and the African American Studies Program. She is a co-editor of *Anthrohistory: Unsettling Knowledge, Questioning Disciplines.*